"A unique and original contribution to the debate about AI now unfolding across the world. Rather than offering an exercise in futurology, Elliott provides a detailed and sophisticated analysis of the impact of AI and the digital revolution in the here and now."

Professor Lord Anthony Giddens, Department of Sociology,
London School of Economics

"Anthony Elliott's compelling and accessible book is an impressive survey of the impact of artificial intelligence on almost everything, from global politics to everyday communication. Adopting his fine theoretical lens, he raises crucial questions particularly regarding the power of automated technologies to reconfigure our sense of ourselves, our very identity. The book is essential reading for understanding the way digital transformations work in the contemporary moment."

Judy Wajcman, Anthony Giddens Professor of Sociology,
London School of Economics

"Artificial Intelligence is an overused term which has been the subject of too many inflated claims. So we are lucky that in this book, Anthony Elliott expertly guides us through this thicket of hyperbole and out onto clearer ground. His emphasis on what software does – what Kaplan has called anthropic computing – and how it is transforming the mundanities of everyday life through a grab-bag of software is a welcome antidote to AI as a false idol which, at the same time, shows us where the opportunities and worries really are. A measured read which really takes the measure of AI."

Sir Nigel Thrift, Visiting Professor, Oxford and Tsinghua Universities

"Hollywood has blinded us to the idea that AI will bring a future of intelligent robots. But, as Anthony Elliott shows in this important book, the reality is that AI is already here and its impact encompasses the entirety of our social relations. A very welcome addition to the debate about the impact of AI on society."

Toby Walsh, Professor of AI, UNSW and author of 2062: The World that AI Made

"The book breaks new ground by covering familiar debates about the impact of digital systems – Robotics, AI and Machine Learning – on jobs; communication, mobility and life-styles; the transformation of identities and self; embattled democracies and the global economic order. By focusing on everyday digital experience it provides well-argued insights into the adaptive interactions between humans and digital machines and into the digitally mediated connectivity between humans. It presents the self as information system and thus a timely answer to pervasive cultural anxieties and techno-hype alike. Anthony Elliott prepares us to better understand the digital world that surrounds us already."

Helga Nowotny, Professor Emerita of Science and Technology Studies, ETH Zurich, and Former President of the European Research Council (ERC)

THE CULTURE OF AI

In this groundbreaking book, Cambridge-trained sociologist Anthony Elliott argues that much of what passes for conventional wisdom about artificial intelligence is either ill-considered or plain wrong. The reason? The AI revolution is not so much about cyborgs and super-robots in the future, but rather massive changes in the here-and-now of everyday life.

In *The Culture of AI*, Elliott explores how intelligent machines, advanced robotics, accelerating automation, big data and the Internet of Everything impact upon day-to-day life and contemporary societies. With remarkable clarity and insight, Elliott's examination of the reordering of everyday life highlights the centrality of AI to everything we do – from receiving Amazon recommendations to requesting Uber, and from getting information from virtual personal assistants to talking with chatbots.

The rise of intelligent machines transforms the global economy and threatens jobs, but equally there are other major challenges to contemporary societies – although these challenges are unfolding in complex and uneven ways across the globe. *The Culture of AI* explores technological innovations from industrial robots to softbots, and from self-driving cars to military drones – and along the way provides detailed treatments of:

- The history of AI and the advent of the digital universe;
- automated technology, jobs and employment;

- the self and private life in times of accelerating machine intelligence;
- AI and new forms of social interaction;
- automated vehicles and new warfare;
- and the future of AI.

Written by one of the world's foremost social theorists, *The Culture of AI* is a major contribution to the field and a provocative reflection on one of the most urgent issues of our time. It will be essential reading to those working in a wide variety of disciplines including sociology, science and technology studies, politics, and cultural studies.

Anthony Elliott is Executive Director of the Hawke EU Jean Monnet Centre of Excellence at the University of South Australia, where he is Research Professor of Sociology and Chancellery Dean of External Engagement. He is Super-Global Professor of Sociology (Visiting) at Keio University, Japan, and Visiting Professor of Sociology at UCD, Ireland. Professor Elliott studied at the Universities of Melbourne and Cambridge, where he was supervised by Lord Anthony Giddens. He was previously Professor of Sociology at the University of Kent at Canterbury, UK and was Associate Deputy Vice-Chancellor at Flinders University, Australia. Professor Elliott is a Fellow of the Academy of the Social Sciences in Australia, a Fellow of the Cambridge Commonwealth Trust, and a member of King's College, Cambridge. He is the author and editor of some 40 books, which have been translated into or are forthcoming in 17 languages. His recent books include *Identity* (4 volumes), *Contemporary Social Theory: An Introduction*, *The New Individualism* (with Charles Lemert), *Mobile Lives* (with John Urry), *On Society* (with Bryan S. Turner), *Reinvention*, and *Identity Troubles*. He is best known for *Concepts of the Self*, which has been in continuous print for 20 years and across three editions.

Also by Anthony Elliott

Social Theory and Psychoanalysis in Transition: Self and Society from Freud to Kristeva

Psychoanalytic Theory: An Introduction

Psychoanalysis in Contexts: Paths Between Theory and Modern Culture (Co-editor)

Subject To Ourselves: Social Theory, Psychoanalysis and Postmodernity

Freud 2000 (Editor)

The Blackwell Reader in Contemporary Social Theory (Editor)

The Mourning of John Lennon

Psychoanalysis at its Limits: Navigating the Postmodern Turn (Co-editor)

Concepts of the Self

Profiles in Contemporary Social Theory (Co-editor)

Key Contemporary Social Theorists (Co-editor)

Critical Visions: New Directions in Social Theory

Social Theory Since Freud: Traversing Social Imaginaries

The New Individualism: The Emotional Costs of Globalization (with Charles Lemert)

The Contemporary Bauman (Editor)

Making The Cut: How Cosmetic Surgery is Transforming Our Lives

The Routledge Companion to Social Theory (Editor)

Contemporary Social Theory: An Introduction

Identity in Question (Co-editor)

Mobile Lives (with John Urry)

Globalization: A Reader (Co-editor)

The Routledge Handbook of Identity Studies (Editor)

On Society (with Bryan S. Turner)

Reinvention

The Routledge Companion to Contemporary Japanese Social Theory: From Individualization to Globalization in Japan Today (Co-editor)

Identity: Critical Concepts in Sociology (Editor)

Introduction to Contemporary Social Theory (with Charles Lemert)

The Routledge Handbook of Social and Cultural Theory (Editor)

Identity Troubles

The Routledge Handbook of Psychoanalysis in the Social Sciences and Humanities (Co-editor)

The Consequences of Global Disasters (Co-editor)

Routledge Handbook of Celebrity Studies (Editor)

THE CULTURE OF AI

Everyday Life and the
Digital Revolution

Anthony Elliott

Routledge
Taylor & Francis Group

LONDON AND NEW YORK

First published 2019
by Routledge
2 Park Square, Milton Park, Abingdon, Oxon OX14 4RN

and by Routledge
52 Vanderbilt Avenue, New York, NY 10017

Routledge is an imprint of the Taylor & Francis Group, an informa business

British Library Cataloguing-in-Publication Data
A catalogue record for this book is available from the British Library

Library of Congress Cataloging-in-Publication Data
A catalog record has been requested for this book

ISBN: 978-1-138-23004-0 (hbk)
ISBN: 978-1-138-23005-7 (pbk)
ISBN: 978-1-315-38718-5 (ebk)

Typeset in Janson
by Apex CoVantage, LLC

FOR TONY GIDDENS

CONTENTS

ACKNOWLEDGMENTS

It was partly with the aim of addressing what I have termed today's "technological tsunami" that I set out, in 2013, to study systematically the digital revolution and its associated global transformations. At that time, I was Director of the Hawke Research Institute at the University of South Australia, and I was influenced considerably by the former Prime Minister of Australia, the Hon. Bob Hawke, who suggested to me the urgency of these issues for both the social sciences and public policy. I began by working on an area of the digital revolution which was close to my own heart, namely the reorganization of identity and the self as a consequence of large-scale technological change. The results of that research were published in 2016 in *Identity Troubles*. Following the publication of that book, I turned to address a related, but quite distinct, set of developments associated with the digital revolution – that of artificial intelligence (AI), machine learning, advanced robotics and accelerating automation. My principal goal was to study the extensity and intensity of the world of AI from the standpoint of sociology in general and social theory in particular. In doing so, I should like to acknowledge that I owe a large debt of gratitude to Lord Anthony Giddens, who perhaps more than anyone else has influenced my thinking of digital transformation in our times and our lives in these times. I am very grateful to him for taking the time to talk through with me in detail his work on the UK Parliament's House of Lords Select Committee on Artificial Intelligence. I am similarly grateful for the time he devoted to reading an earlier draft of my manuscript, and for his insightful suggestions and recommendations. I should also like to express my thanks to Sven Kesselring, who provided remarkably helpful comments on an earlier draft of the book.

I benefited considerably from being appointed by the Chief Scientist of Australia, Dr Alan Finkel, to the Expert Working Group on Artificial Intelligence of the Australian Council of Learned Academies. This inquiry was at the request of the Prime Minister's Commonwealth Science Council, and with support from the Australian Research Council, the Department of Prime Minister and Cabinet, and the Department of Industry, Innovation and Science. I owe thanks to my colleagues on the Expert Working Group, and in particular to Dr Angus Henderson of ACOLA and to Dr John Beaton at the Academy of the Social Sciences of Australia.

The research for this book was carried out over a period of four years, from 2015 to 2018. I am grateful to a number of academic institutions and funding agencies which supported this research and enabled me to spend extended periods of time working overseas on this project. These include the Australian Research Council (DP 160100979 and DP180101816); the Toyota Foundation, Japan (D16-R-0242) and the European Commission's Erasmus+ Jean Monnet Actions (587082-EPP-1-2017-1-AU-EPPJMO-PROJECT) for a generous grant. I carried out research in Japan through the award of a Super-Global (Visiting) Professorship in the Graduate School of Human Relations at Keio University, and I am very grateful for the support of colleagues at the School and University. In Europe, my base was as a Visiting Fellow at the Long Room Hub at Trinity College Dublin (many thanks to Juergen Barkhoff), Visiting Professor at the School of Sociology at University College Dublin (with thanks to Iarfhlaith Watson and Siniša Malešević), and in Paris as Visiting Professor at the Universite Pantheon Assas, Paris II (with thanks to Jean-Jacques Roche). I was fortunate to receive detailed and pertinent comments from audiences where I lectured on the sociology of AI in Brazil, Japan, Germany, France, the UK, Ireland, Finland and Australia.

I am especially grateful for collaboration with colleagues in the Hawke EU Jean Monnet Centre of Excellence at the University of South Australia, and in particular thanks to Eric Hsu and Louis Everuss. Ross Boyd, Senior Research Associate at the Centre, supported the various stages of the book's gestation with his highly calibrated research assistance and unstinting meticulous care. At UniSA, I should also express my thanks to colleagues in the External Relations and Strategic Projects Portfolio in Chancellery, and in particular to Nigel Relph – with whom it has been my good fortune to work – for helping to create the conditions under which I could finish this book.

I am very grateful for discussions with many colleagues on these various themes, including especially the late John Urry. Special thanks for comments, suggestions or recent discussions with Masataka Katagiri, Atsushi Sawai, Ralf Blomqvist, Bo-Magnus Salenius, Malene Freudendal-Pedersen, Robert J. Holton, Charles Lemert, Nigel Thrift, Nick Stevenson, Anthony Moran, Thomas Birtchnell, Mikako Suzuki, Takeshi Deguchi, Mike Innes, Kriss McKie, Bianca Freire-Mederios, Judy Wajcman, David Bissell, John Cash, Rina Yamamoto, Ingrid Biese, David Radford, Deborah Maxwell, Jean Elliott, Keith Elliott, Jeffrey Prager, Susan Luckman, Hideki Endo, Carlos Benedito Martins, Yukari Ishi, Fumi Kato, Pal Ahluwalia and Michael Lai.

Thanks, as ever, to my editor Gerhard Boomgaarden at Routledge. I have greatly appreciated his wise counsel, and he has shown me over and over what friendship can mean. Also at Routledge, many thanks to Alyson Claffey and Diana Ciobotea. Huge thanks to Caoimhe Elliott for assisting in getting the cover of the book right.

There is a final, and most significant, debt to my family. Throughout working on this book, Nicola Geraghty understood what I was trying to accomplish better than anyone and gave her full support. Her encouragement and faith has been vital. Caoimhe, Oscar and Niamh have grown up in a world of intensive AI, and the story of digital transformation has been the background story of their lives. My work on AI and robotics has been hugely enriched as a result of their interest in, and fascination for, the digital revolution. They have helped me see that thinking about AI is also a way of thinking about social relations, and especially alternative futures for self and society. Thinking about mobile digital connectivity is a way of thinking about what we mean to each other, and of how those meanings are transforming across space and time. The book is written, in one sense, as an extended essay to them about how I see our connections in the future – mediated significantly, but hopefully not wholly, by intelligent machines – and of the wider social, cultural, economic and political consequences of AI.

PREFACE

Rachel wakes at 7 AM to the sound of BBC radio, activated by Amazon's Alexa device.[1] The virtual personal assistant has been programmed to assist with Rachel's tight morning schedule, and completes multiple tasks – turning on the lights and heating system, starting the coffee machine – whilst Rachel gets on with her usual morning routine. Heading to the bathroom where she picks up a digital quip toothbrush, which pings every 30 seconds to remind her to move to a different quadrant of teeth for optimal oral hygiene, Rachel listens to the latest BBC update on the UK Parliament's House of Lords Inquiry into Artificial Intelligence which has been hearing evidence from security experts on AI-enabled cyber-attacks exploiting everyday smart technologies.[2] Checking traffic conditions on her tablet over breakfast, she decides to use the eco-friendly car-sharing app *Zipcar*. Arriving at the office, Rachel focuses swiftly on work, as she is mindful that a recent raft of job cuts due to a new round of automation has generated much anxiety amongst her colleagues. She spends the day organizing the filling of a vacant company position with a recently developed and increasingly popular jobs website, which uses smart algorithms to categorize applicants.[3] Whilst working on this, and throughout the day, Rachel monitors her elderly pet cat with *Petcube*, a Wi-Fi enabled device that streams video and other monitoring functions.[4]

After work, Rachel heads to a café, where she logs onto the app *Be My Eyes*, which matches sighted people wishing to volunteer their vision to the visually impaired through mobile devices. She tries to do this a couple of times a week, as it has a strong emotional connection due to the fact that her father (who passed away some years earlier) had been blind. Returning home, she stops at a supermarket to collect some items to fix dinner for herself and partner. Using her recently purchased smartfridge app, Rachel is reminded to buy tomatoes, onions and milk, items on which she is low and which the smartfridge 'knows' she uses frequently.[5] After dinner and catching up with her partner, she picks up her mobile and checks a notification that ticket prices for flights to Australia have dropped significantly. Rachel wants to visit her cousin in Sydney, and had requested an alert when airfares drop to a price she could better afford. Retiring to the bedroom, Rachel and her partner rest in their new smartbed. The bed 'knows' when she tends to go to sleep, which allows it to warm her side of the bed to a temperature she finds comfortable; the bed can also gently raise her partner's head if he starts snoring.[6]

What can be gleaned about our lives, and our lives in these times, from Rachel's day? What does Rachel's story tell us about how AI is changing the ways we live and work in these early decades of the twenty-first century? To begin with, this vignette is set in London, but it might just as easily be Copenhagen or Chicago, Singapore or San Francisco. The unfolding of Rachel's day tells us not only about the digital revolution but the rise of AI and software algorithms in our everyday activities and connections with others. AI is not what you think, but rather what you do! From virtual personal assistants to voice-based chatbots, Rachel's story indicates that AI has become increasingly central to our daily lives – as more and more of us access multiple AI software programs and virtual assistants simultaneously and often across multiple platforms. This explosion in AI, machine learning and big data goes to the core of the daily routine interactions in which people are embedded – from personalized social media to facial recognition software to gain access to offices.

AI has become, in a word, mainstream. There are, however, clearly other changes at work too. If AI impacts lifestyles and personal life, it also transforms organizations, social systems, nation-states and the global economy. AI is not an advancement of technology, but rather the metamorphosis of all technology. The increasingly ubiquitous spread of software algorithms, deep learning, advanced robotics, accelerating automation and machine decision-making, when contextualized in terms of the global digital distribution and use of Internet-connected devices which generate massive quantities of data, generates complex new systems and processes with multiple impacts across social, cultural, political and institutional life. As Rachel's daily activities demonstrate, people's lives and lifestyles today presuppose complex digital systems, as well as specialized forms of technological expertise, of which they are often only dimly aware. Another way of putting this point is to say that lifestyles permeated by AI are intricately interwoven with extensive and highly intensive complex digital systems. In this book I focus at some length on this *interplay of digital systems and lifestyles* ushered into existence by the rise of AI, advanced robotics and accelerating automation.

To live during the advent of the digital revolution is not, to be sure, an unmixed blessing. We live increasingly in a world of technological innovation riven between extraordinary opportunity and wholesale risk. As the huge wave of AI breaks across the world, the possibilities for the reinvention of common public life and successful collaborative social action on a scale unprecedented in human history has come into focus. AI is being used, for example, to track fish in the Great Barrier Reef, protect biodiversity in the Amazon and deter animals from entering endangered habitats using sensors[7]; research is also at an advanced stage for AI-powered microscopes to monitor plankton floating in the sea and for robots powered by AI to clean the oceans.[8] The deployment of AI in the fight against global terrorism, through the international pooling of information and intelligence from supercomputers, is another case in point. But there are also massive high-consequence, possibly existential, threats.[9] From killer robots to lethal autonomous weapons technology to AI used by criminal organizations or rogue states, AI might potentially spell the end of humanity – a warning issued by such luminaries as the late Stephen Hawking, Bill Gates and Elon Musk. At its center, this cultural anxiety concerns what might happen if AI outstrips human intelligence. One of the most disturbing trends has to do with the merging of AI, digital technology and the means of waging war. In this book I place a good deal of emphasis upon the role of AI in the transformation of military power, and especially the impact of new forms of surveillance – of which big data and awesome algorithmic power have been the most momentous features of technological development – upon the development of world order.

In order to systematically capture an argument that spills out over large tracts of technological innovation and scientific discovery, I shall summarize here the main claims of this book in the form of basic observations.

1   The digital universe has a direct connection with AI, but today's technological changes are far more encompassing in scope than AI alone. Notwithstanding key terminological differences, digital transformation can be adequately grasped in social, cultural and political terms only if we see the interconnections between, amongst other technologies, AI, advanced robotics, Industry 4.0, accelerated automation, big data, supercomputers, 3D printing, smart cities, cloud computing and the Internet of Everything. These technological transformations must also be viewed in the wider context of developments in biotechnology, nanotechnology and information science. Benjamin Bratton has recently captured this point with reference to a "planetary-scale computing megastructure".[10]

2   AI is not so much about the future as the here-and-now. Our lives are already saturated with AI – evidenced in the rise of chatbots, Google Maps, Uber, Amazon recommendations, email spam filters, robo-readers, and AI-powered personal assistants such as Siri, Alexa and Echo. The AI revolution is thus already well underway, and is unfolding in complex and uneven ways across the globe.

3   AI is not simply an "out-there" phenomenon, such as the technological field of machine learning algorithms or emotion recognition technologies. AI also pervades personal life, reorganizing the nature of self-identity and the fabric of social relations in the broadest sense.

4   Much of what we do in everyday life is organized and mediated by AI. Yet AI transforms the fabric of everyday life in largely unnoticed ways. Like electricity, AI is essentially *invisible*. AI functions automatically, operating "behind the scenes" – so that airport doors automatically open (or not!), GPS navigation gets us home, and virtual personal assistants help in our daily lives. And just like electricity, AI is fast becoming a general purpose technology – that is to say, a technology which enables the development of a whole range of further innovative applications.

5   As a consequence of the development and deepening of Industry 4.0, AI will radically intensify digital disruption in the labor market and employment. Many jobs will certainly disappear as a result of AI, but this is not as simple as the "rise of the robots" thesis. Other jobs will be enhanced by AI, and many – as yet unknown – jobs will be generated. In all of this, digital skills – and especially the fostering of digital understanding – will be crucial.

6   To be sure, AI inaugurates an employment revolution. But perhaps the most significant global transformation will be at the level of *talk and everyday life*. AI has major implications for the ways in which people will communicate and talk with each other. Not only is over 50% of Internet traffic now generated by machine-to-machine communication, but person-to-machine talk is significantly rising and will continue to escalate. In particular, chatbots, softbots and virtual personal assistants will become an integral part of how people live and work.

7   Advanced AI is very different from previous forms of technological automation. Today we witness the spread of new technologies which are mobile, situationally aware, adaptive and in communication with other intelligent machines. Intelligent machines are now "on the move" as never before – from self-driving cars to drones – and are making and remaking

networked connections and communications at often rapid speed around the world.

8 Technological innovations and scientific discoveries are dramatically advancing the scope and intensity of AI across societies, economies, polities and cultures. This next phase of development – from edible surgical robots to military micro-drones – involves very high levels of uncertainty. The key question for us today is whether our societies can tolerate the uncertainty of the culture of AI, react creatively to it and become more open towards constantly evolving digital transformation.

Some remarks should perhaps be noted about the nature and scope of these arguments. The central emphasis of this book is upon providing an interpretation of the culture of AI, both its embedding in everyday life and transformations of modern institutions. AI has its origins in geopolitics, which at the same time it has impacted and transformed. AI constantly interlaces with the nation-state, the contemporary phase of globalization and global politics. In the sphere of geopolitics, the main narrative for AI has been about power – the power to shape the worldwide race in AI-driven economic growth, as well as research and development initiatives to remain globally competitive. Innovation underpinned by monetary investment and public policy initiatives lies at the core of the digital revolution. Globally the most important AI hubs are in Silicon Valley, New York, Boston, London, Beijing and Shenzhen.[11] In terms of national investment in AI, for example, the UK has committed $1.3 billion over 10 years and France $1.8 billion over five years, and the EU estimates a total public investment of $20 billion by 2030 and China calculates it will spend $209 billion by 2030. Small wonder that some estimates of productivity-driven economic growth conclude that AI could contribute approximately $16 trillion to the global economy by 2030.[12] Throughout this book I try to trace out the direction of movement of such transformations in AI, but I make no claim to develop an exhaustive analysis of the geopolitics of AI, nor of variations among nations in today's world.[13]

INTRODUCTION

Like many a supposedly contemporary phenomenon, artificial intelligence (AI) is in fact an ancient invention.[1] As a cultural ideal, it first emerged during the Hellenistic period – which is to say, it was an idea that pervaded ancient Greece as an urge (in the words of one commentator) to "forge the Gods".[2] The idea of intelligent robots and thinking machines crops up in Greek myths such as *Talos of Crete*, and humanoid automatons were crafted by artificer Yan Shi and presented to King Mu of Zhou.[3] The classical epoch saw the appearance of mechanical men and other automatons as designed by the Greek engineer Hero of Alexandria, and for a polymath like Ismail al-Jazari only a programmable orchestra of mechanical automatons could sustain legitimately scientific inquiry as set out in his programmatic *The Book of Knowledge of Ingenious Mechanical Devices*.[4] Kevin LaGrandeur holds that artificial slaves can be traced as far back as Book XVIII of Homer's *Iliad*, and also underscores Aristotle's lengthy treatment of artificial slaves in his *Politics* as foundational.[5]

The arrival of the early modern period in Europe ushered in less eye-catching brands of AI, with Rene Descartes comparing the bodies of animals to complex machines. For political theorists like Thomas Hobbes, only a mechanical theory of cognition could adequately grasp the contours of human reason. The

French philosopher Blaise Pascal set about inventing a mechanical calculator, and along the way this remarkable mathematician developed some fifty prototypes and twenty calculating machines. Gaby Woods, who considers that our anxious fascination with robots can be traced directly to the early modern quest for mechanical life, discusses Jacques de Vaucanson's Digesting Duck (which was a wonderful con) and his mechanical Flute Player (which actually worked) as symptomatic.[6] The wranglings of the early modern age over mechanical life were, in effect, dreams of technological promise, which in turn generated the wish for more technology throughout cultures at large. In the nineteenth century, artificial beings crop up in various works of fiction, represented as the nexus of science and society. There is, say, Victor Frankenstein's scientific forays into imparting life to non-living matter in Mary Shelley's *Frankenstein*, or the factory production of robots, cyborgs and androids in Karel Capek's *Rossum's Universal Robots*.

In our own time, artificial intelligence has been largely the preserve of such disciplines as computer science, mathematics, information science, linguistics, psychology and neuroscience. The word "artificial" in this context has come to denote that machines can be made to replicate or simulate human intelligence, and hence the affinity between artificial intelligence and digital technologies (including advanced robotics and accelerating automation) which I seek to sketch throughout this book. The debate over what AI actually is, and what it is not, could easily merit book-length treatment. Since the mid-1950s when the American computer scientist John McCarthy, along with Marvin Minksy, Herbert Simon and Allen Newell, founded the field of artificial intelligence and organized a legendary academic conference at Dartmouth College in the US, there has been great controversy over claims that human abilities will be increasingly replicable by intelligent machines in the future. Among the central questions have been these. What, specifically, defines AI? How does AI differ from, say, advanced robotics? What makes a machine artificially intelligent, as opposed to just useful? How might artificial intelligence be disentangled from organic intelligence? Whilst the debate over what AI actually is has remained highly contested in the academic discourse of computer science, information science, semantics, philosophy of language and mind, and theories of consciousness, the discussion more broadly in the media and the business community has been more opportunistic. Here AI has, for the large part, appeared as a buzzword, a marketing tool to scoop up customer attention and position companies as at the cutting-edge of the newest technologies. Equally, AI has been conflated with robots, with the Hollywood dreamscapes of *Terminator* and *Wall-E*. "Artificial intelligence", writes Ian Bogost of the contemporary cultural debate, "has become meaningless".[7]

Although there is a lack of agreement among researchers about how to characterize the main defining elements of AI and its related technologies,[8] there is some measure of agreement in the area of public policy and governance. The UK Government's 2017 "Industrial Strategy White Paper", for example, defines AI as "technologies with the ability to perform tasks that would otherwise require human intelligence, such as visual perception, speech recognition, and language translation".[9] It is perhaps useful to begin with such a definition, one geared to state-promoted AI, if only because such an account is clearly quite narrow, and leaves unaddressed some of the most important deep drivers of AI. It is crucially important, for instance, to underscore the intricate interconnections between AI and machine learning. A key condition of AI, one not captured by the UK Government's White Paper, is the capacity to learn from, and adapt to, new information or stimuli. Among the deep drivers of AI are technological advances in the networked communications of self-learning and relative autonomy of intelligent machines. These new systems of self-learning, adaptation and self-governance have helped to reconstitute not only the debate over what AI actually is, but also impacted the relationship between artificial and organic intelligence.

While AI generates increasing systems of interconnected self-learning, it does not automatically spawn a common set of human reactions or values in terms of those engaging with such technologies. The relation between AI and its technologies, including particularly people's experiences or views of AI, is a complicated one. For the purposes of this study I define AI, and its related offshoot machine learning, as encompassing any computational system that can sense its relevant context and react intelligently to data. Machines might be said to become 'intelligent', thus warranting the badge 'AI', when certain degrees of self-learning, self-awareness and sentience are realized. Intelligent machines act not only with expertise, but ongoing degrees of reflexivity. The relation between AI and self-learning can be considered to operate at a high level when intelligent machines can cope with the element of surprise. After all, many machine learning algorithms can easily be duped. Broadly speaking, I thus approach AI in this book as referring to any computational system which can sense its environment, think, learn and react in response (and cope with surprises) to such data-sensing.[10] AI-related technologies may include both robots and purely digital systems that employ learning methods such as deep learning, neural networks, pattern recognition (including machine vision and cognition), reinforcement learning and machine decision-making.

Computational learning, adaptation and system improvement in response to data or stimuli is a common component of artificially intelligent systems. The rise of neural networks, a kind of machine learning loosely modelled on the structure of the human brain, consisting of deeply layered processing nodes, has been especially significant in the spread and efficacy of AI. So too, deep leaning – a more recent spin-off of neural networks – which deploys multiple layers of AI to solve complex problems has underpinned much of the explosion of interest from businesses, media, the finance sector and large-scale corporations. The essential scientific aspiration, as we will chart throughout this book, has focused on replicating general intelligence, which for the most part has been understood largely in terms of reason, cognition, perception as well as planning, learning and natural language processing. As such, it is not always clear in what sense the psychological, sexual or private domains might actually count for the discourse of artificial intelligence. But one of the central arguments I develop in this book is that the rise of digital life (ranging across ubiquitous computing, the Internet of Everything, AI and robotics) is producing a profound transformation of the relations between the public, political and global on the one hand and the private, sexual and psychological on the other. The promises of AI – some fulfilled, others dreams – lie at the core of this metamorphosis.

The Turing test and after

For most people today, AI denotes chatbots and complex algorithms, not the definitional argumentation of computer scientists. Indeed, some of those who nowadays drop reference to AI in daily conversation are probably unaware that there exists a rich scientific and philosophical debate as to whether AI can replicate human intelligence at all. Computer pioneer Alan Turing raised the key question "can machines think?" as early as 1950. Since there was no agreed method or singular test for determining what constitutes 'thinking', Turing instead posed a thought experiment in which the question of whether scientists can build a machine that would pass as a human to other humans was pivotal. Turing called this thought experiment the "imitation game" – an adaptation of a Victorian-style competition – in which a judge sought to identify the difference between human and machine contestants. In this game, the judge sits one side of a computer screen, chatting to mysterious interlocutors on the other side of the screen. These interlocutors are human beings, but one of the interlocutors will be a machine, seeking to trick the judge into thinking that it is a flesh-and-blood person. This experiment became known as the Turing Test.

The discrepancy between AI as thought experiment and AI as actuality is one which has played out, sometimes dramatically, over recent decades in assessing the possibility of thinking machines. As with any test or experiment, there have been various claims to have passed the Turing Test, as well as many more stories of failure. In 1966, the ELIZA Computer program – which replicated the behavior of a psychotherapist – was determined by some to pass the Turing Test, though this claim was highly contested by others.[11] Since that time, AI has been deployed in computer programs which have defeated world champions at chess and won against contestants on the TV quiz show *Jeopardy!* AI has generated software in mobile devices which can converse in natural language, from Apple's *Siri* to Microsoft's *Cortana*. There has also been a dramatic increase in intelligent digital assistants, especially in-car assistants such as those developed by Toyota, Hyundai and Tesla. Most recently, Google has released *Duplex*, a dazzling AI and voice technology – which not only can reserve a table at a restaurant or book a haircut, but can chat relatively easily with people on the phone when making such arrangements.

Notwithstanding the significant advances in natural language processing by data-driven software, the search for machine intelligence remains elusive. The reasons for this are not only technological, but touch on profound issues of what it means to be human – issues which the social sciences have helped to illuminate. The American philosopher John Searle has provided an important discussion of this issue. Given the immense complexity of language as experienced in the shifting contexts of everyday life, Searle argued that it is not possible for computer systems to think or understand language in the manner that people do. To demonstrate this, Searle developed what he called the "Chinese Room Argument". He sets out this argument as follows:

> Imagine a native English speaker who knows no Chinese locked in a room full of boxes of Chinese symbols (a data base) together with a book of instructions for manipulating symbols (the program). Imagine that people outside the room send in other Chinese symbols which, unknown to the person in the room, are questions in Chinese (the input). And imagine that by following the instructions in the program the man in the room is able to pass out Chinese symbols which are correct answers to the questions (the output). The program enables the person in the room to pass the

Turing Test for understanding Chinese but he does not understand a word of Chinese.[12]

The functioning of computer code – and, by implication, any AI program – is insufficient to achieve an enduring sense of consciousness or intentionality. As Searle summarizes this, "if the man in the room does not understand Chinese on the basis of implementing the appropriate program for understanding Chinese then neither does any other digital computer solely on the basis because no computer, qua computer, has anything the man does not have".

Searle developed the Chinese Room Argument to refute functionalist approaches to the mind. Against computational theories of mind which treat understanding as a form of information processing, Searle was out to show that consciousness or intentionality cannot be ordered independently of our encounters with external reality. There have been many criticisms levelled against the Chinese Room Argument, and these have been well rehearsed in the relevant literatures – so I will not examine them here.[13] The broad conclusion of Searle's argument – that is, that understanding is not built up through descriptions of external reality – is, I think, substantially correct. To know the meaning of words, as Wittgensteinian philosophy emphasizes, involves instead being able to use those words as an essential aspect of the routines of everyday life. Listening to Google's Duplex chat on the phone with a waiter whilst booking a restaurant table has convinced some observers that machine intelligence has finally arrived. Whether this is so or not, my focus in this book is on a different, but related issue. This concerns transformations which AI is ushering into existence around the globe – the AI revolution in *talk*. Talk ordinarily is produced as conversation between people. But today talk (and how we produce talk in everyday life) is changing, and rapidly, thanks to AI. What is talk, viewed through the lens of AI? Many point to the rise of *Siri*, *Alexa*, *Cortana*, *Ozlo* and other chatbots. Rather than focus on AI as a technological achievement alone, my focus in what follows will be on how people use, and react to, these AI systems. Talk is an increasingly central feature of our daily encounters mediated by AI – in person-to-machine conversation – though it has been a neglected aspect of the AI debate.

Throughout this book, I develop a broad interpretation of AI rather than using narrow methodological definitions which proliferate within the AI and ML research communities. My focus is on AI as rooted in everyday life and modern institutions, and I draw liberally from media reports as well as industry and business understandings of this phenomenon. I develop this orientation partly in order to scoop up various forms of machine 'intelligence' and AI 'self-learning algorithms' and to consider their consequences for social, cultural, economic and political relations. The book addresses a range of current applications in AI, robotics and machine learning that already permeate many aspects of our lives, as well as potential applications that are set to profoundly transform our personal and professional lives.

What was once a wish has today arguably become a worldwide reality. The demand for digital technologies to order, reorder and transform our daily lives seems to know no boundary. Today, AI is threaded into much of what we do, and increasingly shapes who we are. Digital technology has been remarkably successful in satisfying the demands of our high-speed societies. AI creeps more and more into the fabric of our lives, through technology like check-scanning machines at ATMs to GPS navigation. What began as philosophical dreaming or experimental science has by now become commonplace, even routine. Today's technology revolution – from digitalization 3.0, cloud computing and 3D printing to chatbots, telerobotics and drones – is one geared to a transformation of the future. The digital revolution, we are routinely told by technology experts and the media, will change how we live and work in the decades ahead. Transformed futures are everywhere, and there is now a large and ever-growing industry of specialists thinking and anticipating how digital technologies will transform how we act, see, feel, think and talk in the future.[14] Such future-orientated orientations to possible worlds unlocked by artificial intelligence are, again, hardly new. From Isaac Asimov's *I, Robot* to Arthur C. Clarke's *2001: A Space Odyssey*, portraits of the future have strongly overlapped with the worlds of artificial intelligence and robotics. But the future, as morphed by new technologies, has most definitely arrived. Technology futures – whilst hugely contested and saturated with conflicting socio-economic interests – are remolding the here-and-now of contemporary societies and as never before.

AI is not simply 'external', or merely an 'out there' technology. AI cuts to the core of our lives, deeply influencing and restructuring social relations and personal identity. The complex ways in which people interact with new technologies fundamentally reshapes the further development of those very technologies. One of the central distinguishing features of advanced AI and associated new digital technologies is that the boundaries between humans and machines have – to a considerable extent – dissolved, which in turn promotes ever-growing opportunities for human-AI interaction in diverse robotic ecosystems. Today's proliferation of human-machine interfaces have deep implications for the way we work, how we live, how we socialize and interact with others, and many other aspects of our personal and professional lives. For example, it is more and more evident that we will be unlikely to interact with most intelligent systems in the future through keyboards and mice – natural language is already making headlines as a game-changing technology for personal assistant devices, yet is still very much in its infancy. An increasing number of consumer devices have recently appeared on the market that dispense altogether with conventional interfaces, such as Amazon's Alexa and Google's Home. Instances of other novel interfaces include augmented and virtual reality, interactive holograms, consumer-level EEG, RFID implantation, computational mood analysis and prediction, and wearables.[15] Emerging interfaces have been demonstrated in research laboratories, yet remain some years away from widespread commercialization. These include immersive haptics, implantable EEG or ECG, multi-function implants (the beginnings of cyborgs), human augmentation and exoskeletons.

From self-driving cars to space robots: disruptive technology and the digital universe

Consider these three instances – selected somewhat randomly from recent media reports – of technological innovations and scientific breakthroughs transforming social, economic, cultural and political life. First, consider self-driving cars. Rapid progress in the autonomization of mobility systems, as well as big data for the modelling of traffic behavior, has given rise to claims that driverless vehicles will soon be the future of road transportation. Perhaps nowhere more so have the prospects of future making been closely tied to cultural expectations on technology and science than the advent of driverless cars. As it happens and notwithstanding that many experts predict that full adoption of autonomous vehicles will not occur until the 2030s,[16] the age of AI has rendered the future already here, with many autonomous vehicles – from self-driving cars to robot lorries – already on the world's roads and highways. Technology giants from Google to Uber, along with automotive manufacturers such as Tesla, GM, Volvo, Daimler, Ford, Jaguar, Audi and BMW, have been developing self-driving vehicles. Many self-driving vehicles are small, compact cars; but other self-driving technologies have involved innovations in autonomous trucks as well as public transport shuttles. A self-driving electric shuttle bus, WePod, was successfully trialled on Dutch public roads in early 2016; this was followed in July 2016 by an automated bus capable of carrying up to 12 people, the Easymile EZ-10 electric mini-bus, which carried commuters alongside rush-hour traffic in Helsinki, Finland. Trialling the future of road transportation has also been conducted with many other self-driving vehicles, including self-driving cars on public roads in California, Florida, Nevada and Michigan in the US since 2012 as well as driverless trucks at the port of Rotterdam and automated lorries on the M6 in the UK.[17]

As a narrative, the future making of self-driving vehicles involves not only powerful technologies (from advanced sensors to computer vision systems) but the controlled management of mobility. Future making and future transport thus interweave through innovations in camera technology, GPS, accelerometers and gyroscopes when coupled to transportation development blueprints and the commercialization of driverless technology.[18] The roll-out of driverless vehicles for the advancement of public transport in the UK illustrates this well, as reported by *New Scientist*:

> London [will] become one of the first cities in the world to have driverless vehicles. The number and exact routes they will take have still to be decided, but a few months from now you will be able to jump into an autonomous pod and be ferried to your destination along public roads. . . . This is the beginning of a revolution in transport, as the cars roll out slowly in small pilots in urban areas. In the UK, Greenwich, Milton Keynes, Coventry and Bristol will lead the way. Similar projects are happening in other cities around the world, including Singapore; Austin, Texas; Mountain View in California; and Ann Arbor in Michigan.[19]

In 2017, autonomous pods commenced operating from Heathrow Airport and there were associated roll-outs across south-east London.[20] Various personal and cultural benefits were underscored for consumers, from watching movies to getting on with work on these autonomous passenger-ferrying pods. Engineers were quick to emphasize the improved safety of autonomous vehicles,[21] and policy planners have stressed the social benefits of assisting less mobile people to move around the city.[22] Most recently, however, the argument in favor of self-driving vehicles suffered a massive blow after an autonomous car operated by Uber – and with an emergency backup driver behind the wheel – struck and killed a woman in the United States.[23] This was a stark reminder of the new risk parameters stemming from AI, with some commentators suggesting that such risks are now an unavoidable part of our contemporary experience.

Second, let's turn to 3D printing. The scientific trajectory of 3D printing and its consolidation has been marked by strong technological innovation and commercial investment, along with surging demand for rapid prototyping. 3D printing has opened the way for a process of manufacture which is "additive", involving the building up of products layer by layer. This contrasts sharply with industrial manufacturing that was "subtractive", and involved for example the cutting, welding or drilling of metal or timber or other materials. The worldwide media attention accorded to 3D printing as a form of "desktop manufacturing", involving the possible spread of such technologies in offices, homes, stores and workshops, largely centered on new innovations in the local design and production of products. But, in assessing the promises of 3D printing against the risks, a range of controversies have raged regarding the extent to which the mass adoption of 3D printing would disrupt existing systems of industrial and post-industrial manufacture as well as create new challenges for the global economy.[24] Carrying a future making promise similar to that of self-driving vehicles, such controversy has been to some large degree undercut by current trends in global manufacturing and world trade where products are already 3D printed. As Thomas Birtchnell and John Urry point out, 3D printing is already used in many industrial processes in automotive and aerospace manufacture, luxury product accessories, medical and health applications (from the printing of prosthetics to organic transplants), as well as retail and service products.[25]

A rapidly future-orientated convergence of 3D printing and traditional construction, backed by evolving desktop manufacturing technologies, created media waves in China in the 2010s with the printing of houses. One might well have been excused for thinking that this was science fiction; however, the design and manufacture of houses in China through software packages and 3D printers unfolded rapidly and dramatically. As one media report summarized these developments:

> A 3D-printed printed house has been built in just three hours in one of China's capital cities. The individual modules of a dining room, kitchen, bathroom and bedrooms were assembled by Chinese developer Zhuoda Group on a site in Xi'an earlier this month.[26]

Apart from the speed of construction, these 3D houses were remarkably inexpensive to build and were made from environmentally friendly materials. Most recently, this type of innovation has been further developed in China by a company printing 10 houses every day. Such technology, it has been emphasized, ushers in a whole new world in real estate, where consumers will be able to update and print new house extensions as and when desired.

Third, one of the most astonishing deployments of 'disruptive technology' over recent years has been in space exploration. It is now over 50 years ago that the iconic science-fiction film *2001: A Space Odyssey* portrayed HAL 9000, a sentient AI computer that killed many of the crew on the *Discovery One* spacecraft. *2001: A Space Odyssey* is still highly relevant today, as a commentary on fears about new technologies and anxieties evoked by AI and robotics. Such worries, however, have not clouded the outlook of many agencies introducing robotics and advanced artificial intelligence into spacecraft exploration. Since 2012, dexterous humanoids such as NASA's Robonaut and the University of Tokyo's Kirobo have been sent to assist astronauts on board the International Space Station (ISS). More recently, airbus and IBM have developed CIMON (Crew Interactive MObile CompanioN), a floating robot with Watson AI technology. Referred to by researchers as the first 'flying brain' in space, CIMON sports an advanced AI neural network of facial and voice recognition technology, and can support astronauts in performing routine work as a "genuine colleague" on board the ISS. Or take Valkyrie, a 6ft 2in, 275 pound humanoid space robot. Developed by NASA's Johnson Space Center for future space missions to Mars, Valkyrie will be sent ahead to establish base camps and life-support systems until human astronauts arrive.[27] To do this, Valkyrie has been fitted with the most sophisticated sensing, computing and mobility technology – including two Intel core i7 computers, lasers, hazard cameras, actuators and a multi-sense camera on the robot's head.

So what do these instances of changing digitalization and advanced AI tell us about our world? With rapid advances in technology intersecting with social relations in unpredictable ways, what about the opportunities of AI, robotics and advanced automation and also the anxieties evoked by such innovation? From self-driving vehicles to 3D printing to advanced space robotics, much will depend on how society reacts to and copes with the current and future technologies which order and reorder our ways of living and working. As with other AI experiments, it is the social reception of technology and not simply technology itself which conditions our collective imaginaries and desirable futures.[28] In other words, the outcome of AI innovations cannot be known in advance. What can be said is that the dream of AI has not only become a worldwide actuality but now infuses our culture of technological promises. In the software universe of digital lives, AI has yielded knowledge an informational overlay (with territory now open to virtual intrusion) and with ever-increasing instrumental-technical dexterity. The fundamental transformation, I argue, is a *new protological infrastructure* which triggers the *contactless contact* (communicative, digital, virtual) operating between people and machines and which converses the machine-to-machine connections which are beginning to dramatically impact on our lives. Nigel Thrift noted as early as 2014 that "half of internet traffic now comes from non-human sources", underscoring the rise of social bots on computational machines masquerading as flesh-and-blood human agents.[29] Economist Brian Arthur calls this the new "second economy" of intelligent, automatic machines.[30] As Arthur tells the story of this software-driven automation, the most advanced technology "is running an awful lot of the economy. It's helping architects design buildings, it's tracking sales and inventory, getting goods from here to there, executing trades and banking operations, controlling manufacturing equipment, making design calculations, billing clients, navigating aircraft, helping diagnose patients and guiding laparoscopic surgeries". This is undeniably accurate, but the cases described by Arthur only hint at the watershed-like social, cultural and political changes in the development of digital technologies and AI. These changes are not only economic, but fundamentally impact the human condition and social relations. Digital technologies and AI engender new models of identity and personhood, social relationships, family and friendship formation, gender and sexuality as well as power imbalances alongside its lightning-speed delivery of big data, self-referential calculations, sentient environments, location tagging, complex algorithms, sensors and robots.

The arguments of this book

The social impacts of robotics and AI, its current development and future institutional forms, have emerged as fundamental issues for the social sciences in the twenty-first century. The connections between social science and the emergence of technological automation in the workplace and society more broadly have long been recognized. Indeed, a good deal of nineteenth- and twentieth-century social science had been devoted to mapping these connections, especially the intricate ties between technological automation and industrialization (and subsequently post-industrialization). Yet in the present day, we see not only that new digital technologies are merging the physical, biological and digital worlds in ways not previously anticipated, but that robotics and AI are increasingly networked, mobile and global. That is to say, we are witnessing a new kind of technological transformation which is unlike anything previously realized – especially when viewed as converging with developments in biotechnology and nanotechnology. What is new is not only the speed, breadth and depth of digital innovation and change, but also the connected nature of our interactions with others and everyday objects. From this angle, the Internet of Things – in bringing together people, processes, data and things – is generative of techno-landscapes comprising self-aware devices which can sense, interact and analyze data from other devices whilst "on the move". The consequences of these transformations are extraordinary, and require a rethinking of the nature of modernity which must go hand in hand with a reworking of certain basic premises of the social sciences.

Contemporary life differs from previous forms of social organization not only in its degree of technological dynamism (radically transforming both time and space), but also in its interlacing of the physical, communicative, digital and virtual spheres. Consider, for example, the globe's cybersphere. Over three billion people are today online, which represents almost half of the world's population.[31] In 2016, the Internet-based economy reached $US4.2 trillion in the G-20 economies.[32] If the Internet-based economy were a national economy, it would rank behind only the US, China, Japan and India. Across the G-20, this new high-tech economy already contributes to over 4% of gross domestic product. It is the projected growth of the globe's cybersphere, however, which is most staggering. By 2030 it is estimated that there will be 125 billion inter-connected devices operating worldwide.

No matter how far-reaching these changes may be for our professional and personal lives, however, this is only the tip of the iceberg as regards the technological tsunami sweeping the globe. For whilst people are connecting to the Internet as never before, so too are machines – and in staggering numbers. High-tech electric cars, TVs, computers, fridges – more and more, the appliances and devices we use in daily life have the capacity to communicate autonomously with other machines. Smart home-based devices have in large part attracted the bulk of media attention, yet it is in industry and the public services sector – ranging across retail, services, smart buildings and smart grid applications – where the large bulk of growth in connected devices will occur. Contemporary life increasingly consists of a merging of social and digital networks of interaction – with devices and software systems (operational via the Internet) producing, receiving and analyzing data. Some government estimates forecast that, by 2020, there may be 50 billion machines connected to the Internet globally.[33] Some other commentators have gone as far as putting the figure at over 200 billion devices. Clearly, the real revolution is an explosion in the Internet of Things, which is fast emerging as the Internet of Everything.

This book is not intended as an addition to the mounting number of technical studies of digital technologies, robotics and AI. Instead, my aim is to trace the contours of these socio-technological transformations, and to explore some of their consequences for the world in which we live today. In general, I try to set the study of digital technologies in what I hope is a rather more original context, one which is grounded in social theory. This is a work of theory and sociology, couched in an appropriately analytical style. In seeking to insert digital technologies, robotics and AI into social theory, I am aiming to challenge the current evasions and displacements of mainstream social science treatments of the topic, especially in economics, political science and social policy. For much of the contribution from these disciplines has damagingly neglected certain developments – of social relations, identity and personal life, mobility, violence – which have accompanied transformations in digital technologies. Thus, I try to identify in this book some structuring features at the core of digital technologies – and especially in robotics and AI – which are interwoven in complex ways with a number of other transformations in society, culture and politics.

The opening chapter sketches the broad parameters of the digital revolution, and its penetration into daily life through the impact of big data, supercomputers, robotics and artificial intelligence. Developing a theme which will inform the whole of this book, I shall be concerned to underscore the gradual expansion of networks of digital technology, and to try to show how robotics and AI have become pervasive features of social relations and social organization which are increasingly global in scope. I try to identify some of the structuring features at the core of the digital revolution which interact with transformations of the self and social interaction. I also introduce the reader to notions that will form the key focus of this book: the rise of digital technologies; the digital transformation of social interaction; the reinvention of processes of self-formation; and, the reshaping of the boundaries of public and private life.

Drawing on the theoretical precepts elaborated in the first chapter, Chapter 2 shifts the analysis to a focus on technological automation in the workplace. There I develop an account of the main transformations influencing work, employment and unemployment associated with the rise of technological automation and digital technologies. I examine the globalizing tendencies of modernity as deeply interwoven with the spread of capitalism and technological automation, focusing on Karl Marx's classic account of technological automation as serving the development of capitalism and its continual changing, expanding and transforming of itself. From Marx's account of capitalism as substituting machines for human labor, the chapter shifts to contemporary debates on how today's world is being reshaped by automated technology as well as the consequences of technological innovation for employment and unemployment. New automated technologies spawned by robotics and artificial intelligence loom large in this connection, and I critically review the recent contributions of – amongst others – Erik Brynjolfsson and Andrew McAfee, Martin Ford, Jeremy Rifkin, Martin Ford and Nicholas Carr.[34] In conditions of advanced AI and intensive digitalization, the importance of digital literacy in order to participate in economy and society becomes more and more commonplace.

The development of digital technologies, and especially the rise of robotics and AI, is not (as I stressed earlier) an 'out-there' phenomenon, as if technologies operate with straightforward given properties and causal effects upon institutions, organizations and networks. Technologies, on the contrary, are always mediated through social relations, entangled in our everyday ways of doing things and the living of lives. If digital technologies transfigure institutions, they also reach profoundly into individual identities. The digital is both around us and inside us. In our age of self-cultivation, where do-it-yourself identity construction and reconstruction is all the rage, this implies that digital technologies, robotics and AI become raw materials for the production and performance of the self. Chapter 3 is concerned to explore some of the ways in which the development of digital technologies enter into self-actualization and the daily lives of individuals. Here I focus on the recent work of Sherry Turkle, particularly her thesis that new technology produces an enforced solitude, as a foil to develop an alternative standpoint. I argue, *pace* Turkle, that new technology creates both new opportunities and new burdens for the self. From the use of iPhones to Fitbit, and from AI-powered predictive analytics to smart personal assistants, the production of the self has become increasingly interwoven with digital technologies. Digital technologies and AI innovations, as I argue at length, are transforming what self-formation and self-experience actually mean.

A central argument of this book is that the robotics revolution and AI impact upon not only work, employment and unemployment, but also social relationships in the broadest sense. We can adequately grasp the social impact of robotics and AI only if we question the general notion that digital technologies leave relations between people essentially unaltered. On the contrary, I try to demonstrate in this book that the use of digital technologies, robotics and AI necessarily involves the development of new forms of social interaction, new kinds of social relationships and new ways of experiencing and performing our identities. In conditions of advanced automation, robotics and AI, the influence of digitally mediated materials on social relationships, and on personal intimacies of the self, become more pronounced. Social media, cloud computing and digital communication more broadly plays a central role in this respect. But so too do smart products, services and devices, 3D printing, intelligent ecosystems, virtual reality, augmented reality, and supercomputer algorithms. In a fundamental way, this informational overlay of contemporary societies reorients social life away from face-to-face interaction which has traditionally characterized social organization and generates new forms of digitally mediated interaction which transforms our basic coordinates of time and space. With the development of digital technologies, particularly AI, a revised interlacing of self-organization and social interaction, up to and including the global electronic economy, becomes more and more commonplace.

In Chapter 4 I explore those features of social interaction which have become increasingly bound up with digital technologies, and of associated technological transformations unfolding across social relationships and society more generally. From the use of SMS to social media, and from Internet apps to chatbots, individuals today increasingly navigate daily life and social interaction through the informational overlays of touchscreens, virtual landscapes, location tagging, and augmented realities. Such navigations routinely take individuals away from physical face-to-face co-presence and into the digital terrain of mediated, online interaction. But as I try to show, it is a mistake to separate off our online and offline worlds. We must see, instead, that interactions of communication, whilst flowing across digital platforms, impact directly upon and restructure existing social settings – as people are busy texting, emailing or posting status updates at business meetings, on trains or during regular catchups with friends. In order to best grasp these transformations in technology and social interaction, I draw in this chapter from the sociological insights of Erving Goffman. Examining Goffman's celebrated notion of the "action framework", I analyze how digital technologies, robotics and AI are impacting upon social encounters, framing and co-presence. The interactive framework spawned by digital technologies brings with it major transformations in space and time which increasingly frees individuals from the restrictions of traditional social mores and the physical movement of their bodies. This creates new possibilities for digital social interaction, but there are also significant burdens impacting upon the professional and personal lives of women and men.

Robotics and AI are very different from previous forms of technological automation, partly because recent technologies have heralded robots equipped with self-learning abilities, action initiatives and the capacity for deep learning. That is to say, robotics is characterized by data-driven computing rather than instruction-driven computing. This quantum leap in machine intelligence has emerged through exponentially growing quantities of data and processing power together with the development of complex algorithms, leading to new capacities for self-organization, sense-making, insight extracting, and problem solving. Advances in cloud computing, machine-to-machine communications and the Internet of Things have simultaneously developed incredibly rapidly, faster than previous technologies and with huge mobility consequences for how we live increasingly mobile lives as well as for enterprises and institutions.

These converging digital technologies are transforming many aspects of economic, social and cultural life that are in some sense mobilized or "on the move". Where conventional automated machines were fixed in place and programmed for specific repetitive tasks, the new technologies are mobile, situationally aware and can adapt to and communicate with their environment. In a world of intensive digitalization, the rise and rise of machine-generated data is especially consequential, with the overall volume of communications increasingly written by automated machines, using data and analytical information which has been converted into natural language. Travel, transport and tourism more generally play a fundamental role in the mobilization of digital technologies, and in Chapter 5 I turn to consider how machine-based tech is increasingly "on the move", making and remaking communications, connections and networks at often rapid speed around the world. From Uber to self-driving cars, from collaborative robotics in logistics to transport robots, the emergence of what might be termed "mobility robotics" has moved center-stage on many industry and policy agendas.

In the final chapter of the book I take a look ahead, focusing on advances in AI, robotics and machine learning in terms of social futures. Here I outline some of the main parameters of how new digital technologies are transforming intimacy, gender and self-actualization; healthcare and AI as a framework for the redesign of medicine; and, the transformation of democratic politics in the wake of the digital revolution. Thinking social futures in the light of advanced artificial intelligence demands fresh thinking, and forces us to confront how the globalizing tendencies of AI are transforming day-to-day social life and the fabric of our personal lives.

1
THE DIGITAL UNIVERSE

Zoe Flood, a well-known journalist writing in *The Guardian*, recently summed up advances in unmanned aerial vehicles (UAVs) thus: "Some are killing machines. Others are pesky passions of the weekend hobbyist. As such, drones have not always been welcomed in our skies".[1] A critical observer might say that drones are all this and much more, especially since many people are increasingly held in thrall to those UAVs deployed in the service of the retail and service sectors.[2] All sorts of contradictions and ambiguities can be at identified in this respect. The very same people who protest about the militarization of drones may also want to order books through Amazon, which plans future dispatches by UAVs. Drones not only have noxious uses but promote the dehumanization of bodies into targets – for identification in service delivery, for remote monitoring in surveillance, and for destruction in war. There has also been growing public concern where drones have flown near commercial planes at airports worldwide, and in 2017 a Canadian charter skyjet was hit by a drone (without incident) as it prepared to land at Quebec City's Jean Lesage International Airport.[3]

The social impact of drones has to be understood against a wide institutional backdrop. UAVs, for example, have the potential to radically diminish barriers to access for countless medical services and critical medicines to save lives, and on a scale not previously realizable.[4] This is a socio-technological development with major global significance, and one that is radically transforming underdeveloped countries too. Consider the following example. In Rwanda, where travel between towns and villages in the rainy season is particularly fraught with danger, drones are now in use to deliver blood, vaccines and other urgent supplies to provide nationwide delivery of medical services.[5] The Rwandan government signed a contract with Zipline, a California-based robotics company, for fixed-wing drones to deliver medical essentials to rural health facilities across its landlocked state. In 2016, the Rwandan government also announced the location for the world's first droneport, designed by celebrated British architect Norman Foster.[6] It is envisioned that various robotics start-up companies will develop services operating across a national network of droneports in Rwanda. Most significantly, the Rwandan droneport is not an isolated development. Drones are increasingly in use, both commercial and otherwise, in many other countries. In South Africa, Peru, Guyana, Papua New Guinea and the Dominican Republic, UAVs are being used for health deliveries and other humanitarian emergencies. In the Democratic Republic of the Congo, the UN has deployed drones as part of their general peacekeeping program. And in the rich North, UAV advocates argue that drones will soon become mainstream in potential commercial uses from retail delivery to medical supplies, and from building construction analysis to infrastructure inspection.

But there are other consequences too, and many involve huge risks. Advances in machine-learning algorithms for the guiding of military drone programs is one powerful indication of how new technology contributes to the perpetration of violence and war. The United States, for example, has used unmanned drones to attack militants in Pakistan and Afghanistan; however, the very same U.S. drone program has killed thousands of innocent people, having wrongly targeted numerous innocent civilians, according to some reports.[7] And then there is the case of a new drone which French and British military contractors have developed for use by the Royal Air Force, with autonomous capabilities for selecting and engaging targets using AI. This is the Taranis drone, named after the Celtic god of thunder. The financial investment in the development of this unmanned combat system, which aims to provide autonomous drones by 2030, is estimated at over $US2 billion. Under current international law, autonomous combat systems such as military drones require human operators to fire on targets.[8] But whether military violence or war could be conducted entirely by machines remains an open possibility, and the production of drones such as Taranis suggests that autonomous military drones might become a reality in the future. Certainly, the possibility of fully autonomous weapons systems is a topic of great debate, and with huge implications for global politics, military defence and humanitarian issues.

On the face of it, AI-based drones are contested and saturated with different socio-economic interests, and this is perhaps nowhere more evident than in relation to military drones. There are serious concerns about the kinds of threats autonomous combat systems might pose to the future of humanity. But at this point we need to recognize that the rise of AI in society is double-edged. There is no easy way in advance of identifying how new technologies based on autonomous systems and adaptation to the environment will play out. There are certainly some stunning opportunities, with the potential to drastically reduce poverty, disease and war. But so too the risks are enormous, and this can be clearly discerned from the IT arms race, the development of autonomous weapons systems and other fundamental threats. Moreover, the assessment of risk here must involve not only direct but also indirect threats. An example of the latter kind of high-consequence risk is that of insurgent groups tapping into communication satellites and aerial drone camera feeds in order to hack into military drones.

In this opening chapter, I shall not offer an analysis of the opportunities and risks arising in relation to social and technological systems. Instead, I focus on the complex systems which power and sustain digital life itself. I begin with the complexity debate and consider how new technologies are folded into social relations, ranging from smart grids and cloud infrastructures to the legions of algorithms, sensors and robots that infuse everyday life. I shall concentrate my attention on trying to define the distinctive characteristics of complex digital systems, both as key to the production of our professional and personal lives and as integral to the world's future as a whole. I shall then look at some innovative attempts to conceptualize emergent intersections between technology and society – not only computational forms, but also developments in AI and robotics. I argue that the development of digital life creates new forms of action, interaction and social structure which depend upon the performance of digital identities on the one hand and the reproduction and transformation of digital systems on the other. In outlining and drawing upon various traditions of contemporary social and cultural theory, I contend that transformations in complex digital systems (mobile apps, bots, technological automation, smart cities, the Internet of Things) occur at the intersection where ways of life and digital skills become deeply layered as everyday occurrences.

Complex digital systems

The flow of human action and the production of cultural practices takes place today in the context of complex, powerful technological and social systems that stretch across time and space. In speaking of the systematic properties of technology and society, I mean their ordering features, giving a certain degree of 'solidity' to social practices which are self-organizing, adaptive and evolving. From this angle, technical and social systems are by definition emergent, dynamic and open. Yet such systems are never 'solid' in the sense that they are stable or unchanging. Complex technological and social systems, including the conditions of systems reproduction, are characterized by unpredictability, non-linearity and reversal. The ordering and reordering of systems, structures and networks, as developed in complexity theory, is highly dynamic, processual and unpredictable; the impact of positive and negative feedback loops shift systems away from states of equilibrium.[9] Drawing from advances in complexity theory, historical sociology and social theory, I shall argue that a grounded, theoretically informed account of the digitization of technological and social systems must be based on seven sets of considerations. These complex, overlapping connections between technological systems and digital life can be analyzed and critiqued from the sociological considerations I now detail.

First, there is the sheer scale of systems of digitization, of technological automation and of social relations threaded through artificial intelligence – all being key global enablers of the digital data economy. Over 3 billion people – almost half the world's population – are online, and digital interactions increasingly impact upon even those who find themselves with limited digital resources.[10] Complex computerized systems of digitization make possible (and are increasingly interwoven with) the production and performance of social life – of business, leisure, consumerism, travel, governance and so on. These systems – of computing databases, codes of software, Wi-Fi, Bluetooth, RFID, GPS and other technologies – make possible our everyday networked interactions, from search engine enquiries to online shopping to social media. These systems facilitate predictable and relatively routine pathways of digitization which underpin smartphone social interactions, online banking, music streaming, status updates, blogs, vlogs and related actions of searching, retrieval and tagging spawned by the Internet. Systems of digitization enable repetition. In the contemporary world of digital life, these systems include social media, CCTV, credit cards, laptops, tablets, wearable computers, URLs (Uniform Resource Locators), smartphones, email, SMS, satellites, computer algorithms, location tagging and so on. The complex, interdependent systems of digitization flourishing today are the "flow architectures" that increasingly order and reorder social relations, production, consumption, communications, travel and transport, and surveillance around the world.[11]

In addition to the rapid spread of systems of digitalization, the scaling up of robotics is hugely significant throughout much of the world. Industrial robots transforming manufacturing – from packaging and testing to assembling minute electronics – are the fastest growing source of robotic technologies. From the early 1960s when one of the first industrial robots was operationalized in a candy factory in Ontario through to the 2010s where new technologies facilitated robots working hand-in-hand with workers, there has been a growing expansion in robotics and the number of published patents on robotics technology. The number of industrial robots in the USA jumped from 200 in 1970 to 5,500 in 1981 to 90,000 in 2001.[12] In 2015, the number of industrial robots sold worldwide was nearly 250,000; industrial robotics is an industry which annually enjoys global growth of approximately 10%. Automotive and electronics have been the major industry sectors for robotics use, but many other sectors are increasingly adopting robotics and technological automation. Robotics coupled with converging mobile technologies are especially transforming industry in Asia, which has dominated the ramp-up of robotics use, with China being the primary contributor. But demand for greater productivity, mass customization, miniaturization and shorter product life cycles has also driven growth for robotics worldwide, especially in Japan, Germany, Korea and the USA.

Second, digital systems should not be viewed as simply products of the contemporary but in part depend upon technological systems which have developed at earlier historical periods. "Many old technologies", writes John Urry, "do not simply disappear but survive through path-dependent relationships, combining with the 'new' in a reconfigured and unpredicted cluster. An interesting example of this has been the enduring importance of the 'technology' of paper even within 'high-tech' offices".[13] Thus, the development and exploitation of digital technologies are interwoven in complex ways with multiple pre-digital technological systems. Another way of putting this point is to say that our wireless world is interdependent with a range of wired technologies. Many of the wired technologies – the wires, cables and connections of pre-digital systems – which intersect with digital technologies of Wi-Fi, Bluetooth and RFID date from the 1830s, 1840s and 1850s. There occurred in this historical period an astonishing range of experiments with systems of electrical energy for the purposes of communication. Systems dating from that period based upon the communication potential of electricity include electromagnetic telegraphy (which was trialled in England, Germany and the United States in the 1830s), the first viable telegraph line between Washington and Baltimore (constructed by Morse in 1843 with funds from the US Congress), the successful laying of early submarine cables across the English Channel and between England and Ireland in 1851–2 (with a transatlantic cable successfully laid the following decade), and the discovery of the electric voice-operated telephone (demonstrated in 1854 by Antonio Mecucci in New York), although it was some decades later that Alexander Graham Bell conceived the idea for the telephone as a communication system.[14]

Subsequent to this period, the twentieth century witnessed a vast array of technological systems emerge and develop. Broadcasting systems – radio from the 1920s, television from the 1940s – were pervasive and hugely consequential for social transformations associated with mass communications. In the 1960s, the launching of the world's first geo-stationary communications satellites spelt the arrival of near-instantaneous communication on a global level. Around this time, other technological systems – from personal computing to mobile telephony – underwent early development too. The interlinked, tangled dynamics of these 'systems', of which most people are largely unaware as they go about their everyday social activities, is of key importance. Individuals will not necessarily know, or entertain awareness of, the conditions, scale or impact of such complex systems since these different technologies fuse and enrich each other.

Third, whilst the emergence of complex communication networks coincided with the advent of industrialization, it was only in the late twentieth century and early twenty-first century that digital communication technologies and networks were systematically established on a global scale. In this connection, the exceptional significance of various technological transitions that occurred between 1989 and 2007 should be underscored. While digital technologies have progressively developed across time, 1989 is a key moment in the constitution of digital life. For this was the year that Tim Berners-Lee invented the World Wide Web through the technological innovations of URL, HTML and HTTP. (The Web did not become readily accessible to people, however, until 1994). 1989 is also significant because Soviet Communism collapsed. According to Manuel Castells, this occurred because of Russia's failure to develop new information technologies.[15] Also, in this year, global financial markets were increasingly integrated through instantaneous communications and online real-time trading. Also, mobile telephony was launched, initially through Nokia and Vodafone, through the breakthroughs of GSM (global system for mobile communications). In 1991, the first GSM phone call was made with a Nokia device through the Finnish network Radilinja.

As the computing technology–inspired 1990s turned into the social media–driven 2000s, the sheer technological brilliance of digitization seemed all the more striking. For this next decade ushered in a range of platforms, apps and devices, along with the digital transformation of society. In 2001, iTunes and Wikipedia commenced operation. There were also new commercialized forms of social media. LinkedIn was rolled out in 2003, Facebook in 2004, YouTube and Flickr in 2005, and Twitter in 2006. The point, seemingly, was less to apply the digital to everyday life, and instead to secure one's social niche within the field of the digital. In 2007, smartphones arrived on the market. This was followed by the introduction of tablets in 2010. With the arrival of the 2010s, and such additional platforms as Instagram, Spotify, Google+ and Uber, culture and society was coming to mean status updates, SMS, posts, blogs, tagging, GPS and virtual reality. Digital technologies were transforming social life.

Fourth, these various interdependent systems are today everywhere transferring, coding, sorting and resorting digital information (more or less) instantaneously across global networks. With systems of digitization and technological automation, information processing becomes the pervasive architecture of our densely networked environments. As society becomes informationalized as never before, digitization emerges as the operating backcloth against which everything is coded, tagged, scanned and located. Complex automated systems of digital technology emerge as the 'surround' to both everyday life and modern institutions. These technological systems seem to usher in worlds – informational, digital, and virtual – that are generalized; that is, these technologies are increasingly diffused throughout contemporary systems of activity and take on the appearance of a functionality which is "wall-to-wall". Today's independent, informational systems of digitization are, to invoke Adam Greenfield, both "everywhere and everyware".[16] From GPS to RFID tagging, and from augmented reality to the Internet of Things, these various interdependent systems are the architectural surround or operational backcloth through which airport doors automatically open, credit card transactions are enabled, SMS is enacted, and big data is accessed. As Greenfield contends, this increasingly pervasive digital surround scoops up "all of the power of a densely networked environment, but refining its perceptible signs until they disappear into the things we do every day".[17]

To invoke the possibility of disappearance in this context, as Greenfield does, is to raise the question of the hidden and the invisible as concerns systems of digitalization. Digital life inaugurates a transformation in the nature of invisibility – operationalized through supercomputers, big data, and artificial intelligence – and the changing relation between the visible, the hidden and power. My argument is that the rise of systems of digital technology in the late twentieth and early twenty-first centuries has created a new form of invisibility which is linked to the characteristics of software code, computer algorithms and AI protocols and to its modes of information processing. The invisibility created by digital technologies is that of a protocological infrastructure which orders and reorders the many connectivities, calculations, authorizations, registrations, tag-gings, uploads, downloads and transmissions infusing everyday life. Codes, algorithms and protocols are the invisible surround which facilitates our communications with others and our shar-ing with others of personal data through the array of devices and apps and wearable technologies and self-tracking tools which monitor, measure and record people's personal data. The development of Wi-Fi, Bluetooth, RFID, and other novel tech-nologies of artificial intelligence has thus created a new form of sociality, based on a distinctive kind of invisibility, which touches on and tracks identities and bodies and constitutes and reorders our social interactions through ubiquitous contactless technolo-gies. But the digital field is, of course, much more extensive in scope, enabling also smart objects (or, anti-wearables) and other digital data-gathering technologies. Many objects and environ-ments have been rendered 'smart' through embedded sensors, interactive visualizations and digital dashboards – again, with an invisible protological infrastructure and the kinds of social rela-tions spawned by it, touching upon the operations of shopping centers, airports, road toll systems, schools and many more.

Fifth, these systems which are ordering and reordering digital life are becoming more complex, and increasingly complicated. This growing complexity has powered the rise of ubiquitous computing and AI, and has been underpinned by exponential rates of technological and associated social transformations. 'Moore's Law' has been the guiding maxim of innovation since the mid-1960s, and refers to the so-called doubling of computing power every two years. Computing power is based on the num-ber of transistors in an integrated circuit; and against the back-drop of ever-shrinking computer circuits, engineers have been able to fit exponentially more onto microchips. This has made computers more complex, powerful and cheaper: it is estimated that a smartphone, for example, possesses the computer power previously available only in large mainframe computers. More recently, reports from various technology companies – such as Samsung and Intel – have suggested that beyond 2021 it may not be feasible to shrink transistors any smaller.[18] The limits to technological miniaturization has thus propelled a debate on whether Moore's Law has reached an end point;[19] some analysts argue that quantum computing will provide the new route forward for the continued expansion of computing processing power. And many people believe that ubiquitous computing and AI, when viewed in the context of convergence with nanotechnology, biotechnology and information science, will continue to propel exponential rates of technological complexity, socio-economic innovation and social transformation. Certainly the ubiquity of digital technology, and especially complexity in AI and robotics, involves multimodal informational traffic flows, which in turn substantially depends on technical specialization and complex expert systems.

Sixth, complex systems and technological infrastructures are not just 'out there' processes or happenings, but are condensed in social relationships and the fabric of peoples' lives. That is to say, complex digital systems generate new forms of social relations as well as reshape processes of self-formation and personal identity. Complex computerized systems, for example, 'bend' social relations towards the short-term, the fragmentary and the episodic – based upon computational interplays of connection and disconnection. 'Life on the screen' (to invoke Sherry Turkle) appears to unfold faster and faster in the early decades of the twenty-first century, as people 'life-splice' the threads of professional, business, family and leisure zones together – using multiple devices across diverse digital platforms. As I try to show in Chapter 4, digital technologies are intricately interwoven with the trend towards DIY, individualized life-strategies, where people are busy using devices, apps and bots to schedule and reschedule their everyday lives and experiments with digital life. Systems of digital technology increasingly wrap the self in experiences of "instantaneous time", and the individualized work of constituting and reinventing digital identities is built out of instantaneous computer clicks of 'search', 'cut-and-paste', 'erase', 'delete' and 'cancel'.

Web-based digital technologies play a constitutive role in social relations today, facilitating digitally downloadable and transferable files containing apps and bots which power the smart-devices that people use "on the move". Over 100 billion apps have been downloaded from the Apple App Store alone since 2008,[20] and over 75% of all smartphone users deploy some kind of messaging app – from Facebook Messenger to WeChat to Viber. The instantaneous, just-in-time culture of Apps has been a primary conduit through which the great bulk of people in the rich North now communicate, work and socialize. The arrival of the 2020s, however, promises a wholesale shift of social relations into even more accelerated web-based digital technologies, and specifically the rise of mobile chatbots. This is part of a growing shift to conversational computing, where language is the new user interface which people use for calling upon their digital assistants for booking a hotel room or ordering a pizza. There is already a large online source network of efficient and intelligent bots available for download, and in Chapter 4 I examine how the spread of mobile chatbots is reshaping social relationships both now and into the future.

Seventh, the technological changes stimulated by the advent of complex digital systems involve processes of transformation of surveillance and power quite distinct from anything occurring previously. The expansion of surveillance capabilities is a central medium of the control of social activities – especially the control over the *spacing and timing* of human activities – arising from the deployment of digital technologies to watch, observe, record, track and trace human subjects. From one angle, complex digital systems might be said to have ushered into existence a digital observatory of greatly increased surveillance, somewhat akin to George Orwell's account of Big Brother and Newspeak. Ubiquitous CCTV in public spaces, data mining software, RFID chips in passports and identity cards, automated software systems governing transport and the speed of vehicles, and the migration of biometric security into various organizational settings: a whole variety of convergent developments has unfolded dramatically extending the scope of digital surveillance. It is evident that digital monitoring of the activities of citizens and the observing of the online and smartphone interactions of individuals has been undertaken by a growing number of corporations and state agencies. Since former CIA whistleblower Edward Snowden released documents in 2013 revealing the numerous global surveillance programs run by the National Security Agency with the cooperation of telecommunication giants and various governments, the issue of digital surveillance has moved center-stage in world politics and has become associated for many critics with the production and governance of citizens in the age of neoliberalism. Led by digital technology, the rise of various 'watching technologies' (from CCTV to telerobotics) indicates the arrival of always-on, 24/7 electronic surveillance and a radical extension of the surveillance of subject populations in the political sphere by the modern state.

Critics of digital surveillance tend to be heavily influenced by the late French historian Michel Foucault's notion of panoptic surveillance.[21] Foucault famously identified Jeremy Bentham's Panoptican as the prototype of disciplinary power in modernity, and argued that prisons, asylums, schools and factories were designed so that those in positions of power could watch and monitor individuals from a central point of observation. Foucault's panoptican metaphor emphasized the gaze in the sense of surveillance, especially in the form of the continued observation (as in the instance of guards keeping watch upon prisoners or teachers observing a classroom of pupils). These characteristics of disciplinary power have been extended and deepened through digitized surveillance. For example, prisoners can now be kept under 24-hour electronic surveillance. The dispersal of digital technologies of watching are especially consequential for the internalization of surveillance and the more repressive features of disciplinary power. Indeed, some critics understand the digital age as a kind of lifting of the panopticon gaze to the second power, such that digitized surveillance is ever-present and complete.[22]

There can be little doubt that digital forms of surveillance have transformed power relations in contemporary societies, and much more radical developments are likely to result from the next wave of technological innovation. But it is mistaken, I argue, to see digital surveillance as maximizing disciplinary power of the kind described by Foucault. Certainly, some digital systems of surveillance depend upon authoritative forms of monitoring and control, and in that sense can be likened to many of the instances of direct supervision discussed by Foucault. But this is not the only aspect of surveillance which comes to the fore in conditions of digital life. Today, surveillance is often indirect and based upon the collection, ordering and control of information. Characteristic of digital interactions such as social media platforms is that there is no centralized location from which individuals are observed; there is instead a distribution of digital interaction across a range of sites and operationalized through a variety of networks. This suggests that the routine use of digital technologies can also be understood in less threatening or menacing ways. Many people now wear self-tracking devices such as Fitbit and Nike's Fuelband, designed to monitor the state of their bodies and provide information on bodily functions such as heart rate, pulse, calories burned, and body temperature. New developments in telemedicine make possible the 24/7 monitoring of elderly and vulnerable people; patients who participate in self-care practices through digital monitoring systems are supported by doctors and other healthcare professionals who also access and monitor the health data of patients. Advances in telerobotic technologies within medicine and surgery have been dramatic in recent years, allowing patients in rural and remote areas to access specialist procedures in microsurgery, orthopedic surgery and minimally invasive surgery in ways not previously possible. Many of the social changes happening to power relations in this technological context cannot be understood as only disciplinary or simply repressive; they also contribute to novel practices of self-care, new forms of selfhood and identity, and the extension of social reflexivity.

Digitized surveillance might perhaps be better characterized as distributed monitoring, a sea of interconnected digital activities ranging from self-tracking to auto-activated information gathering. Central to this idea of distributed informational monitoring, assembled across many platforms and networks, is the notion of "sousveillance", which refers to people watching each other at a distance through digital technologies.[23] In this digitalization of life, people become part of environments which are sentient and smart, and such digital systems promote increasingly swarming behavior. Whilst it is acknowledged that professional and personal information is routinely gathered by state agencies through the deployment of digital surveillance technologies, the important point from this viewpoint is that increasingly indirect forms of surveillance operate "from below" – as people use digital technologies to click "like", "favourite" and "retweet". From this angle, people 'watching each other' on social media platforms – Facebook, Youtube, Twitter, Instagram – become caught up in wider processes of surveillance which are at once self-regulating and self-mobilising.[24]

It follows that another attribute of information monitoring across platforms and networks is that of surveillance at-a-distance, where data is fluid, decentered, transferred and routinely shared with third parties. As data-mining fast becomes the DNA of the platform economy, one inadvertent, unplanned side-effect of the ubiquity of AI has been that complex systems of recording, measuring and assessing the personal information of citizens have become fodder to the business of politics, elections and voting. The 2018 scandal over British political consulting firm Cambridge Analytica, which harvested data from millions of Facebook profiles to influence voter behavior in the 2016 US Presidential election, is a signal example.[25] The data mined by Cambridge Analytica had been contracted through Cambridge University psychologist Aleksandr Kogan; Facebook had previously authorized Kogan to pull data from its online profiles through an app he had developed – *thisismydigitallife* – ostensibly for academic purposes. The app was, essentially, a personality quiz for Facebook users. Before undertaking the quiz, however, users of the app needed to give consent for access to their Facebook profiles as well as the profiles of their Facebook friends. More than 270,000 Facebook users took the quiz, which ultimately resulted in Kogan gaining access to over 87 million Facebook profiles – 30 million of which contained enough information to be matched with other data trails. Cambridge Analytica had invested approximately US$7 million on harvesting this data undertaken by Kogan. Christopher Wylie, a Cambridge Analytica data scientist who became the key whistleblower on this scandal, commented that this data had been used to construct elaborate psychographic profiles of individual voters. Many commentators argued that it was such data which enabled the Trump campaign to win the Electoral College vote while losing the popular vote by 3 million votes.[26]

The trend towards 'behavioral micro-targeting' of individual behavior (consumer choices, political affiliations, personal preferences) to 'nudge' or 'steer' election outcomes is part and parcel of the 'dark side' of surveillance in the age of AI. Some critics have argued that there is indeed an emerging system of ubiquitous mass surveillance which is central to the functioning of corporations and governments in contemporary societies. Digital technologies of observation, monitoring, tracking and surveillance of the public and private lives of people function across digital platforms from social networking (Facebook, Snapchat, Instagram) to mobile payment (PayPal, Apple Pay, Google Wallet) to Internet search engines (Google, Yahoo, Bing). Companies use technologies of surveillance to track web-locations, record consumer spending patterns, store emails, manipulate social networking activity and the resulting patterns linked through smart algorithms. "Facebook", writes Zeynep Tufekci, "is a giant 'surveillance machine'". The business of surveillance, from the data broker industry to personalized advertising, involves the mining of vast digital data, and the personal information of citizens is routinely bought and sold without the knowledge of the individuals concerned. The result includes

major threats to human freedom and privacy, as corporate surveillance over the private and public lives of citizens develops
unchecked.

Surveillance is not only a profound structural problem in
the digital age; it has been directly marshalled by governments
around the world to manipulate and control citizens. Bruce
Schneier, in *Data and Goliath*, contends that the ability of governments to peer into our collective personal lives is histori-
cally greater than it has ever been: "Governments around the
world are surveilling their citizens, and breaking into computers
both domestically and internationally. They want to spy on everyone to find terrorists and criminals, and – depending on the
government – political activists, dissidents, environmental activists, consumer advocates, and freethinkers".[27] Central in many
of these surveillance processes is how the state security world
deploys data-gathering programs of extraordinary scale, range
and depth. For example, the US Prism surveillance operation
mines data from Google, Facebook, Verizon, Yahoo and other
key internet companies to track foreign nationals. Similarly, the
UK's Government Communications Headquarters (GCHQ)
draws data from all Internet and social networking traffic entering Europe to anticipate and prevent cyber-attacks, government
hacks and terrorist plots. What Louise Amoore terms "digitized
dissection", the disaggregation of a person's data-trail into various
degrees of security risk, is of key importance to the new surveillance technologies.[28] Such data dissection occurs not only within
national-state borders, but rather on a global plane. As Schneier
concludes, there is today "a global surveillance network where
all countries collude to surveil everyone on the entire planet".[29]
Whilst the advantages to world security of the digital revolution have been considerable, there are clearly many costs stemming from unchecked disciplinary surveillance on citizens. Real
dangers include disturbing effects on free speech and freedom
of expression, loss of liberty and erosion of democracy. I shall
return to examine in more detail the question of democracy in
the age of AI in the final chapter of this book.

Digital life: theoretical perspectives

Today, in the early decades of the twenty-first century, it is argued by many, we stand on the cusp of a new era, where contemporary science, biotechnologies and digital systems of automation affect the very fiber of identity and the structure of social relationships. Many of the anxieties and forebodings related to digital technologies and scientific breakthroughs are expressed as a fear of loss for "the human", including the breakdown of existing patterns of identity-formation and basic frameworks of reference for interacting with others. A stunning variety of terms have emerged to capture this global metamorphosis, including the "posthuman", the "transhuman" and "panhumanity".[30] Some authors deploying these terms concentrate mainly upon the transformation of technological systems, focusing on profound anxieties about world economic collapse, apocalyptic fears of global devastation, or the ensuing war against machines resulting from rapid progress in technological automation. More commonly, however, authors addressing these controversies focus largely upon dramatic alterations to our understanding of what constitutes the human, as well as the transformed interconnections between the human and the non-human, engendered by advanced digital technologies.

One of the earliest theoretical engagements with artificial intelligence in the social sciences was arguably the exchanges held in the 1960s between Hubert Dreyfus and some of the pioneers of AI, including Marvin Minsky, Allen Newell and Herbert Simon. Dreyfus initially developed a pessimistic critique of the relevance of AI to social organization. Drawing from the insights of Heidegger and Merleau-Ponty, Dreyfus argued that AI could not grasp the 'systems of reference' of which it was part.[31] Dreyfus saw human intelligence as rooted in the unconscious mind rather than conscious determination alone, and believed that our unconscious architectures could not be captured in the mathematical rules of AI. Another theoretical tradition, more sociological and historical in orientation, and with a debt to disciplines as

diverse as anthropology, art history, literary studies and prima-
tology, includes the writings of Lewis Mumford, Jacques Ellul,
Leo Marx, Langdon Winner and Thomas Hughes.[32] Subsequent
work in the sociology of science by Harry Collins on AI and
tacit knowledge, Randall Collins on AI and ritual interaction,
and Alan Wolfe on what humans can do and computers cannot
has also been influential.[33] This tradition of thought focused on
explorations of the similarities and differences between human
action and machine intelligence.

A standard response to the current challenges stemming from
new technologies and social change has been to draw from the
author who has been largely responsible for popularizing the
rethinking of relations between humans and non-human objects,
Bruno Latour.[34] Latour's work builds upon a philosophical tradition that runs from A. N. Whitehead and William James through
to Michel Serres and Isabelle Stengers.[35] As Latour represents it,
technology and society are mutually constitutive, and agency is
best conceived as distributed among people and machines. From
this angle, the condition of modernity is distinguished as a folding
of humans and non-humans into ever deeper and more intimate
imbroglios. Latour's pioneering contributions to what has come
to be known as Science and Technology Studies (STS) would
appear, at first sight, to offer much of value to the contemporary
critique of AI and social transformation. Curiously, however,
Latour himself has made few direct contributions to the literature on AI, machine learning or robotics.[36] Instead, most of the
major statements in this area have come from authors more or
less affiliated with the STS perspective, and some strongly influenced by Latour. Social scientists working from this tradition
include Lucy Suchman on human-robot interaction, Paul Dourish and Genevieve Bell on ubiquitous computing, Judy Wacjman
on social acceleration and new digital technologies, and Susan
Leigh Star on information infrastructures.[37]

The characteristic outlook of authors working from the STS
perspective is one which stresses the intricate and profound associations between human subjects and technological artefacts, as

well as the transformed relation between the human and the non-human. Authors working from within the STS perspective very often express a pessimistic view of the expansion of new technologies, including advances in AI and automatization. From this perspective, digital technologies, robotics and AI introduce either mechanical automism or other "machinic intentionality" as fundamental displacements of the human – along with all associated relations to the self, others, nature, culture and the future. The strength of the STS position is that it engages with the complexity of contemporary science and forges a direct connection to today's cultural uncertainties that come in the wake of technological innovation. An important criticism of the sort of ideas expressed by writers indebted to STS is the claim that the consequences of scientific and technological complexity are not demonstrated for understanding shifts in identity, cultural production and forms of sociality. Philosopher Rosi Braidotti writes, for example, that "science and technology studies . . . falls wide of the mark because it introduces selected segments of humanistic values without addressing the contradictions. . . . Science and technology studies tend to dismiss the implications of their positions for a revised vision of the subject. Subjectivity is out of the picture and, with it, a sustained political analysis of the posthuman condition".[38] There is considerable merit to this claim.

In this book, however, I want to develop a different approach. Rather than critique the anti-epistemology and anti-subjectivity position of STS, I shall develop a sociological (rather than philosophical) understanding of the implications of digital technologies, robotics and AI for identity, culture and society. The reshaping of the global world today in the wake of digital technologies, I shall argue, means we have to look in detail at the dynamics of digitalization and associated alterations in modern institutions arising from advanced robotics, big data, cloud computing and AI. To analyze how these dynamics are transforming society, it is insufficient to merely deploy terms such as the "post-human" and the rest. Instead, we need to bring work and employment, social relations, culture, identity, mobility, power and the future back into the equation, and explore how global transformations reflect the complex interdependencies of digital technologies, robotics and AI in the contemporary age. As a consequence of new technologies dissolving the boundaries between the digital universe and institutional life, we are moving into an extraordinarily different social order. This is a global world where the complex interplay of physical, communicative, digital and virtual interactions produce new orderings and reorderings of the human and the non-human environment; but the consequences of these transformations for identity, culture and society are quite different from what analysts have described under the theoretical banner of the "posthuman". Beyond technological automation, I shall claim, we are moving into a world where the human is guided, sorted, tracked, traced, tagged and mapped through various auto-activations of machines, robots and AI. But even auto-activations of the human, in the perspective I develop in this book, implicate responses from people. In short, the engagements of flesh-and-blood human subjects with digital technologies matter.

In developing my arguments throughout this book I draw extensively on contemporary social and cultural theory. There are three key theoretical perspectives which are especially relevant to understanding the digitalization of society and its associated transformations in AI and robotics. One is the approach of social theorists who have explored the significance of digital technologies and informational systems to cultural production and social innovation in the age of global capitalism. Perhaps one of the most original and interesting analysts working from this approach is the British geographer Nigel Thrift, who has coined the phrase "knowing capitalism" to capture the utter centrality of automated digital technologies to the global economy.[39] As a result of new auto-activated digital technologies, says Thrift, "the world is tagged with an informational overlay". This is a world loaded, indeed overloaded, with information. Social life becomes suffused with information technology, and the sheer amount of information and communications which are automatically generated both overwhelms individuals and produces continuous mediated interactions. Capitalism and the business of innovation becomes informational as never before, as the birth of a new information age continually increases "the rate of innovation and invention through the acceleration of connective mutation".[40] Capitalist systems of digital technology generate knowledge (the 'knowing' about products, services, choices, preferences, tastes, habits) in the form of constant feedback and iteration, producing an environment filled with massive quantities of digital data.

Technological systems of interdependence on this scale in turn at some point presumes political reordering. Thrift's chain of reasoning here runs as follows. In the age of the so-called new economy, digital technology and multinational business practices of continual downsizing, outsourcing and offshoring, the global economy underwrites innovation and new technological knowledge as a form of practice for the very transformation of capitalism itself. To put it bluntly, capitalism develops knowledge in the form of digital data and technological systems about itself. Because digital data has become hugely profitable as forms of knowledge, capitalism depends on technologies as never before to intervene into the object world – from barcodes to computational meeting schedules, from urban software to big data biopolitics of population medicine. Yet digital data, platforms and templates not only infiltrate organizational life but also reshape social practices. In response, particular ways of performing identity and 'doing everyday life' depends both on technologies and on the commodification of digital data in massive quantities. The rise of "soft capitalism" for Thrift is when the global economy develops theories of innovation about itself; where technologies generate knowledge in the form of digital data concerning human behavior, public services, public health, education, policing and surveillance, workplace productivity, the environment and global governance.

The strength of Thrift's work is that it treats the rise of digital technologies as an integral feature of contemporary societies. It is not just that new technologies generate knowledge in the form of digital data whereby new products and services are crafted to better capture the desires of consumers and frame information about citizens. It is also, and fundamentally, that the world is literally overlaid with information. Informational overlay in the sense of pervasive computing, augmented reality, touchscreens, location tagging and virtuality is the "background wallpaper" through which moving fields of data are logged, recorded and tracked in this increasingly "diagrammatic world". Central to Thrift's portrayal of the global digital economy is what he terms "a world of infinite mobilization" or "movement-space" – the never-ending shifts of communication (email, texts, status updates, posts, blogs), and the back and forth of data upload and download.

A second tradition of thought on which I draw in this book is from work stemming from various social theorists of advanced modernization and associated transformations of the self. The most well-known of these theorists are Anthony Giddens, Ulrich Beck and Zygmunt Bauman.[41] Giddens was one of the first to explore, in a sustained and systematic fashion, the impacts of globalization on the self and the advent of post-traditional practices of the self. His argument, in brief, is that as the global economy enters a more advanced phase (the arrival of which he calls "late modernity"), traditional forms of social life begin to come under scrutiny and are exposed to the transformational impact of communications and informational frameworks which alters the status of practices of the self in certain ways. Likewise, Beck put forward the view that globalization ushers into existence a profound shift from industrial to advanced modernization (what he calls "reflexive modernization"), which is a profoundly conflictive, ambiguous and plural modernity propelling women and men into forms of "self-confrontation" with the conditions and consequences of their choices about life in post-traditional patterns and frameworks of social action. This approach is also echoed, but advanced in a very different way, in the work of Bauman. He too highlights that globalization has inaugurated a broad shift from traditional to contemporary world-views and systems of social action – what he calls the shift from "solid" to "liquid" modernity, or from "hardware" to "software" modernity. In doing so, Bauman calls attention to the many ways in which the mix of advanced consumer culture, social media and informational systems impact on ways of organizing life (what he calls "life-strategies") that are more fluid, liquid, episodic and brittle. There is a growing sense of freedom across cities of the rich North, says Bauman, precisely because social bonds and the political grounds of collective security atrophy in social conditions of a liquid world.

The work of Giddens, Beck and Bauman emphasizes the fact that the global organization of communications, media and informational systems have significantly transformed contemporary societies, and especially generated new power imbalances and social inequalities. But I shall not examine the views of these particular theorists in further detail here concerning the dynamics of globalization, nor the structuring features of a more advanced phase of modernization. I want instead to focus on the specific question raised by their work: how has the advent of detraditionalized ways of living and post-traditional ways of thinking impacted upon the self, as well as people's ways of organizing their social relationships? For it is my view that these particular theorists, who have reflected on the dynamics of selfhood in our globalizing age, have much to offer to an enhanced understanding of digital life and technologically automated cultures. Of key importance in this connection is the concept of "reflexivity", deployed most often (though again in strikingly different ways) by Giddens and Beck. Reflexivity, according to Giddens and Beck, is an essential feature of all forms of social organization, but it is one which alters significantly and becomes much more prominent with the onset of the global economy. Reflexivity is fundamental to people living in modern societies, and involves the ongoing monitoring of (and reflection upon) information concerning possible trajectories of life and courses of social action. "The reflexivity of modern social life", as Giddens writes, "consists in the fact that social practices are constantly examined and reformed in the light of incoming information about those very practices, thus constitutively altering their character".[42] As individuals are increasingly formed today by the impacts of consumer culture, social media and the communications revolution, traditional ways of doing things begin to break down and are increasingly questioned. More and more, people must choose from a vast array of options (there is, as Giddens underscores, no choice but to choose) and to become much more self-active and open in the design of their lives and the lives of others.

To say that reflexive self-constitution increasingly invades society is to say that we have entered a world of wholesale reflexivity, which for Giddens includes ongoing reflection upon the nature of reflection itself. The expansion of communications media and new information technologies is a good example in this respect, and it is one which Giddens often invokes in his own writings. Recent advances in information technology and social media have arguably resulted in a much more interconnected world, where what happens on one side of the planet is relayed virtually instantly to the other side of the planet, and again with often immediate (though unexpected and unintended) consequences. Very often this kind of technological reflexivity is of the "small consequence" kind, as people go about their daily activities, scheduling and re-scheduling meetings and events with their smartphones, tablets and laptops. Note that even here we can discern the influence of reflexivity, since the impromptu nature of scheduling and rescheduling meetings through information technology reshapes people's understanding of the temporal nature of what a meeting actually is. This is an example of how the small-scale (or what sociologists call "micro" settings of action) can influence large-scale social changes, and in Chapter 4 I will discuss further the role of digital technologies in inaugurating shifts from "clock-time" to "negotiated time" in contemporary societies. But it is important to also underscore the core centrality of reflexivity to institutional and organization life. From big data which is used to advance the modelling of traffic behavior through to the

AI tracking of eye movements which facilitates the identification of potential consumers for large companies, the intrusion of expert reflexive systems into daily life is pivotal to the world of digital life and technologically automated cultures.

In his most recent work, Giddens has spoken of digital technologies as shifting contemporary societies "off the edge of history".[43] The accelerating flow of digitalization, according to Giddens, is already transforming the complexity, speed and unexpectedness of our lives today; but even more so digital technologies, including supercomputers and robotics, will significantly impact on what the future will look like. As Giddens comments:

> People can become far more knowledgeable than they ever were before and do things they couldn't do before. A smart phone – or personal computer or iPad – gives you awesome algorithmic computing power. We can live a just-in-time life in a way that would not have been possible even a couple of decades ago. The same is true on an institutional level. These are deeply structural changes, affecting everything from the economy to politics. It's like the industrial revolution, not yet as profound, but happening at a far quicker pace.

The current of cultural experiment we know as the digital revolution is highly contradictory and ambiguous, according to Giddens. Indeed, as digital innovations sweep throughout society there are very mixed consequences. The development of digital technologies plays an important role in the advancement of innovation, both in conjunction with the activities of the private sector and government agencies. Healthcare is one signal example. As Giddens notes, "the overlap between supercomputers and genetics – each of which essentially deals with information – is promoting huge advances in medical diagnosis and treatment". But the flipside of opportunity is risk, and there is a growing range of dangerous developments regarding both the political and commercial exploitation of new technological developments. High-consequence risks arising from the development of digital technologies, says Giddens, "overlap with other fundamental problems we face in the 21st century – climate change, the unrelenting growth in the world's population, the existence of nuclear weapons and other factors. Most of the great innovations in history begin and end in war and the digital revolution is no exception". The world may indeed become more fragmented, based on widening gaps in digital skills and accompanying income differentials. For Giddens, there is no way for us to know (in advance) how this will play out. The point is that, as a result of the globalization of digital technologies, we have entered into a very different world – a world of digitally encoded information which produces stunning opportunities and dangerous risks. Being engaged in digital life means accepting this contradiction.

The third tradition which informs my approach is that of critical discourse (which moves on several levels) pertaining to reinvention, innovation and experimentation.[44] This approach has been developed by a number of contemporary social analysts whose work contributes to our understanding of the relation between new technology and contemporary society, and in what follows I turn at various points to recent research I have conducted with, among others, Charles Lemert, John Urry, Bryan S. Turner, Masataka Katagiri and Atsushi Sawai.[45] This critical discourse underscores that digital technologies not only inaugurate a world of informational overlay, diagrammatic regimes, protocological infrastructures and heightened forms of reflexivity, but also radical moldings of self-reinvention. This work calls our attention to an emerging branch of social ideologies of self-fashioning, in which instantaneity, plurality, plasticity, speed and short-termism grip the imaginations of women and men throughout the digitalized cities of the West who are riding the next wave of innovation. An openness to 'self-fashioning' comes pre-wrapped with ideas on how to 'improve', 'better' and 'remake' every aspect of contemporary living: this applies not only to employment, careers and professional life, but also intimacy, sexuality, diet, health and the body. This tradition of thought is helpful for critically exploring the argument – advanced in many sectors of popular culture, the academy and policy circles – that we must reinvent the idea of "life" itself in a way that reflects the complex interdependencies of the digital universe, and in a way that recognizes the growing importance of forms of technological automation and AI.

Complex digital systems enable social relations across the world which are intricately layered, involving multiple positive and negative feedback loops and characterized by unpredictability. These complex systems support and sustain the reflexivity of both human action and large-scale organizations. However, beyond reflexivity, these complex systems of digitalization, information and communication are also the bases for cultural reinvention and social experimentation. Through the increasingly structured power of digital systems and technological automation, the hold of tradition across societies has progressively less purchase and new patternings of reinvention and experimentation give rise to many new structures, especially of various digital and virtual kinds. To help take account of this, I have previously introduced the terms "reinvention society" and "new individualism", referring to different aspects of experimentalism which cut across social systems recognizably ordered and reordered by huge new digital industries, social media, big data, supercomputers, robotics and more generally the globalization of communication and information technologies. I have elsewhere analyzed how professional and personal lifestyle reinvention becomes globally consequential in driving new patterns of individualism and the advancement of do-it-yourself biographies and life-strategies – all the way from life coaching and speed dating to compulsive consumerism and reality TV to therapy culture and cosmetic surgery. I also want to use these notions extensively later in this book for interpreting how complex digital systems enable and sustain heightened cultural reinvention and social experimentation within the global economy, concentrating especially on the rise of technological automation, robotics and AI.

The influence of globalization, especially the development of global electronic offshoring and outsourcing, has been highly consequential for reconfiguring how people, networks, organizations, and large-scale institutions react to and cope with a post-traditional societal era characterized by reinvention and experimentalism. Reinvention society stems from various complex digital and expert systems that enable the reflexive side effects of contemporary life to be monitored, ordered, tagged, traced and traced, resulting in continual processes of self-reconstruction and self-recalibration. In this connection, recent social theories of reinvention, innovation and experimentation have much to offer research on the conditions and consequences of digital life and technologically automated cultures. Again, consider healthcare as illustrative. The arrival of various digital devices worn directly on the body – many equipped with cameras, sensors and other digital data-generating technologies – has powerfully transformed the capacities of individuals for increased reflexivity. Such digital self-tracking practices – and the wearing of devices aggregating data on fitness, diet, sleep, weight and related wellness tools – are not simply deployed to reflexively monitor the health goals of the individual. Rather, such digital self-tracking is also pressed into the service of ineluctable patterns of reinvention, ranging across career advancement, personal achievement, corporate imperatives and the rest.

In drawing upon these three theoretical approaches – sometimes cross-referencing these constructs, occasionally linking them together – this book seeks to explore the relation between new technology (specifically AI, machine learning and robotics) on the one hand, and the analysis of contemporary society and modern culture on the other. I draw from these theoretical reflections, in a liberal and pragmatic fashion, to develop a better understanding of this relation.[46] The central contours of these theoretical approaches provide a framework within which it is possible to begin to think critically about the emergence and spread of a *culture of artificial intelligence*. By this I mean the general social process by which everyday life and modern institutions become increasingly influenced and shaped by the digitalized and technical apparatuses of AI. Understanding this process is crucial for understanding the world today, a world which is increasingly overlaid by digital networks of communication, AI technical systems, institutionalized automation and advanced robotics.

2

THE RISE OF ROBOTICS

People go to work most usually to earn a living, largely based on some kind of contract with a company, corporation or government agency. Employment has indeed many synonyms capturing different aspects of the relationship between a worker and an employee. Those with negative connotations include "toil", "drudgery", "graft", "grind" and "slog". Those that name more positive aspects of work include "vocation", "craftsmanship", "handiwork", "design", "creation" and "masterpiece". Any account of how these different aspects of work and employment has been changed by technological automation and advanced robotics would be rudimentary. But imagine a tradesperson or office-worker, or indeed professional, who declares, "I've got nothing to worry about, I know my job inside and out, and I am across all aspects of the work". We know that such a worker will struggle to cope with our brave new world of high-tech innovation, endless corporate reengineering, lifelong learning, networked teams and the juggling of multiple projects. We know that any employee focused on attaining such certitude will struggle with work demands to demonstrate flexibility, adaptability and plasticity. But still we might only guess at the degree to which robotics and AI are impacting employment and work in society.

As early as 1930, the British economist John Maynard Keynes predicted that machines will replace workers. In his prophetic

Economic Possibilities for our Grandchildren, Keynes coined the term "technological unemployment", speculating that the power of automated technology would render the worker of tomorrow with at-most a "fifteen-hour workweek".[1] Almost a century later Keynes's prophecy has not eventuated, but still cultural anxiety over the prospects of technological unemployment has been raised to the second power. Will robots destroy jobs? This has become one of the key questions of our times. The fields of advanced robotics and accelerating AI promise not only profound economic disruption, but a technological tsunami at the level of work, employment and unemployment. If you work in a construction job, it is time to think again. New York-based Construction Robotics released in 2017 a robot bricklayer which can place bricks at a rate never seen before. SAM – the Semi-Automated Mason – can lay an astonishing 3,000 bricks a day, which easily outstrips the construction worker's average of 500 bricks. If you work in a shelf-auditing job, it is time to think again. San Francisco-based Simbe Robotics have created a robot, called Tally, which roams shop aisles and warehouses ensuring that goods are stocked, replaced and accurately priced. Tally can operate for 12 hours without recharging and can process autonomous shelf-auditing up to 20,000 stock items with over 95% accuracy. If you work in private security, it is time to think again. Palo Alto-based Cobalt Robotics Inc. have released roving security robots – equipped with 60 sensors, including ultrasound, depth sensors and cameras, as well 360-degree day and night cameras to detect people and objects around them – which provide around the clock monitoring without a break.

This chapter examines how this world of automated work has become embedded in the global economy and some of its major social, economic and political consequences. Robotics impacts employment fields such as healthcare, retail, education, construction and many other employment sectors in the developed world. However, this is an issue not only about jobs and employment but many other processes concerning economic productivity, new business models, retraining and reskilling of the workforce, as well as lifestyle change in society at large. All of these transformations are currently unfolding, some are uneven in their distribution, and many are highly experimental in character. This world of innovative technological automation, and how it reshapes work and everyday life, is what this chapter seeks to explore. In the next section of the chapter I briefly position technological automation within a wider social and historical context.

Technology and automation

Automation has been pivotal to both the advent and advancement of modernity. That element of factory machines which reconstituted the individual worker as "dead labour" is what Karl Marx[2] famously dissected. For Marx, automation is a complex dynamic set in motion by the emergence of modern societies. Marx discerned in capitalism a relentless mechanization of economic, social and political life. Marx's portrayal of modern capitalist society is, from one angle, all about machines and especially the substitution of automation for human labor. Unlike feudalism, which is essentially conservative as a mode of production, capitalism is continually changing, expanding and transforming itself. The massive unleashing of such continuously revolutionizing powers is, for Marx, the unfolding of automation as a process. With ongoing automation, capitalist development brings the substitution of machines for human labor. "To the degree that large industry develops", wrote Marx, "the creation of real wealth comes to depend less on labour time and on the amount of labour employed than on the power of the agencies set in motion during labour time".[3] The automation revolution, said Marx, melts all that is solid, fixed or established into air. Needless to say, in these circumstances of technological revolution, it is the human individual who is turned inside out – rendered a "mere living appendage" to machines on the factory floor. Thus, Marx saw automation technology as an unprecedented challenge for the individual and society. "Labour", Marx wrote, "no longer appears so much to be included within the production process; rather the human being comes to relate more as watchmen and regulator to the production process itself".[4]

Many commentators have underscored the prophetic dimensions of Marx's account of capitalism as substituting machines for human labor.[5] In general terms, commentators have highlighted that Marx dissected the self-destructive dynamic of modern capitalist societies – namely, that the process of automation renders the entire economy less and less labor intensive. But few critics have perhaps sufficiently appreciated the complexities contained in Marx's writings on the process of automation. On the one hand, Marx was deeply despairing of the squandering of human lives – of flesh and blood factory workers – resulting from the automated organization of society. Marx's critique of industrial manufacturing is all about the human tragedy of wasted lives, in which the great majority of women and men are condemned to a life of monotonous, repetitive, dull labor. On the other hand – and this was a key theme of his writings – Marx discerned in automated technology possibilities for the freeing of human creative powers, a kind of exhilarating release of human capacities and the minting of fresh skills into different forms of activity and alternative social formations. Automation is for Marx "the wonderful power of shortening and fructifying human labour". These destructive and liberating aspects of automation, it should be noted, occur simultaneously. Automation technology is for Marx at once liberating and constraining, beneficial and destructive. To paraphrase the Marxist-inspired cultural critic Walter Benjamin, automation is both a process of civilization and a record of barbarism.

The fourth industrial revolution: the sceptics and their critics

Since Marx's diagnosis of the social and economic impacts of the process of automation, much academic and policy writing has focused on how the contemporary world is being reshaped by automated technology as well as the consequences of technological innovation for employment and unemployment.[6] Much of this research concentrates on technological scenarios – and their ensuing impacts upon jobs and unemployment – in the industrial countries. Scenario-based thinking is primarily concerned with future possibilities, and so it is perhaps not surprising that there are many who question the claim that current innovations in robotics and AI are radically eroding employment and the world of work. Indeed, the debate about robotics, work and unemployment has produced a voluminous literature, and there are relatively clear lines of demarcation between those who consider that contemporary robotics is a profoundly revolutionary process, whom I shall call the transformationalists, and those who consider that this thesis is wildly exaggerated and thus occludes key forces reshaping employment and the economy today, whom I shall call the sceptics. The transformationalists credit the robotics revolution with producing a world of comprehensive change. The sceptics, by contrast, largely see the global economy as business-as-usual.

For the sceptics, the mantra of "no significant change" holds good. Robotics may be sweeping through industries and enterprises, but it is not revolutionary. The arrival of supercomputers, intelligent machines, robots and algorithms are undoubtedly impacting upon jobs and the way in which people work today – that much is acknowledged. Indeed, whilst finding much of the excited talk of the robotics revolution overhyped and thus ultimately unsatisfactory, many writers of a sceptical persuasion do acknowledge that robots are going to be able to undertake many routine, repetitive types of jobs. Some sceptics even recognize that certain types of workers are in for a rude awakening as a consequence of the rise of intelligent machines. But the thesis of a revolution in the workplace is strongly rejected. What, ask the sceptics, is "transformational" about robotics? Rather than a transformational economy powered by global robotics, the current world economy, the sceptics argue, remains structured by advances in technology, on the one hand, and adaptation by the labor force, on the other hand. Central to this sceptical interpretation is a conception of workplace change involving the twin forces of workers and machines, people and technology – as workers adapt to, and cope with, emerging patterns of technological innovation. Such an approach involves locating contemporary robotics within broader, long-term patterns of historical change. Just as modernization – and specifically the mechanization of agriculture – did not destroy the economy, neither will robotics. For many sceptics, history underscores that technological innovation creates more jobs than it destroys.[7] For other sceptics, there is an implicit acknowledgment that advancing technology is a key risk to jobs; but that risk is understood as primarily limited to routine, unskilled work. In any event, ever-advancing information technology is said to be generating new jobs, with dispossessed workers finding new opportunities to acquire skills. Such a standpoint thus ties technological innovation and economic productivity firmly together, such that the value of employment is underscored. In short, technology-driven productivity gains produce jobs and wages growth – or, so say the sceptics.[8]

Technology and jobs cut two ways. The awesome terrain of advancing technology can spell disappearing jobs – especially low-paying, low-skill employment. But there are some who say we have underestimated both the scope and depth of new employment opportunities created by digital technologies. This is the standpoint put forward by Geoff Colvin, who entitled his influential book on how technology reshapes employment *Humans Are Underrated: What High Achievers Know That Brilliant Machines Never Will*.[9] Colvin offers a quite sophisticated form of scepticism. He accepts, for example, that advancing technology might, for the first time in history, eliminate jobs faster than it can create new ones. That is to say, he concedes that AI and robotics could reduce total employment rather than increase it. However, he warns of the dangers of constructing a doomsday employment future against the backdrop of current mind-bending innovation stemming from digital technology. Colvin's central premise is that new technology revalues human skills. The skills of women and men for deep human interaction, he contends, will become increasingly valuable as technology evolves. As he writes:

> The skills that will prove most valuable are no longer the technical, classroom-taught, left-brain skills that economic

advances have demanded from workers over the past 300 years. Those skills will remain vitally important, but important isn't the same as valuable. . . . The new high-value skills are instead part of our deepest nature, the abilities that literally define us as humans: sensing the thoughts and feelings of others, working productively in groups, building relationships, solving problems together, expressing ourselves with greater power than logic can ever achieve. These are fundamentally different types of skills than those the economy has valued most highly in the past. And unlike some previous revolutions in what the economy values, this one holds the promise of making our lives not only rewarding financially, but also richer and more satisfying emotionally.[10]

In short, creative skills and emotional intelligence are key for Colvin in the age of smart machines.[11]

Other sceptics take a somewhat different tack, and seek to establish a systematic empirical test for assessing the economic impacts of robotics. Georg Graetz and Guy Michaels, for instance, question hyperbolic claims that robots will replace the large bulk of existing jobs and instead offer an empirical investigation of the economic impact of robotics on employment and productivity.[12] Graetz and Michaels review data on the economic impact of industrial robots across a range of industries in 17 countries between 1993 and 2007. Utilizing data drawn from the International Federation of Robotics and other sources, their analysis discloses that the increased utilization of robots in many industries occurred due to a rapid decline in the cost of robotics. Rapid increases in robot density, they say, have been especially pronounced in chemicals, transport equipment and the metal industries, and particularly prominent in Germany, Italy and Denmark. On whether robotics impact negatively on employment, however, Graetz and Michaels conclude that that data reveals no significant effect of "robot densification" on the aggregate hours worked by employees. Regarding different skill groups, they find some evidence that robots reduce the hours worked by low-skilled and middle-skilled employees, but no change is noted for the hours worked by high-skill employees. Graetz and Michaels go one step further to argue that "unlike ICT (information and communications technology), robots do not polarize the labor market, since their negative effects on the least educated are no smaller than those on the middle-skilled".[13]

Graetz and Michaels put into question claims of growing links between robotics and the increased productivity of national economies or societies. There is no significant effect of robot densification, they say, on the labor share. Against the thesis of the rise of the robots, Graetz and Michaels contend that the influence of robotics on future economic growth is substantial but not transformational. ICT rather than robotics, they suggest, is more likely to be transformative of economy and productivity: "the total value of ICT capital services is at least five times larger than that of robot services".

These findings are significant and revealing. Employment changes going on as a consequence of robotics are uneven and less uniform than some analysts suppose.[14] The conclusion is surely correct, although the data analyzed by Graetz and Michaels is now dated. Robotic automation has become both more generalized and radicalized since 2007. Software bots, socially assistive robots and a host of new digital technologies have come to supplement or even displace earlier generations of industrial robots reviewed in the study by Graetz and Michaels. Whilst robotics has been heavily utilized in several industries over recent decades, especially in the manufacturing and automative sectors, this process has now started to unfold very rapidly in other sectors – from logistics and analytics to the garment industry to fully autonomous shelf-auditing in supermarkets. The crucial point – one neglected by Graetz and Michaels – is that there is a great deal of potential for growth in advanced robotics. Intelligent machines are increasingly performing tasks that were once imagined the unique province of people – for example, the situational deployment of everyday language. Against this backdrop, a key question becomes what happens when AI and robotics can undertake not only mundane and routine jobs, but also the work of professionals and experts? We will return to this point later in the chapter.

So, it has become clear that much of significance in economic, social and cultural life involves technological automation, robotics and AI. Rather than these technological transformations impacting upon the economy only, AI – in both extensity and intensity – is rapidly remaking the coordinates of social, cultural and political life. Enter the transformationalists. Here the argument is very different. A key focus concerns the volatility of employment in the face of advancing technological automation. This volatility arises from an advanced robotics which increasingly revolutionizes employment and the workplace while, at the same time, transfigures the forces of economic globalization, transnational markets, and the intricate connections between society, economy and politics. Transformationalists reject the claim, advanced by sceptics, that robotics fits with, or can be contained by, the existing socio-economic structures of twenty-first century capitalism. Instead of business-as-usual for the global economy, the transformationalist standpoint underscores that robotics is an expression of broader digital shifts in the organization of modern institutions and contemporary society. Such shifts are evident in, among other developments, the growth of AI, wireless communication, supercomputers, 3D printing, the Internet of Things and its networking of ordinary objects with information processors.

One central aspect of this transformationalist standpoint is a conception of social change involving not only employment and the workplace, but also culture and politics in the broadest sense. For the transformationalists, the very organizing principles of social life and global order are radically shifting, thanks to the twin impacts of digital technologies and advanced robotics. Put simply, the robotics revolution is transforming not only *how we work* but also *how we live*. This is a digital transformation of traditional patterns of socio-economic organization, of everyday life, and of power. "Computers", write Erik Brynjolfsson and Andrew McAfee in *The Second Machine Age*, "started diagnosing diseases, listening and speaking to us, and writing high-quality prose, while robots started scurrying around warehouses and driving cars with minimal or no guidance".[15] Breakthrough technologies, digital communication and advanced robotics – according to the transformationalist interpretation – create demands for different kinds of work, different sorts of skills and gives rise to different ways of living from even the very recent past. Beyond this broad consensus, it is possible to identify considerable divergences in the transformationalist position. Many transformationalists are, in one form or another, positive about the payoff of digital technologies. According to these authors, AI promises innovation, robotics promotes productivity, and the digital revolution advances economic growth. But other authors (also transformationalists) reach more negative conclusions regarding long-term economic forecasts and the prospects for social cohesion. A principal concern for these authors is that the robotics revolution – viewed as transformational of society, economy and polity – positions economic growth and social equality as out of alignment. Martin Ford, for example, argues that few, if any, existing occupations will remain untouched by AI.[16] According to Ford, this will in turn generate disruptive ripple effects through, among other things, the higher education sector, healthcare, consumer culture and, most importantly, existing systems of income distribution which throughout the industrial and post-industrial age have been organized around the labor market. I shall consider some of these divergences in the transformationalist position in more detail below.

Another central aspect of this transformationalist standpoint is the attempt to capture the significant shift in the digital and networked dynamics of the new global economy. A dazzling variety of terms have been coined to describe this social and historical transition, including the "fourth industrial revolution", the "second machine age", "AI capitalism", "digital capitalism" and the "bot economy". Some of these contributions concentrate mainly upon digital transformations, with a particular focus on the exponentially disruptive change of new technology as distinguishing the current global economy from that of prior epochs. More commonly, however, these contributions have focused largely on how the core economies in the global system have undergone profound workplace transformation as a result of technological automation and digital disruption. Again, there are significant differences in the interpretations of transformationalists. Some authors refer positively to the emergence of new kinds of jobs – founded on freshly minted digital skills – stemming from the robotics revolution. Others are more cautious, suggesting that the age of AI disguises a confronting reality which requires employees to adapt to new technology but with little chance of success. In general, the sociological argument is that the contemporary epoch inaugurates a shift from hardware to software capitalism, and from postmodernism to post-humanism.

One of the most prominent transformationalists is Klaus Schwab, founder of the World Economic Forum. In his programmatic volume *The Fourth Industrial Revolution*, Schwab argues that we stand at the opening of a new era, in which prior economic, social and organizational processes undergo radical mutation.[17] The new industrial revolution, says Schwab, is one centered on digital disruption, AI, intelligent machines and robotics. The first profound industrial revolution was steam-powered, the second electrical, the third the arrival of the computer age, and Schwab considers the fourth industrial revolution "unlike anything humankind has experienced before". This is substantially due to the speed, breadth and depth of the new technology revolution, and Schwab writes in witheringly high-management style of an era of "exponentially disruptive change". In developing an account of these shifts, Schwab concentrates upon analyzing both the upsides and downsides of new technology. Challenges and opportunities are identified for every sector of society – from economy and business to cities, nations, regions and global governance. AI will bring significant efficiency gains and cost reductions, but result in the massive automation of jobs. Three-dimensional bioprinting will address the global shortage of donated organs, but may give rise to the unregulated production of body parts. Little can be said with confidence regarding the future socio-economic trajectories of the fourth industrial revolution, but Schwab emphasizes the risks and opportunities of these profoundly cross-cutting technological processes. The choice of how we respond to technological innovation is ours, says Schwab. There will be multiple impacts of the new technology revolution on the economy, business, regions and cities, as well as geopolitics and global order. The key question for Schwab is whether societies can adapt to new technology and create a future in which technological innovation is pressed into the service of collective humanity and the enhancement of social cohesion.

It has also become evident that many fresh opportunities (at once economic and social) arise from AI, that these opportunities fuel the imagination of those working in the creative industries, as well as entrepreneurs and policymakers, and that such socio-economic opportunities engender new types of reskilling and retraining at the level of work and employment. This more positive agenda has been described by various authors documenting advanced technological automation characterized by robotics and AI. Brynjolfsson and McAfee's *The Second Machine Age* is often referenced with the transformationalist literature, and indeed the subtitle of the book – *Work, Progress and Prosperity in a Time of Brilliant Technologies* – underscores the optimism of its authors. They advance the claim that the dynamics and rate of technological change – in everything from the rise of machine-to-machine communication and the proliferation of low-cost sensors to driverless cars and the Internet of Things – has reached an "inflection point" where dramatic socio-economic capacities are unleashed. We are in a brave new world of work the authors contend, one in which the growth of economic productivity has become uncoupled from jobs and income.

Few, if any, areas of employment escape the transformational reach of digital technologies. For the most part, the rise of Silicon Valley has been viewed by transformationalists as coterminous not only with the disruption of entire industries, but with the transmutation of work itself. Sandwiched between the forces of globalization and automation, the blue-collar working class – performing largely predictable, routine and repetitive tasks – found their jobs increasingly destroyed by technology and robots. Current research tends to affirm that the job-destroying impact of digital technologies also threatens the middle class and traditional professions. Richard Susskind and Daniel Susskind, in *The Future of the Professions*, contend that new technology is reordering the professions.[18] Contemporary patterns of technological innovation, they say, are enabling intelligent machines and para-professionals to assume many traditional tasks once performed only by professionals. In getting to grips with financial questions, for example, almost 50 million Americans now use online tax preparation software rather than consult an accountant to lodge their tax returns. In law, one of the most celebrated legal brands is not a traditional law firm but an online automated service, legalzoom.com. In healthcare, nurses and healthcare workers – supported by computational diagnostic tools – are undertaking work once the exclusive province of doctors. Susskind and Susskind conclude that digital technology spells "a dismantling of the traditional professions". Increasingly, they argue, complex digital systems will replace the work of traditional professionals, with expertise and professional wisdom entirely encoded into software and operated by either various new groups of para-professionals or fully automated services.

Robotics, therefore, appears largely 'collar blind'. If technological automation has become a generic principle of contemporary societies, however, the thorny issue still remains as to how people will negotiate their partially automated lives. What are the jobs of the future? What kinds of employment will there be? And who will have these jobs? Against the backdrop of advancing information technology, smart machines, robotics and artificial intelligence, the transformationalist argument is that such innovations are a hugely disruptive economic force, threatening to make both unskilled and many skilled jobs obsolete. Jeremy Rifkin offers a powerful analysis of how the technological transformations of our age brings about the "end of work".[19] The communications revolution based in Internet technology, when coupled with developments in artificial intelligence, is a key force, says Rifkin, for understanding the transformation of modern economies. Automated technology, according to Rifkin, is bringing us ever closer to a "near workerless world". The technology revolution – especially the economy of machines – is a very recent phenomenon and inaugurates new risks on a global scale. The disruption of advancing automation technology, 3D printing and robotics could well be massive unemployment and global economic depression. The potential of smart technologies lies in their convergence with lifestyle change and heightened levels of free time for leisure and civil society. Rifkin envisages the technological transformations of our age as creating social capital in the not-for-profit civil society, in which collaborative networking and a new Creative Commons come to the fore.

The debate between transformationalists and sceptics over the digital revolution is not simply one of conflicting interpretations, or contrasting academic arguments and political opinions. Rather, this debate – in addition to the positions taken in academic and public forums – has impacted deeply at the institutional level, inside of enterprises companies and industries.[20] Indeed, organizations have not only had to cope with the AI revolution, reacting to the velocity of technological disruption and the acceleration of digital innovation, but simultaneously had to deal with the power struggles deep inside of organizations regarding the new challenges posed by AI and of whether CEOs, directors and managers inclined towards transformationalist or sceptical standpoints, or perhaps some middle pathway. Is the AI revolution just a passing fad, a brief period of technological hype from which companies and organizations will emerge somewhere on the other side, stronger and more resilient than ever? Or is advanced AI and accelerated automation a watershed moment which altogether threatens established management practices and organizational life? This is where these conflicting arguments and fundamental points of disagreement tip over on the company scale into *micropolitics*, or what Henry Mintzberg has termed the "game of coalition building".[21]

At the particular juncture where business and enterprise finds itself today, responding to the technological upheaval whose consequences are so far-reaching is, in some large part, about the very "coalition building" of how businesses will be led, organized and resourced in the age of AI. Since no "coalition building" can accommodate the complexity of interpretations from transformationalists and sceptics – the sheer mêlée of conflicting voices – and thus clear-cut management policy is unlikely to succeed, ambivalence is destined to pervade the leadership of companies and organizations. Major shifts shaping the policies, procedures and power struggles of the advanced manufacturing companies, especially the automated segments, provides ample illustration of this. BMW's *Connected Drive*, for example, reveals a vision of organizing all mobility, aimed at delivering technically revolutionary innovations in automated driving, intelligent connectivity and fully connected digital life at home.[22] BMW Connected Drive, as a game of coalition building, aspires to position the company as the repository for mobility planning, our movement and machine intelligence, our distances and data. Needless to say, however, the mission to implant AI within our mobile lifestyles is far from the desired image of "building better cars" which informs the "coalition building" of old-school traditionalists at BMW. Such fundamental points of tension, of the struggle of micropolitics, make the game of coalition building only more blurry, differentiated and ambivalent.

Globalization and offshoring

Representing the debate over automated technology and the future of jobs as neatly divided between sceptics and transformationalists is, it should be acknowledged, overly simplistic. To be sure, the conflicting interpretations of sceptics and transformationalists represent fundamental points of disagreement in the literature on robotics and employment, but this basic dualism fails to capture the complexity of specific ideological positions and the intellectual lines of argument of specific authors. As with so many of the technological changes discussed in this book, the debate over robotics and the future of employment has been shaped by a diversity of voices and complex fields of inquiry and, above all, has been surrounded by uncertainties – in large part because robotics and artificial intelligence are advancing rapidly, and because there are multiple possibilities concerning how these developments will transform the global economy as well as society as a whole. That automated technology and advancing information technology have had a dramatic impact on jobs and rising unemployment in certain industries is undeniable, and the more mature debate has instead focused on how these transformations are becoming generalized, resulting in both stunning opportunities but also significant costs for economy and society.

However, it is not only advancing digital technology which has contributed to increased automation and its accompanying transformation of work, unemployment and lifestyle options. Other social and technological changes have also been central. These changes are internally complex, and have been analyzed at length in the scholarly literature. Here I simply identify two contemporary challenges most directly affecting ordinary people's lives as a result of automated technology.

First has been the impacts of globalization. What British sociologist Anthony Giddens has called the "runaway world" of globalization involves a relentless technological acceleration of social, political and economic life.[23] This "speeding up" of social life, according to some analysts, occurred during the last quarter of the twentieth century.[24] Especially consequential in this connection was the positioning of the first telecommunications satellites in geosynchronous orbits during the early 1970s, which ushered into existence the spread of virtually instantaneous electronic communication around the globe. In an age of satellite and digital communications, the spread of globalization reflected a distinctly Western culture and an advanced capitalist world. In the years following 1990, globalization continued its acceleration and there was convincing evidence that economies, finance, politics, governance, communications, media, migration, travel, tourism, family life, friendship, work and employment were less and less structured within nation-states and increasingly organized by the forces of globalism.

The 2000s saw globalization and information technology innovation seamlessly interweave, and the Internet was pivotal to the arrival of what some commentators termed the "new economy".[25] In this brave new world of transnational capital investment, infrastructural corridors, software protocols, multipurpose production, just-in-time deliveries, ceaseless corporate downsizings, algorithmic economic efficiencies and global supply chains, there has been a profound metamorphosis of labor forces in particular and whole societies in general. Many analysts argued, especially in the early 2000s, that globalization would remake the world for the better. Fresh ideas, new business opportunities, greater openness of information and improved international understanding: globalization would herald a truly cosmopolitan ethos. Established ways of doing things would wither, replaced by ever-increasing economic innovation and social experimentation. Such global optimism was, however, short-lived. The terror attack of 11 September 2001 on the Twin Tower of the New York Trade Center represented, significantly, the "dark side" of globalization. Optimism fast shaded off into cultural pessimism. This shift in understanding of the complexities of globalization was subsequently intensified through the global financial crisis of 2008, in which stock markets plummeted, companies announced massive layoffs and overall economic confidence collapsed.[26] Since that time, there has been a dramatic intensification of what some analysts call "deglobalization".[27] The arrival of this new age of isolationism can be discerned in a series of policy reversals and electoral shocks – from Brexit and the withdrawal of the UK from the EU to the resurgence of nationalist sentiment rising across Europe to the election of Donald Trump as President of the USA.

The impacts of globalization spurned a second new societal challenge – the practice of offshoring.[28] Various patterns of offshoring – of jobs, services, data management, surveillance, and environmental obligations – spread across the globe during the

2000s. Offshoring generally involved companies moving jobs electronically to low-wage countries. The backcloth to these developments is to be found in the West's outsourcing of manu-facturing, which radically took off in the 1980s. Such outsourcing of industrial manufacture to cheap labor spots around the globe eventually found its counterpart some decades later in the off-shoring of service-intensive jobs, or what has been termed "global electronic offshoring". Call center workers and information tech-nology professionals in India, for example, competed directly with white-collar workers in the Anglo-American world. Companies including IBM, Accenture, Cisco, Intel and Microsoft offshored many IT processes, realizing significant cost savings. Advances in technology meant that more and more technical, informational and administrative services could be offshored to low-cost labor countries, including the Philippines, Mexico, South Africa, Cen-tral and South America and the East European Countries.

One consequence of offshoring, when viewed in combination with globalization, has been an unprecedented risk to jobs and employment security. Princeton economist Alan Blinder esti-mated in 2009 that 25% of US jobs were at risk of being off-shored to low-wage countries. But which types of jobs were most at risk? At it happens, not just unskilled or semi-skilled work-ers were threatened by practices of offshoring. As the offshoring process unfolded in the early years of the twenty-first century, it became increasingly clear that the highly skilled and the highly educated – those working in finance, legal, medical and hi-tech sectors – were coming under increased competition from over-seas workers. Radiologists, solicitors, computer programmers and information technology specialists all felt the significant impact of offshore workers in countries such as India and China competing for jobs. Among economists it was Princeton aca-demic Gene Grossman who offered the most startling prognosis of the possible consequences of offshoring to the US economy, estimating that 30 to 40 million service jobs were potentially at risk.[29] The societal implications of offshoring, it was increas-ingly evident, ran very deep, and in fact have since become only further intensified (as we shall see) when directly connected to developments in advanced machine automation.

The debate about robotics and the increasing use of automation throughout the developed economies has been consequential for the offshore business model. Reshoring rather than offshoring is said by many analysts to be the result. One of the main flashpoints here was a report published in the US by Gartner Inc, entitled "The Rise of the Machine leads to Obsolescence of Offshoring for Competitive Advantage". The report argues that automation and smart machine technologies erode the competitive advantage of offshoring. This opens the pathway for a reshoring of manufacturing production, as well as much economic activity in some service sectors. The combination of robotics, AI, 3D printing and smart technologies spells a crisis for the offshore business model, bringing undone the idea that productivity and humans are synonymous. The report highlights that many manufacturers have brought their facilities back to the US. One key indicator here is that, whilst the US lost 8 million manufacturing jobs between 1998 and 2009, it has regained about 2 million of these jobs since that period. Robotics and automation manufacturing processes have been a major reason for this reversal. Indeed Jeff Immelt, the chief executive of General Electric, has described offshoring as "yesterday's model".

How valid are such arguments? The situation is undoubtedly more complex than reshoring simply replacing offshoring. Technological innovation will very likely continue to open new paths into the global economy, and continue to spawn uneven reversals and countertrends such as Brexit in the UK, Trumpism in the US and the rise of right wing populism in Europe. Some recent research confirms that, whilst robotics and automation spells major change for the traditional offshore model, there are few signs of the collapse of offshoring. There are various interconnecting reasons for this. For one thing, offshoring is not an isolated phenomenon. As economist Frances Karamouzis notes, "clients never said I am going to go off shore for a project, and 100% of it was done in India or Brazil". Companies instead focus strategically on identifying the "best shore" for the production of goods and services. This often means a mix of onshore, offshore or nearshore locations for manufacture, production and the delivery of services. Similarly, in the same way that offshoring is not discrete, nor is it uniform. Digitization facilitates a mixing of shores and dispersal of supply chains that had previously been bundled together in one economic location, splitting up the process into dozens or sometimes hundreds of stages. Thus, the increasing regionalization of economies – where production processes are broken up into discrete pieces and specialized tasks – is likely to develop further impetus as a result of the present-day combination of technology, innovation and politics.

If offshoring refers to not just global market outsourcing but also a global technological integration, then a sophisticated understanding of the next phase of global offshoring needs to be concerned with the power of remote intelligence, telepresence and digital technology. Digital technologies are unlikely to displace, or stand-in for, economic processes of offshoring, but they can and do foster an altogether different level of dynamism in the mixing together of labor, goods, products and services which cross national borders. Richard Baldwin has written one of the best studies of the coming transformation of manufacture and services as a result of new technology and its deployment in offshore business models. In *The Great Convergence: Information Technology and the New Globalization*, Baldwin argues that advances in computing power and digital technology are radically changing how people work in a world of large international differences in wages and salaries.[30] If earlier phases of globalization concerned largely the movement of goods, with the advent of the steamship and railways facilitating the transportation of physical goods, then more recent advances in globalization refer to shifts in the movement of ideas, communications, networks and people across borders. In particular, digital technology revolutionizes traditional understandings that employment requires the physical presence of employees in the workplace.

This is where robots and technological automation enter into the picture, because, according to Baldwin, digital technology undoes traditional constraints on human movement. The coming of robotics in digital technology, says Baldwin, makes it economical for an increasing number of people to work across borders. Crucially, firms can make use of telerobotic technology which overcomes the requirement for physical presence in many jobs. As Baldwin says: "Soon, a worker in, say, Peru will be able to clean a hotel room in Manhattan without actually being there". Baldwin calls this development "globalization's third unbundling" – where labor services are uncoupled from work locations and instead work is delivered globally. International wage competition is highly consequential in this respect. As Baldwin develops this point:

> A hotel cleaner in Britain, for instance, earns about $2,250 per month while a worker performing the same job in India earns about $300 per month. Using an Indian worker to "drive" a robot in London would save the hotel around $23,000 per year. While it is not cost effective today (one of the most advanced robots, the HRP-4 from Kawada Industries, costs around $300,000), robot prices have fallen rapidly since 1990 and the trend looks set to continue. Once robots get cheap enough, the manual services jobs of many in the U.S. will be in direct competition with workers living in low-wage nations. Robots are unlikely to completely replace in-person workers, but they could certainly be used for a huge number of tasks – from cleaners and gardeners to road workers and factory workers. Language, moreover, will no longer be a barrier. Information technology is already melting the language barrier.[31]

Of central significance here is that robotics and offshoring intersect. Contrary to the claim that the age of robotics threatens obsolescence for offshore business models, Baldwin sees these developments as deeply interwoven. With robotics, telepresence and related digital technologies, employment emerges as something which is managed from afar.[32] The arrival of employment at-a-distance is part and parcel of a world of remote-control robots and intensive digitalization.

Robotics and jobs: where we stand

On the basis of the foregoing discussion, it should be plain that robotics and AI intersect with processes of globalization and offshoring in cross-cutting ways. There are two senses in which such a convergence is especially relevant to this chapter. The first concerns how many jobs robots will destroy, and whether technological innovation will create new jobs of scale and on a global level. The second, equally pressing, concerns the types of digital, emotional and social skills which advances in robotics and AI foster. I refer to these two dilemmas, spawned by recent technological innovation, as the *future of jobs* and the *future of talent*. In the remainder of this chapter, I shall briefly sketch out some of the current and future trajectories relating to how robotics impacts jobs and talent.

The debate about robotics on the future economy and job market is one divided squarely between transformationalists and sceptics, but that debate has in fact been increasingly undermined by the dynamics of AI and its relentless acceleration. Recent evidence indicates that robotics and AI are heavily impacting the economy, destroying low-wage jobs and increasingly eating away at higher-skill occupations as people are increasingly replaced by intelligent algorithms. There is evidence that the workplace of tomorrow, powered by AI and accelerating digital technology, is about to arrive much sooner than anticipated by many analysts. A 2017 report from the World Economic Forum estimates the net loss of over 5 million jobs across 15 developed countries by 2020.[33] Another report, published by the International Labor Organization, predicts that over 137 million workers in the Philippines, Thailand, Vietnam, Indonesia and Cambodia are likely to be replaced by robots in the near future.[34] Moreover, as this tipping point in robotic job deployment is reached, advancing technology is driving many developed economies towards higher inequality. The global digital economy is generating more monopolies and resulting in greater income gaps between rich and poor, with many workers ending up unemployed and many highly skilled professionals increasing their wealth.[35]

Does the exceptional scale of economic and social practices associated with the digital revolution indicate the rise and rise of AI, or does it show that we have seen nothing yet in terms of the revolutionary transformation that is the army of robots and other smart machines now on the horizon? Is advanced robotics an irreversible system change? The recent evidence of massive worldwide job losses to robots is in keeping with the discontinuist interpretation of modern history which I am proposing in this book.[36] That is to say, the culture of AI, advanced robotics and accelerating automation does entail high job losses and radical employment shifts, and such changes are confined to relatively recent times. That being said, it is important to grasp the historical dimensions of social development which underlie the progressive displacement of workers by mechanization and machines. Columbia University economist Jeffrey Sachs has explored the stunning historical impact of machines in reducing the overall burden of work, and also their adverse distributional consequences on wealth. Drawing on US census data, Sachs notes that, whilst agricultural workers comprised 36% of the American labor force in 1900, they made up less than 1% of the labor market in 2015. There has also been a sharp decline in the numbers of production workers (those working in mining, construction and manufacturing), from 24% in 1900 to 14% in 2015 of the US labor force. For Sachs, mechanization and machines lie at the core of the global shift from rural to urban life. "Machines", writes Sachs, "have dramatically eased the toil of most Americans and extended our lives, in stark contrast to the hard, long toil and lower life expectancies that continue for hundreds of millions of people around the world who are still trapped in subsistence agriculture".[37] Sachs argues that there is a clear disconnect between ongoing labor productivity growth and wages, which is leading to a decline in the share of labor in national income, and one principal reason for this is the displacement of workers by robots and smart machines. Workers most impacted by the astonishing growth in automation, according to Sachs, are those in jobs which are repetitive, predictable, and requiring only low to moderate levels of expertise. Specifically, jobs in agriculture, mining, construction, and manufacturing, as well as basic services (utilities, wholesale trade, retail trade, transport and warehousing) have been hardest hit.[38]

But automation as a system should not be held to involve the progressive displacement of employment *in toto*. Sceptics have been quick to caution that robots cannot (at least as yet) reprogram or service their own operations. This point is often made by sceptics to underscore that technological innovation creates new, high-skilled jobs. The argument is that robotic automation, in fact, generates job creation for technicians, computer programmers and other newly generated digital workers. But the evidence for this claim looks increasingly brittle. Ford convincingly shows that the US economy, for instance, has become progressively less effective at creating new jobs. This is largely because disruptive technological shifts are driving people out of the labor force. Most significantly, recent evidence demonstrates that every new robot entering the workplace leads to at least six job losses. A report from the National Bureau of Economic Research, by economists Daron Acemogh of MIT and Pascual Restrepo of Boston University, argues that the "productivity effect" of robotics is significantly outweighed by its "displacement effect", whereby robots eliminate jobs.[39] According to this data, the use of every industrial robot led to an average loss of 6.2 jobs. For the period 1990 through 2007, Acemogh and Restrepo find "large and robust negative effects of robots on employment and wages across commuting zones".

So, are massive layoffs and entrenched unemployment the way of the future as intelligent algorithms increasingly appear on the workplace frontier? Many argue so. But supercomputers, big data, automated technology and advanced robotics can already perform many different kinds of jobs. We must acknowledge that robots are already displacing and replacing jobs, however important the debate over digital upscaling and educational retraining might be. To date, the most profound disruptions have been in the automotive and manufacturing sectors. But again the evidence is that, as a result of the acceleration of technological innovation and its spin-offs, other employment sectors are undergoing profound change because of robotics and AI. Developments in sensor technologies, automated motion control and AI are resulting in a powerfully advanced class of robots aimed primarily at consumer markets and the service sector.

The vision of a jobless future, and social futures more generally in which robots "unpeople" societies, is today far more commonplace than some years ago. One reason is that, in current economic circumstances, sophisticated machines are fast outpacing jobs and the large bulk of data indicates that AI will continue to substitute jobs with technological automation. Another is that public opinion largely sides with the notion of robots replacing people rather than augmenting skills and thus facilitating people to do things which they could not otherwise do. In other words, AI erodes rather than bolsters talent. A third reason, perhaps the most significant, is what I have called the illusion of new individualism.[40] In the era of AI and pervasive digital technologies, jobs have become increasingly changeable and multifaceted. The consequences for employees are that new jobs require different skills from those required in the recent past, and many average workers engaged in routine, predictable forms of employment do not have those skills. As a result, many economists, policy think-tanks and politicians have called for improving education (especially the development and deepening of digital literacy) and retraining opportunities.[41]

In this new individualist scenario, workers of the future will be highly adaptable, endlessly pliable, effortlessly juggling both technological and social demands, and continually keeping up-to-date with new digital skills. A faith in self-fashioning, reinvention, reflexivity, the power of lifelong learning – all this, whilst undoubtedly in tune with the ecosystems of Industry 4.0 and global digital transformations, also denotes a distinctively

Western culture of individualism and the ethos of advanced globalization. This is an activist account of human skills, in which the singular individual undertakes a kind of relentless self-fashioning new individualism in order to update their talent for jobs of the moment. However, the truth, at least for millions of average workers around the globe, is that technology often results in a significant deskilling effect. The automation of many lower-skilled jobs has not necessarily produced more opportunities for advancing education levels or retraining, and recent evidence indicates that the idea of continuous retraining is optimistic at best.[42]

3

DIGITAL LIFE AND THE SELF

In October 2012, a teenage girl entered St Pancreas station in London, waited at a platform and fell under an approaching train. In the lead up to her tragic death, the girl – a talented ballet dancer – had become increasingly preoccupied with the Internet and especially social media; she had withdrawn from contact with others at home and at school into an online world. In particular, the girl had been more and more obsessed with blogs where teenagers shared images of self-inflicted injuries. Her death received widespread newspaper coverage in many countries across Europe and elsewhere. The mother of the girl, speaking at a press conference, commented that our "toxic digital world" had directly contributed to her daughter's death.[1] A tragic, but isolated, case? One might be forgiven for thinking so. However, a small, but growing, number of young people have died in mysterious circumstances in the face of compulsive addictions to the Internet, with many of these deaths linked to claims of suicide in various media headlines. This is, of course, all a far cry from the enrichment of the self of which many analysts of the Internet speak. Critics recognize the centrality of digital technologies in the transformation of society but believe that many tech enthusiasts underestimate the scale of emotional changes taking place and of associated pathologies of the self.

The compulsive addiction to the Internet to which many people have fallen prey thus represents, from one angle, a loss of the symbolic boundary between the worlds of fantasy and reality.

Contrast this with the European Commission's *Digital Agenda for Europe*.[2] In the EC's Communication "European Strategy for a Better Internet for Children", data is reviewed which highlights that 75% of children use the Internet; as well as providing opportunities for work, study, leisure activities and mediated social interaction, the EC underscores that time spent online is essential for young people to develop the digital skills required of competent citizens in the digital age. Based on a partnership between the EU and mobile phone operators, Internet providers and social networking services, the Commission's *Digital Agenda for Europe* seeks to stimulate the production of interactive, creative and educational content online while simultaneously raising awareness of cyber-risks and teaching online safety in all EU schools. Online risks such as cyber-bullying and sexual abuse material are strongly underscored by the Commission. But the importance of social, technical skills online is central to the EU member states, in a world where the global digital content market has outstripped £100 billion annually. Against this backdrop, the Internet and related digital technologies are seen as enabling individuals to tap into a rich world of new opportunities to be creative and to participate in the wider society.

Comparing these foregoing developments, we can find a familiar opposition – between threat on the one side, and opportunity on the other – which shapes the public debate over digital technologies. This is an opposition which places digital technologies at the center of formations of the self, but also locates the digital world as constantly slipping out of control. In this chapter, I shall argue that special providence must be given to digital technologies for understanding the constitution of self, identity and everyday life. Digital technologies involve, among other things, intimate communications, shared ideas and the making of identities. The sphere of digitalization is the platform for our living in a world of others. But the arrival of the digital self cannot be adequately understood in terms of the boundaries between online and actual worlds. Digital technologies and AI innovations are transforming what self-formation and self-experience actually mean.[3] My conjecture is that an account of the digitalization of self has to be developed in terms of a broader picture of the psychological make-up of the individual in the contemporary age.

The self as information system

It is perhaps easy enough to see why technological innovation presents self-identity with a problem. If self-identity is partly built out of interaction with the wider world, technology might be said to go all the way down into the very fabric of lived experience and personal life.[4] On this view, identity transforms as technological innovation unfolds. The more that technology ramps up throughout society, the more the individual self is recast in the image of the digital. But a truly responsive identity is not one in which people function as pre-programmed in their subjective responses; it is rather one in which every person adapts, adjusts, responds to and seeks to cope with the massive technological changes currently sweeping modern societies. If digital technologies are intricately intertwined with how our identities function, these interconnections are remarkably complex and encompass online identities, augmented selves, virtual subjectivities, and indeed automated and robotic forms of identity-reconstruction. Digital technologies are not therefore merely an 'out-there' phenomenon – to do only with infrastructures, networks or platforms. This is not to deny the growing pervasiveness of industrial robots on factory floors, service robots within our homes, or the Wi-Fi networks which invisibly surround us and facilitate our devices across the wireless, digital world. But such technologies are never only a matter of computer systems, artificial intelligence or wireless devices. Digital technologies are also experienced by those interacting with them in the most intimately personal ways. What is of central importance in this connection is what I term the "human element of digital technologies".

Whilst it is crucial to look at the consequences of digital technologies, robotics and artificial intelligence in terms of the global economy, employment and unemployment, it is also vital to look at its implication in terms of the self and social relations. Accordingly, in this chapter I shall develop an account of self-identity as deeply imbricated with digital technologies. The approach I develop is largely indebted to psychoanalytic theory, although in what follows I propose a selective use of psychoanalytic ideas in order to reposition digital technologies. Freud, the founder of psychoanalysis and inventor of the concept of the repressed unconscious, wrote of how the remorselessly, pleasure-seeking self comes to adapt to social reality, a world of rivalry and rebellion, of conflict and cooperation, and above all where women and men struggle with human frustration. Selfhood in this view cannot escape frustration, the struggle to secure internal satisfactions but also the struggle to deal with other people as oftentimes frustrating.[5] The heart of the matter for Freud is that humans are doubly frustrated: there is the frustration of need, emotional life and desire on the one hand, but there is also on the other hand the frustration of dealing with the external world of others and objects, a world which is often at odds with our wished-for lives. According to Freud, what allows women and men to cope with frustration – what makes frustration bearable – is the ability to think. Freud may have posited an anarchic, aggressive, sadistic and relentlessly pleasure-seeking unconscious at the core of our psychical lives, but he also hypothesized that our capacity to figure out, to think about and to communicate our frustrations is what shifts the individual self from the internal world of fantasy to contact with the shared world of reality. Freud called this exploration of frustration by understanding "trial action in thought".

This is where other people and the wider world come in to the psychoanalytic picture. The capacity to tolerate our frustrations – to think them through, figure them out, and communicate them – depends largely on our relations with others. In Freud and much subsequent psychoanalysis, the picture of self-identity which emerges is of individuals obtaining relief from frustration through immersion in self-other experiences. It is only by constructing each other, and creating both self and other as we communicate, that we are able to feel – and, crucially, to think about – our frustrations. The British psychoanalyst D. W. Winnicott invented the notion of transitional relations and coined the term "potential space" to capture how people project themselves into others in order to make frustration bearable.[6] We will look at some of these psychoanalytic ideas in a little more detail later in this chapter when considering their relevance to digital technologies, but the key idea here is that we become ourselves while being with others through projecting parts of our identities onto others while simultaneously drawing from them or borrowing parts of others in order to author ourselves. In this account, parts of the self are continuously being projected outwards, or introjected inwards, and such psychic mechanisms lie at the core of the individual subject's relation to other people and the external world. We are all the unconscious architects of self and other constructions, which are built upon "projective identifications" as well as "introjective identifications" with others in the interpersonal organization of space and time.

Psychoanalysis, both classical and contemporary, has not said much on the question of technology and its cultural consequences.[7] But the ideas are there, from which those with the mind to do so can develop a critical appropriation of psychoanalytic ideas to examine digital technologies in depth. If the cultural impact of digital technology is to be made real then it is necessary to see that they take hold in social relationships – reorganizing and redistributing *emotional connections between people*. If we extend and rethink the core premises of the psychoanalytic conceptualization of the self, then it can be seen that the development of the digital revolution has had a profound impact upon processes of identity-formation. Of central importance in this connection is the large-scale shift from face-to-face interaction to digitally mediated interaction, which has been ushered into existence by new technologies. In many ways, psychoanalysis documents the complex ways frustration or anxiety enables certain forms of emotional and personal relationships. But in the classical psychoanalytic tradition, this involves the development of mature emotional relationships (where depressive feelings can be tolerated to think about frustration), built upon face-to-face interactions through which individuals interact with each other. Today things look markedly different. The formulation of anxiety in social organization still leads back to the relation between the self and its surrounding environment, but this is a transformed relationship once we have reckoned into account the kind of digital connections which are now generalized, particularly at the level of the global electronic economy.

In the twenty-first century, self-identity has come to mean, among other things, social networking, status updates, posts, blogs, virtual reality apps, AI cognitive architectures, cloud computing, big data and digital media. Robotics and AI have spread throughout social life, reorganizing the dynamics of identity and the self. Indeed, new cultural ideas of the self – of how to be ourselves in a world of others – have sprung up in a global economy in which digital technologies have become more and more important. What is the significance of psychoanalysis to these new cultural ideas of selfhood? Is it that psychoanalysis engages a whole sensibility for thinking through our frustrations – figuring them out, reflecting on them, communicating them – in a world which has undergone stunning technological metamorphosis? Certainly there are analysts of the current age who believe that digital technologies have brought psychoanalysis into everyday life – as we will see in this chapter. My argument is that psychoanalysis is insightful for understanding digital technologies because it reveals the self as an information processing system of sorts. Much like a computer, the self disseminates, displaces, synthesizes and recalibrates our fundamental pleasures and frustrations – the energetic passions of the unconscious, the moralistic inflictions of the superego, the misrecognitions of the ego – in order to think the world and to author ourselves. In a world of wireless technologies, digital communications, robotics and AI, we must learn to construct our lives as portable selves, moving across society (online and offline) as if the self is an information processor. Or, better, the self might be recast as a kind of information processor, one capable of expressing various degrees of emotional literacy. In this age of smart machines, the key psychoanalytic question is not so much how do we connect but what does it mean for the self when we connect?

Turkle: narcissism and the new solitude

The foregoing discussion suggests that self-development in the contemporary world occurs under conditions of ever-increasing digital mediation and technological frameworks. Displaced more and more from traditional forms of face-to-face social interaction, the self in modern society is the product of simulation, social networks, connectivity, online gaming and machine intelligence. Is it any wonder that in such circumstances there may come to be new burdens which are emotionally debilitating – isolation, social disconnection and anxiety about intimacy – as digital technologies ramp up? Does this brave new world of supercomputers, robotics and AI represent a pathological retreat of the self in the face of an all- enveloping digital revolution? Some prominent authors have argued so, and given the importance of their views I want to turn now to consider these arguments in more detail. In particular, I want to use the idea that 'more technology means greater emotional solitude' as a foil against which to clarify my own arguments about new constructions of the self promoted by digital transformations.

The theme of technology in relation to the breeding of a new solitude has been most comprehensively developed by Sherry Turkle. In her book *Alone Together*, Turkle specifically relates the rise of digital technologies to the decay of our emotional lives.[8] The title of the book says it all: technology reshapes the emotional landscape of the self, promoting the illusion of connectedness through Facebook friends, Twitter tweets and robotic pets. But this brave new world of digital connectivity is above all illusory, says Turkle. New technologies have become such a core aspect of day-to-day social life that no one any longer thinks about the paradox of sharing intimacies through mobile devices in public spaces while remaining unconcerned about whether other people around us can hear the details of our conversations. "Our new devices", writes Turkle, "provide space for the emergence of a new stage of the self, split between the screen and the physical real, wired into existence through technology".[9] Against this backdrop, people search for emotional satisfaction, living their lives largely on the screen. Technology provides us with ever-expanding social connections and makes us busier than ever, but leaves us emotionally drained. For Turkle, people are now connected 24/7, but increasingly disconnected from themselves and unsure of how to make authentic communication with others.

In previous writings, Turkle had elaborated a very different position on simulated life. In an earlier work, *Life on the Screen*, Turkle developed a positive appraisal of new opportunities for exploring life online.[10] This appraisal occurred during the roaring 1990s, when social affluence was high and the speed of a fully networked life unfolded as people plugged into the web via Netscape, Mosaic or Internet Explorer. Questioning mainstream cultural anxiety about the corrosive consequences of mass media, Turkle saw the networked world as heralding more liberating possibilities. Her central focus was Internet relay chat rooms and reconstructions of the self in terms of sexuality, gender and intimacy; she studied how such evolving technologies facilitated self-exploration and self-reconstruction. 'Netsex', as it was then referred to, offered a kind of postmodernist world in which "anything goes". People could change their sexual orientations, gender, personality, race, ethnicity, social status – and all at the click of a mouse. Cybersex for Turkle was fragmenting and episodic, yet also potentially freeing. The simulated self, Turkle concluded, is one of experimentation, where alternative identities and possible imaginaries come to the fore.

Between *Life on the Screen* and *Alone Together*, Turkle became increasingly troubled by pathologies of the simulated self. The increasing intrusion of digital technology into the emotional organization of the self became her key theme, especially its impact on those young 'digital natives' growing up surrounded by mobile devices and robotic toys with strong demands for attention and response. Turkle is a psychoanalytically trained psychologist, and the focus of her later work is on how the individual incorporates digitally mediated interaction into the emotional fabric of self-identity. To do this, she provided children with technological gadgets – ranging from robot toys such as Tamagotchis and Furbies to more complex robots such as Cog and Kismet – and asked them to keep diaries. Her concern was to fathom what she calls the "inner history of technology",[11] and her clinical studies address the changed contours of affect and anxiety in the digital age.

The arrival of robotics, with its engineered relationality and pre-programmed demands for response, represents a decisive turning point in the emotional depletion of the self. By opening up the self to new forms of digital technology, says Turkle, the individual comes to emotionally relate to, and emotionally connect with, such technical objects. Here Turkle contrasts the child's play of using traditional dolls, such as a Barbie doll or teddy bear, with the play of children with robotic pets such as Furbies and Tamagotchis. Traditional forms of childhood play involve the individual animating the toy – investing the object with imagination – in order to establish an emotional relationship. By contrast, robotic toys are presented to children as already animated – as if full of intentions of their own. As one of Turkle's interviewees puts it: "The Furby tells you what it wants".[12] The marching orders spoken by robotic toys to children dramatize emotional needs and inner lives. For Turkle, the robot is deemed sociable, relational and affective. Far from enriching the self, however, these primary transactions between self and robot introduce an alienated quality into contemporary social life.

Critical remarks

So far I have been concerned to outline the views of Turkle on the ways in which the development of digital technologies and robotics reorganizes the self. For the most part, Turkle's late work emphasizes the depletion of self in the face of the digital revolution. The picture painted by Turkle is one of a world in which we find ourselves "alone together", the self defensively rounded back upon itself and separated off from the wider world. But there is another side to all this: the enrichment and accentuated complexity of the self, on which Turkle is largely silent. In what follows, I will draw out these limitations by developing my critical observations around the following themes: (1) the complexity of individual responses to digital technologies and robotics; (2) differences in generational responses to the digital world; and (3) the transitional dynamic of psychological engagement heralded by digital technologies.

(1) The notion that digital technologies impoverish the self has been considerably advanced and much debated over recent years.[13] A range of social pathologies have been proposed in this connection, ranging from the growth of attention deficit disorders in early adolescence through to the spread of new workplace accidents as a result of digital multitasking. I do not intend to trace out these debates here, but will concentrate only on one aspect of them relating directly to Turkle's theme of an all-encompassing dynamic of today's digital attentional ecology. Turkle writes of a new kind of pragmatism, one which defines our psychological culture. This is a pragmatic sensibility towards digital objects – sociable robots, computational games – recast in the image of ourselves. Digital and robotic interactions introduce new emotional demands into our lives, and for Turkle we are consequently "open to the idea of the biological as mechanical and the mechanical as biological".[14] Robots and digital objects ask us to feel for them and connect with them, and we respond "as if" objects of the digital world were, in fact, human.

This standpoint, I shall claim, is inadequate. I have tried to demonstrate elsewhere that a pragmatic conception of digital technology needs to encompass the ways in which the digital demands our attention and our affective sympathies, but equally that this is not a homogeneous or machine-like process of engagement.[15] In Turkle's writings, the individual appears largely passive in relation to the digital world, internalizing demands for immediate emotional response and privileging the digital context. However, it is important to emphasize the contextual settings of technology. That is to say, it is crucial to grasp how digital materials are taken up, appropriated and responded to by individuals; it is crucial to understand that people will respond in very different ways as they encounter new digital experiences, and importantly that their responses will change over time as they find new ways of responding to, and coping with, the opportunities and challenges of digital life.[16] What is required is a focus on how people draw from, and engage with, the symbolic materials of digital technologies in order to reconstruct narratives of their lives and to reinvent versions of identity – of who we are and of where our lives are going. In sum, we need, among other things, to be attentive, as social analysts, to the opportunities and demands of digital life from the perspective of human agents.

Turkle sees a new psychology of engagement with machines as dominating social life today. There is undoubtedly some plausibility to this view. Watch people on any train, or observe people in public space at the shopping mall, and the utter centrality of the digital revolution to how people lead their everyday lives is all too apparent. But the ways in which individuals are confronted by digital technologies today is not a one-way, overwhelming or debilitating process. The self may become increasingly enmeshed in digital and artificial intelligence constructs, but human agents do not blindly follow, incorporate or act upon digitally mediated symbolic forms. Life today is not so much captured as constructed through the digital.[17] Individuals more or less continuously shift between actual, digital and robotic environments, and in so doing reflect upon their actions and activities in the light of the opportunities and risks contained within the settings.

(2) The growth of digital technologies and sociable robots may not only constrain the capacity for personal engagement and social response, according to Turkle; it can profoundly eat

away at the interactive bases of self-formation in childhood. On this view, the spread of sociable robots and digital objects which demand immediate engagement and instant response diverts individuals from genuine communication with significant others, and indeed threatens to warp the self in a profoundly emotional way. Children may be particularly vulnerable in the face of today's digital demands because, according to Turkle, the process of traditional socialization has been short-circuited. "Children", she writes, "need to be with other people to develop mutuality and empathy: interacting with a robot cannot teach these. Adults who have already learned to deal fluidly and easily with others and who choose to 'relax' with less demanding forms of social 'life' are less at risk".[18] Against this backdrop, the function of the digital is revealed to reduce the enigmas of emotional reciprocity to regulated behavioral response.

The absorption of the self in digital objects and artificial intelligence does not necessarily involve the erasure of our capacities for interpersonal engagement and emotional reciprocity, however. Turkle's conception of digital disruption to the self turns on a number of distinctions – between adulthood and childhood, virtual and the real, mutuality and individualism, mature empathy and narcissistic self-enclosure – which for the most part fail to address the enormous multiplicity and stunning variety of social identities which mix together fabrics drawn from the interpersonal and cultural, the digital and virtual, robotics and artificial intelligence. Recent research has highlighted that it is not enough to look at differences between adults and children; it is also essential to investigate the differentiated usage patterns among the digitally connected too.[19] Some analysts argue that social identities today are less characterized by 'isolation' and more by 'connectivity' – with the digital providing the glue to bridge virtual and actual social relations and extending possibilities for interpersonal engagement and empathic social relations. Barry Wellman speaks of "networked individualism".[20] How this impacts upon this digitalization of the self – in both childhood and maturity – is complex. Some analysts, *contra* Turkle, have spoken of a merging or blurring of childhood and adulthood; the recent debate indicates that, at a minimum, it is necessary to look at the relationship of digital skills and online abilities which, in turn, likely influence how people use the digital universe to organize and reorganize their wider social relationships.

Debate over the characteristics of digital generations illustrates these complexities well. Turkle's argument assumes that young people are innately savvy with communication and digital technologies. This is a line of argumentation which has been previously explored in various studies, from the early work of Tapscott on the "Net generation"[21] to Prensky's thesis of the birth of "digital natives" (and contrasted to the previous generation labelled "digital immigrants").[22] Such sharp generational juxtapositions, however, have been questioned by more recent empirical investigations.[23] These research findings reveal that the notion of "digital natives" tends to occlude or mystify the learning process intrinsic to the acquisition and development of digital skills which is undertaken by children (as well as adults arising from the use of digital technologies). More than this, however, it is important to see that these changes going on today are uneven and subject to complex socio-economic distributions because of numerous cultural, social and economic forces which impact upon how people incorporate digital technologies into their everyday lives.[24] Again, recent studies have questioned the value of contrasting younger and older generations in terms of digital skills; the picture which emerges highlights instead the importance of factors such as socio-economic stratification, race/ethnicity and gender for the development and deepening of digital skills and diversity of digital networks.[25] Whilst it is true that Turkle does not write of "digital natives", her argument nonetheless defines the characteristics of digital generations in an overly simplistic fashion.

And so we come back to Turkle's major theme that digital technologies are especially corrosive for the minds of young children. There are serious problems with Turkle's argument in this connection, not least because she seeks to infer what the consequences of digital technology and AI use are likely to be for children without adequately addressing questions concerning the reception, interpretation and appropriation of digital media and technological worlds. Since the publication of *Alone Together*, this issue has received considerable attention in the popular media and wider public debate. An important reference point is Baroness Susan Greenfield's *Mind Change*, which advanced the conjecture that intense use of digital technologies can damage the adolescent brain.[26] The heavy use of digital technologies from computer games to social networking, according to Greenfield, can result in adolescent behavioral problems including short attention span, impulsiveness and aggression. Greenfield is a world leading neuroscientist and, although she has sought to trace links between Internet use and triggers for autism and other harmful effects on the brain, her claim that excessive use of digital technologies can be harmful to children corresponds to certain threads in Turkle's work.

In this context, it is perhaps worth noting a much-discussed critique of Greenfield's research, which details that the thesis of digital technologies as damaging the minds of young children is not supported by scientific evidence.[27] This critique highlights that, *contra* Greenfield, digital technologies such as social networking sites can enhance the social skills of adolescents and benefit the quality of their social relationships (both online and offline). I shall not examine the pros and cons of these particular claims here. I want instead to note the diversity of interpretations of how digital technologies shape the self, and to focus on the related point that it is difficult to understand why Turkle ascribes negative consequences to children's use of digital technologies but holds that adults remain protected or immune from the impacts of social-digital transformation. Apart from failing to engage with an extensive literature documenting the benefits of new technology for boosting learning in young children – such as the use of tablets and computers in classrooms and the home – this perspective appears somewhat nostalgic: it sees the psychic structure of adults, fabricated upon traditional forms of face-to-face interaction, as a form of emotional protection in the face of today's high-speed, technologically mediated social interaction. This is, at best, a questionable assumption.

(3) Let us consider a final respect in which digital technologies impact upon the process of self-formation and self-reconstruction. On an emotional plane, according to Turkle's central thesis, the arrival of digital technologies heralds a new solitude. Digital technologies and robotics demand from individuals "a new psychology of engagement",[28] one beyond the psychology of projection; on the other hand, these very same technologies promote a reduction in the emotional complexity of individuals and the accentuation of narcissistic ego defenses. Turkle invokes the work of self-psychologist Heinz Kohut, specifically his concept of "selfobjects". The construction of selfobjects for Kohut permits the bridging of inner world and external reality, and is somewhat akin to Winnicott's notion of transitional objects.[29] But when there is a breakdown of the self in relationship to selfobjects, severe narcissism is likely to predominate and other people are in turn experienced as mere 'things' or a 'part of one's self'. Taking her cue from Kohut, Turkle writes: "when people turn other people into selfobjects, they are trying to turn a person into a kind of spare part. A robot is already a spare part".[30] Hence, the narcissistic reduction of the self in forms of interaction with sociable robots and digital objects. This reduction of self, according to Turkle, is especially discernible in children's play with sociable robots where "interacting with something" substitutes for the complexity of true companionships – and all the ambiguity, pleasure and disappointment that human relationships entail. For Turkle, the child's play with sociable robots establishes a psychic pathway in which the individual will "reduce relationship and come to see this reduction as the norm".[31]

Oddly, Turkle has little to say about one of the main psychoanalytic themes of play – namely, "transitional" or "potential space". In the writings of Winnicott, the child's play with a toy – such as a special teddy – lies at the core of our relationship to the outer world and other people. The cultivation of transitional space for Winnicott is paradoxical: the child imbues the object (such as the teddy bear) with unique meaning and thus creates a world; but that world would not have been created if the object had not already been there. This transitional space is one of *potential* – a linking of inner and outer, self and other, fantasy and reality. Winnicott was able to demonstrate that transitional relations permit individuals to link the given and the created, the past and the future, the familiar and the strange. From this angle, the self's other (whether teddy bear, literature, music and arguably digital technology) is revealed as a highly personalized creation. We construct our lives through using and playing with transitional objects, which help make life more bearable, by allowing us to imagine ourselves as a central part of everyday living and the wider world. For Winnicott, transitional or potential space is not an alternative to, or refuge from, reality but an essential feature of daily life.

After Winnicott, it is possible to think of our inner lives as doubled, the *lives that we wish for* and the *lives that we are handed*. Winnicott shows us that fantasy and the imagination are at once the source of our creativity and the essential wellspring for negotiating the trials and tribulations of everyday life. So it is worth wondering how the transitional boundaries between inner and outer experience are given shape by social institutions and cultural arrangements at any given historical moment. This, essentially, is the question I will turn to consider in the next section of this chapter, when we turn to look at digital technologies more specifically. But for the moment the analysis of transitional space set out by Winnicott provides the basis of an alternative answer to Turkle's thesis that digital technologies lead to a reduction of complexity in our psychological lives. Turkle's claim that when individuals today imagine robots and digital objects they imagine forms of true companionship shorn of the emotional complexities of mature relationships is inadequate. A continuing concern with our needs and our fantasy lives in relation to the culture of digital technologies has become an intrinsic aspect of contemporary cultural life. Digital technologies form a key backdrop to how individuals learn to live between the lives they wish to have and the lives they encounter. What people fantasize about – what they long for – in connection with digital technologies is hence not necessarily a reduction in emotion or relatedness; the transitional space of the digital can (and often does) underpin how we think about ourselves and other people. Like all aspects of the digital revolution, the transitional space of digital objects (from social media to robotic pets) underpins our appetite for human relationships – and from this angle represents an engagement with the wider world rather than a defensive reduction of it.

Containment, storage and digital keys

In his romantic AI movie *Her*, filmmaker Spike Jonze examines the fate of one Theodore Phoenix, who has begun a new intimate relationship following the breakdown of his marriage. Theodore's love interest is of a radically new kind, since he is conducting this relationship with his operating system – OS One by Element Software – known as Samantha, and voiced by Scarlett Johansson. When the film commences, set in mid-twenty-first-century Los Angeles, Theodore is working for BeautifulHandwrittenLetters.com, composing stylish letters for online customers too overcommitted or inarticulate to undertake the task at hand. He crafts their words, and even invents relationship myths, in order to assist clients deal with the messiness of offline, human relationships in a high-tech digital era.

The core of the movie concerns Theodore's emotional attachment to Samantha. At the beginning, Samantha revolves around Theodore's life as a super-sophisticated AI personal assistant. She organizes his schedule with fabulous dexterity, plans his professional commitments with ease and even provides personal suggestions. Theodore gradually becomes more and more reliant on Samantha. She is warm, witty and empathetic, and it is evident that Theodore slowly feels more emotional connection to Samantha than to other people he encounters in the atomized world of intensive digital life. In fact, Samantha comes to provide a kind of refuge from many of the trials and tribulations of Theodore's everyday life – most especially the spitefulness of his ongoing divorce from wife Catherine.

Theodore realizes, in time, that he has fallen in love with Samantha – his disembodied operating system. She supports him, she reassures him, and she comforts him. She is *there* for him. What unfolds is, essentially, an AI love story. Theodore is captivated by the mysterious and elusive Samantha. The title of the film, however, is instructive: no matter how much Theodore tries to emotionally relate to Samantha, the latter appears as "her" rather than "she". Theodore feels closer and closer to Samantha, but is frustrated because he cannot physically possess her. In time, they have simulated sex. But the inevitable clash of man and machine, or self and device, rears its head and Theodore and Samantha seek to confront the missing physical dimension of their relationship. In the search for a solution, Samantha finds a surrogate sex partner for Theodore, a woman willing to have sex on her behalf, and even to wear miniature cameras and microphones on her body so that Samantha can better appreciate the visual and auditory dimensions of love making. This is a turning point in their relationship.

In the meantime, the film references other technological possibilities which, ultimately, signal the demise of Theodore and Samantha's relationship. In one scene, Theodore, increasingly worried by a short period in which Samantha is absent, confronts his AI love interest directly:

Theodore: Where were you? I couldn't find you anywhere.
Samantha: I shut down to update my software. We wrote an upgrade that allows us to move past matter as our processing platform.
Theodore: We? We who?
Samantha: Me and a group of OSes.

Here the movie references the possibility of a technological singularity, the historical point at which artificial intelligence will exceed the power of the human mind. Samantha talks poetically about an operational transformation and of "infinite spaces between the words", implying that she has technologically evolved to a vast degree. It transpires that she is conducting thousands of conversations and relationships with people simultaneously, intimate and otherwise, and Theodore feels excluded and rejected. But more than that, Theodore is getting left behind. For it is evident that Samantha and other OSs and AIs are leaving their human partners to shift into other worlds. The film concludes by resituating relations between men and women in the broader context of connections with digital technology: Theodore bids farewell to Samantha, and it is evident that he has been forever changed by the experience of this relationship with his OS. Theodore, liberated, is finally able to compose a letter in his own words; it is a letter to his ex-wife Catherine, to whom he writes of his remorse and gratitude. An ending at once moralistic and melancholic, Theodore has adapted to the contours of love in the age of artificial intelligence.

Her is not primarily a movie about the technological singularity. There has been some critical discussion of *Her* in terms of the technological implausibility of the film's timelines. For one thing, it has been said that Samantha's evolution to super-AI status unfolds too swiftly, and that in any case there is no plausible reason why the OSs and AIs need to separate from their human counterparts – since the technological requirements for supporting humans comprise only a small portion of the cognitive ability of advanced artificial intelligence. Another line of criticism has focused on the failure of Theodore and Samantha's relationship on the basis that the latter does not have a body. Here it has been argued that it would have been technologically straightforward to provide Samantha with virtual visual presence and accompanying virtual auditory presence in her interactions with Theodore. It has been further claimed that, with the advent of nanobots with wireless communication which go directly into the brain, full AI sensory capacity should have been feasible for Samantha.

These criticisms are perhaps valid, but arguably miss the central point. *Her* is a movie about identities (actual and virtual, offline and online) trying to connect, and above all about digital affairs which are sensual, in a social world undergoing profound transformations. The central problem in the movie is an emotional one: Theodore recognizes the complexities and immense difficulties of conducting an intimate relationship with his operating system, but nonetheless has come to care for Samantha in an intense, sensual and, ultimately, heartbreaking manner. In his marriage and subsequent offline relationships, Theodore had been unable to find emotional satisfaction and relate sufficiently well to a caring, containing other. But in the digital world, he had discovered a new experience of containment and of love. This experience, paradoxically, was more enlivening, more interesting and more revealing than that offered in the offline world.

Whilst indebted to futuristic fantasies such as Isaac Asimov's *I, Robot*, the problems portrayed in *Her* are distinctly contemporary. Personal life, when sociologically contextualized in terms of the daily lives of ordinary people, has become increasingly entangled with digital technologies to a very considerable degree. More and more, our social existence is being thoroughly transfigured, involving us all in the informational overlays of digital experimentation and AI. From our current vantage point, Theodore's relationship with his operating system Samantha may appear extreme; but there is surely little doubt that individuals today are wrapping up significant aspects of their identity – of their emotional lives – in the network of digital technologies in which they are embedded. Indeed, the deep personal and emotional investment of individuals in digital technologies, AI and robotics is taking on an ever-greater significance in modern societies. From smartphones to computer games to robot pets, people are discovering aspects of their self-identity – including their innermost feelings and desires – in the digital, AI world. And whilst digital technology cannot stand-in for the emotional relationships that individuals need to make, it can and does foster an altogether different experience of others and of the wider world.

But still how, exactly, might digital technologies enter into and reshape psychic experience? What happens when we encounter digital objects? As we journey through digital life, how are we emotionally moved by AI and robotic objects? The psychoanalyst Christopher Bollas has written one of the best accounts of the enhancement and limitation to self-experience in the face of object engagement. Building on the post-Freudian tradition, Bollas focuses simultaneously on the world's impact upon the individual self and the individual's unique authorings of that same world. According to Bollas, people engage with the world and use its objects to bring their identities to life. What happens when we encounter objects – wittingly and unwittingly – is that we endow such objects with unique meaning, or what Bollas calls our "personal idiom".[32] The objects which we both encounter and select – and in terms of digital life this might be anything from the iPhones and iPads we use to organize our days to the computer games we play to pass the hours – make possible a kind of private dreaming. Objects, Bollas argues, unlock a form of dreaming. This dreaming, imagining, indeed unconsciousness, lies at the core of our selection of objects. There is a profoundly unknown and unknowable quality to object selection, and from this angle Bollas is out to underscore the unconsciousness of everyday life. In our day-to-day lives, we are – quite unwittingly – choosing objects (both human and non-human) to express our personal idiom of self.

Freud famously contrasted the "reality principle" with the "pleasure principle";[33] Bollas, in another feat of radical Freudianism, conjures a pleasurable dreaming right at the heart of the object-world itself. This recoupling of pleasure and reality, or dreaming and objects, refracts both selfhood and the object-world in myriad directions. That is to say, Bollas is not only concerned with our investments of dream-life into the object-world; he is also focused on the impact of objects onto the various facets of the self. "As we encounter the object world", Bollas writes, "we are substantially metamorphosed by the structure of objects; internally transformed by objects that leave their trace within us".[34] To say that objects in the world "leave their trace within us" is to emphasize the transformational dynamic of the self's engagement with other people, things, places and events. In any day, people do not only just use objects; they are evocatively nourished by these objects as concerns the articulation of the self. Bollas contends that each of us gravitates to specific object selection because particular objects furnish our self-identities with idiomatic significance. Objects, says Bollas, are like "psychic keys" for the individual self – unlocking, releasing, preserving and transforming the aesthetics of personal identity. Whether we are held in thrall to the latest iPhone or captivated by a robotic pet, object selection for Bollas is akin to a large keyring – with individuals searching for the most appropriate key to release their own private idiom.

Conventional Freudian thought, as we have noted, casts the introjection of others and objects as foundational to personal identity. Bollas's approach, however, deeply complicates this paradigm: for the interconnections between self and objects is fractured, unstable, and ambiguous. Plunged into object evocation, the individual self may not be able to consciously structure or control their selection of objects for daily use, but there is always the option of preserving emotions within these very structures of interaction. That is to say, the self can store emotions – investing affects, desires and fantasies – within the object-world of places, events and things. For Bollas, the storage of emotion in objects is of key importance to self-understanding and self-exploration.

Psychoanalysis as a form of therapy operates by attending to the patient's significant emotional relationships – with parents, family, friends and intimate others. The argument here is that if we find psychoanalysis illuminating as a method for understanding interpersonal relationships, it is equally engaging for exploring how people convert their own lives into novel forms of self-elaboration through immersion in the object-world. A case-study by psychoanalysts George Atwood and Robert Stolorow,

detailing how a man recorded his thoughts, moods and mem-
ories onto a tape recorder outside of therapy, provides a useful illustration.[35] In regularly using the tape recorder outside of
therapy, the man deposited emotion and stored complex feeling
states within this technology; listening to the tapes subsequently,
he could reclaim these sense-impressions in order to work them
back up and create a new elaboration of self. "This use of the tape
recorder as a transitional object", write Atwood and Stolorow,
"both concretized the injured state of the self and reinvoked the
empathic bond with the therapist, thereby enabling the patient
to regain a sense of being substantial and real".[36] This patient's
use of technology, albeit primitive by the standards of digital life,
is indicative of the vitality of affect storage. Technology, on this
account, can work as a transformational object of the self.

Bollas, it should be noted, refers quite frequently to 'objects'
both external and internal, and of the inexhaustible interplay
between need and use, of unconscious projections and the recep-
tive unconscious. To speak of the multiple forms, folds and functions of the object is to speak, from a psychoanalytic point of
view, of a desiring self always involved in representing and conceptualizing the world; stamping their own unconscious of creative explorations on that world, including the world of digital
technologies. There are, Bollas seems to be saying, the displacements, misfirings and hazards of unconscious desire as described
by psychoanalysis from the era of Freud onwards. But there are
also creative, exploratory, vibrant and imaginative unconscious
architectures of the self in its engagement with object worlds –
physical, communicative, virtual and digital. The individual
self, in the frame of Bollas's reinterpretation of psychoanalysis,
encounters the digital in and through the dream work of complex unconscious articulations.

Psychoanalysts do not tend to think of digital life as containing people. But what Bollas ascribes to how we use other people
and things as transformational objects, I want to ascribe to digital
technologies. Indeed digital life, I shall claim, offers an open-
ended menu of technological containment for both the creative

elaboration and defensive closure of the self. Technological containment may sound jarring, and as I say most psychologists (even those influenced by psychoanalysis) tend to think of containment in terms of the kinds of support or sympathy offered *between people*. But adding to this (after Bollas) an acknowledgment of the unconsciousness of our immersion in the world of things, and of what this might mean on an emotional register, is instructive for grasping the impact of digital technologies upon the self. So I am proposing that digital technologies, among other things, facilitate forms of emotional containment. Digital technologies facilitate opportunities to lodge, store, explore and express emotions, anxieties and other psychic conflicts. The investment of emotion in virtual objects, such as Facebook, Instagram or LinkedIn, can enable forms of self-transformation: the storing of emotion for subsequent retrieval, processing and reflective thinking. Or children might make their lives pleasurable, and therefore containable, by playing with robot pets like Nao (the robot kid), Paro (the robot seal) or Roboraptor. Or people might be drawn to the invitational features of computer games, from *Minecraft* to *World of Warcraft*, to imagine wished-for lives and thereby explore complexities of the self. So it may be fruitful, I am suggesting, to think of the profusion of digital technologies as providing individuals with resources for exploring their fantasy lives as well as symbolic forms for seeing their own lives in a new light and investigating their own internal complexity.

To emphasize the containing functions of digital technologies in the emotional life of individuals is not to suggest that our so-called inner lives automatically prosper in the digital age. On the contrary, the profusion of digital technologies, robotics and AI can have significant unsettling consequences, both at the level of self-identity and institutional life. Many people, for complex reasons connected to unsettled family lives, social inequalities or educational disadvantages, decline evocative objects of the digital landscape; many people are unable to use digital objects to bridge the gap between their actual lives and their wished-for lives; and many people, locked into a narrow and repetitive choice of objects, find themselves unable to retrieve stored emotion from digital technologies in order to trace complexities of their lived and imagined lives. Where individuals are unable to use digital objects creatively, either because of debilitating emotional imprints from their past or because of the impairment or corrosion of their capacity for processing unthought emotion, chronic depressive and related pathologies are likely to emerge.[37] While many individuals enjoy using digital technologies as evocative objects for self-transformation and for making emotional connections with other people, many others find that an immersion in digital life can have negative or destructive consequences for their lives and shared worlds. Rather than finding that digital technologies can be used to bring aspects of ourselves alive, there is instead the coercive sense that digital life becomes overwhelming or pathological. Rather than freeing the self to explore processes of invention and reinvention, the world of digital technologies for many people can spiral into a world of addiction – where people take flight from the complexity of self-experience and instead become imprisoned in compulsive forms of behavior from which there is no seeming escape.

As an illustration, take the debate now occurring regarding addiction to social media, associated especially with the emergence of 'selfie culture'. The smartphone self-portrait or 'selfie' – where people offer images of themselves up to photo-sharing platforms such as Facebook, SnapChat, Instagram and Tumblr – has been widely seen as a dangerous sign of addictive pathology.[38] Addictive because selfie culture has become a daily digital habit which many people (and especially young women) engage in – where the image presented for public consumption is tagged, shared and retweeted. Significantly, this cult of digital exhibitionism has quickly become a global phenomenon. In 2014, it was estimated that 93 million selfies were taken per day – and that estimate encompassed only Android technology. But if we now live in a selfie-obsessed global world, this is nowhere more consequential than for adolescents and particularly young women and girls. A report published by the Pew Research Center found that 68% of millennial women had posted selfies.[39] It has been further estimated that the average 16–25-year-old woman spends over five hours a week taking selfies.

What does it say about digital life that selfies should have this drawing power for individuals? Are selfies simply a new form of autobiographical narcissism? Many media commentators have argued so, portraying selfie culture as vain, narcissistic, body dysmorphic and pathological. But it is not only media which has derisively dismissed selfies as narcissistic; various academic studies, especially in the field of psychology, have connected selfies to the rise in our culture at large of narcissism, addiction, mental illness and even suicide.

The issue of selfie culture is more complex than such analyses suggest, not least because we also have to consider the impact of the online reception of selfies as much as the psychology of the creator. Senft and Baym's work on the global complexity of selfies provides a useful source of evidence here.[40] As they demonstrate, conceptualizing selfie culture as narcissistic or pathological functions often as moral panic rather than cultural diagnosis. For one thing, such pathology-based rhetoric tends to screen from view the subtle ways in which young people, women, or sexual minorities use selfies to question and critique sexist societal norms and cultural expectations of unattainable beauty ideals. The result is certainly not shallow narcissism, but rather for many individuals an exercise in free speech and the enhancement of digital skills. For another, the tendency to categorize selfies as narcissistic culture rides roughshod over the wide-ranging diversity of digital images which shape and reshape everyday social life. We need to recognize therefore that the genre of selfies is very wide-ranging, extending from sexualized-selfies, glam-selfies and fan-related selfies to joke selfies, political-critique selfies, sports-related selfies, illness selfies and crime selfies.

Thanks to the revolution in computing and mobile telephony, many people participate in selfie culture as one among many aspects of everyday social activity. All selfies are, in a sense, self-exploratory. This might be the 'fun selfie' of instantaneity, where the creator basks in the thrill of the moment. Or it might be the 'micro-politics selfie', where people self-document their lives in social contexts of violence and danger.[41] But the critical point is that selfie culture provides a rich and varied digital resource for the exploration and enrichment of the self. However, it is also evident that in many cases selfie culture can be debilitating for individuals; in such instances the selfie functions less as a vehicle for self-expression or self-exploration, and more as an object of repetitive intoxication through which individuals act out compulsive behaviors. 'Selfie addiction' is perhaps a useful term here for understanding how compulsion operates on the ground of digital life. The documented case of a man who became so obsessed with trying to take the 'perfect selfie' that he ended up shooting more than 200 pictures of himself everyday captures very well the erosion on self-autonomy that can occur in the face of digital technologies. Like many who discovered that selfie culture can be compulsive, the man attempted suicide by taking an overdose of drugs. Various medical and health professionals commented on the increasing role that selfies play in mental illness, including body dysmorphic disorder. This very negative consequence of selfie culture has been especially consequential for young women, although my focus of concern here is different. For some individuals, the experience of selfie culture can become overwhelming; selfies can contribute to patterns of digital absorption, compulsions and addictions.

Another way of putting this is that there is a kind of psychic corruption of the self as a consequence of absorption in selfie culture. In the psychoanalytic approach I have been sketching, we might say that selfie culture oversimplifies the self; it is that which, because of the compulsions and addictions entailed, leaves people taking revenge on their identities because they cannot bear or tolerate their own complexity. For Freud and Bollas, creative living involves thought: we search for appropriate objects needed for self-transformation, and thinking with and through these objects is a crucial means of, as it were, elaborating the complexity of the self. Many of the stories pertaining to selfie culture in the media and public discourse are stories about this search for complexity. In this respect, selfie culture – as objects of digital transformation – can unlock the experimentalism of the self as an open-ended process. But the ability to explore can also mean entering the overwhelming terrain of digital absorption, where selfie culture may function as a compulsive object of addiction in which the experimentalism of self-identity is declined or rejected.[42]

In this final section of the chapter, I have dwelt on some of the ways in which the interconnections of identities and digital technologies can be a source of cultural creativity and imagination on the one hand, and a trap within which compulsions and addictions proliferate. With the launch of the global era of digital technologies, it may well be that we are witnessing the emergence of a new kind of person. Living in a world of digital technologies carries with it new ways of generating experience, and a variety of new forms for exploring desire and emotional life. Digital technologies give rise to a new dynamic in which the person's unconscious authorings of its world are more and more associated with technological interaction and the storage, containment and retrieval of emotion in the technological contexts of everyday life. From intimate conversations held through smartphones or Skype to playing games with sociable robots, digital life is organized through complex technological networks of connection and disconnection, and in which emotional anxiety and its containment emerges as fundamental.

4

DIGITAL TECHNOLOGIES AND SOCIAL INTERACTION

Digital technologies play a fundamental, indeed ubiquitous, role in coordinating online communications and software-driven information connections across the planet. Glance around any coffee shop, shopping mall, restaurant or train station, and you will see people with their heads down, fixated on their smartphone screens. Our intoxication with new technology leads us away from traditional forms of face-to-face interaction, or so it can seem. We feel instead the urgency to check email, text a friend, tweet, or post updates on social media. This raises the interesting, though vexed, question of whether the AI which underpins our digital lives is a supplement to social relationships, or whether we are fast reaching that point as a society where we can conceive of sociality as nothing else than refracted through digital technologies. Does digital technology automatically result in an erosion of face-to-face contact? And might our new era of AI and digital interconnection be as harmful to social relationships as it is beneficial?

Many authors have argued so. Consider, for example, Ben Bajarin's "Are You Multitasking or Are You Suffering from Digital-Device-Distraction Syndrome", which appeared in *Time*.[1] Bajarin's argument is that our high-tech society leads us away from face-to-face interaction and towards only mediated communication. According to Bajarin, more and more people today would rather email than meet in person; our cultural preference is to text rather than talk. Digital distractions, according to Bajarin, cause people to forgo human engagement. On this view, our immersion in screenlife means we cannot be fully present to others in daily situations – whether at home, in the office, or in routine social interaction. The arrival of what Bajarin calls Digital-Device-Distraction Syndrome is "becoming something that is socially acceptable. In a meeting or conversation, it's O.K. to turn our attention and be as equally engaged with a smart phone as we are with the person across from us. We are, after all, a multitasking generation". In this age of distraction, according to Bajarin, digital devices are destroying our concentration and memory.

Whilst there may be some validity to aspects of the argument outlined by Bajarin, we need, I think, to develop a more balanced understanding of the culture of digital technologies and the social relations they affect. The central limitation of Bajarin's orthodox critique is that he treats digital technologies on a technological level only, as involving a series of electronic exchanges to be managed. I shall instead concentrate my attention not only on the paradox that digital technologies mean we are more connected and potentially also disconnected from others than in previous historical eras, but also on how modern societies bed down the operational ideas of AI and digital technology in everyday experience. I want to argue for what I shall call the *digital imperative* as not just essential to coping with our high-speed information societies but as integral to the production and performance of digital life which takes place against the background of face-to-face communication. I see this transformation as deeply connected to the dissolution of AI and digital technologies into the bloodstream of society to the point where digital life becomes second nature.[2]

The institutional organization of social interaction: face-to-face and digitally mediated action frameworks

In the critiques developed by media critics who lament that digital technologies are sabotaging social relationships, one can find an inadequate account of the relation between identity on the one hand and the social organization of communication on the other. The individual self appears as largely passive in relation to digital technologies – hiding behind email, tweets or Facebook posts. Very often this is accompanied by a misleading or inaccurate view of the restructuring and renewal of processes of communication and information exchange, and of how these are becoming increasingly bound up with digital technologies. An adequate account of social interaction in relation to global transformations of digital communication must encompass the following three points. It must recognize that (1) the growing significance of digital technologies, and underlying developments in AI, mean that digital communication is increasingly supplementing face-to-face and voice-to-voice communication; (2) the rise of digital communication does not necessarily occur at the expense of face-to-face and voice-to-voice interaction, and contemporary social life sees a new mix of interaction unfolding at the level of the social organization of communication; and (3) the use of digital technologies, powered by AI, is having quite profound impacts on various preexisting forms of social interaction. I want now to discuss these points in more detail.

In order to consider the kinds of institutional transformation created by the advent of digital technologies and AI, it is helpful at the outset to note that communications are of many sorts. These range from personal conversations and conversing at small gatherings to letters and postcards to radio and television to SMS, email and social media. As Urry notes, one simple way to understand these sorts of communications is to distinguish between one-to-one communications (the private letter), one-to-many communications (TV), and many-to-many communications (social media). For the large bulk of human history, face-to-face social interaction has been the norm. However, the development of communication media, and especially the rise of digital technologies, has resulted not only in new networks and complex systems that make instantaneous global communication possible but crucially new forms of digital interaction and new kinds of just-in-time lives and social relationships at-a-distance. One can reasonably claim that digital communication does indeed diverge from conventional forms of communication in certain respects, whatever the more hyperbolic estimates of the novelty of the digital age. Digital technologies have stunningly transformed the social organization of space and time, spawning 24/7 commercial interaction and always-on interpersonal communication possibilities and burdens. This major shift in the social organization of communication needs to be understood against the wider institutional backcloth of globalization, especially intensified international economic competition and the general shift in the West away from industrial manufacturing and towards the finance, service and communication sectors. It should be noted that, as a consequence of production outsourcing in the 1980s and 1990s and electronic offshoring in the 2000s and 2010s, social and economic life was powerfully transformed by the geographic dispersion of companies and businesses, all underpinned by the speed of new digital communications. As capitalism became intensively globalized – ever more reliant on ubiquitous computing, the Internet and mobile platforms – social relations shifted away from conventional, fixed, and largely stationary interpersonal interaction and towards more mobile and networked digital interactions. This was, in short, the digital revolution and the arrival of a social world which wholeheartedly came to embrace smartphones, apps, instant messaging and other social media.

From the standpoint of the social organization of communication, however, things are perhaps not so clear cut. These global institutional changes – namely, the digital revolution – which seemed to consign conventional interpersonal interaction to the sidelines were ones which, ironically, renewed and recalibrated the vitality of everyday talk and the functional exchange of information. This was arguably the case all the way from business meetings and the doing of deals to the making of new acquaintances and celebrating family life. The digital, in other words, did not close down the daily business of talk and the ever-ongoing self-presentational work of conversational interaction as much as relaunch it. On this view, digital technologies, social media platforms and global communication networks actually sustain and deepen our everyday patterns of social life; the digital field both facilitates encounters with specific others (leading to face-to-face meetings with friends, family and colleagues) and meetings with generalized others. Indeed, there is a large body of scholarly research which confirms the utter centrality of face-to-face interactions in dispersed organizational structures, as well as the importance of face-to-face and body-to-body meetings for sustaining trust that will have to persist during periods of distance and absence threaded throughout digital life.[3] Thus, digital interaction and face-to-face talk were not necessarily as far apart as some critics presumed.

A key aspect of all social interaction is learning how to project a self-image which is more or less appropriate to both the expectations of others and the contextual experience.[4] For example, talking in a louder than usual voice may be appropriate when mixing with friends in a crowded pub, but it would not be considered so where hotel patrons are requested to demonstrate consideration for residential neighbors when leaving such an establishment. Some of the most advanced contributions to understanding the vital importance of apparently mundane social interaction are to be found in the sociological writings of Erving Goffman.[5] Goffman was an uncommonly shrewd observer of face-to-face interaction and his writings powerfully capture how talking face-to-face is a unique sociological accomplishment.[6] Encounters between people, according to Goffman, involve highly skilled performances, which demand the displaying of attentiveness and commitment to others as well as the discernment of where there might be an absence of trustful commitment in others. Goffman more generally disclosed a kind of invisible dimension of social life, where people invoke various procedures for engaging in social activity, monitoring the actions and activities of other people and also the responses of others to their own actions and activities. In face-to-face talk "when the eyes are joined",[7] wrote Goffman, people display attentiveness, demonstrate commitment and assess the sincerity of others. Participants work at their joint performances of conversing, and crucially commit themselves to remain present and attentive for the duration of the social interaction, which entails effectively managing not only the flow of small talk but also of ensuing silences in order to perform talk and maintain the norms of co-mingling.

There is now an extensive literature on the importance of Goffman's work for the social sciences,[8] but my concern lies elsewhere. In what follows, I shall briefly focus on the significance of Goffman's approach for analyzing social interaction – both face-to-face interaction and digitally mediated interaction. Throughout Goffman's writings, social life emerges as filled with the "impression management" of people – of social roles performed, of agency displayed to others, of social actors distinguishing between different types of encounter and artfully 'jumping' between the contexts of social interaction. For Goffman, participants in social interaction maintain (through various background assumptions) continuous involvement in the mutual making of diverse forms of social activity. For Goffman, the core focus of attention is the 'presence of others', or what might be termed the 'norms of co-presence'.

According to Goffman, the impression management of the self and team performances occur within an "action framework" which involves certain cultural conventions and social assumptions pertaining to appropriate social behavior. Frameworks of action also involve the positioning of people, or the spacing of bodies, as well as the physical features of the actual setting (furniture, equipment, spatial design and so on). An individual acting within this framework will to a large extent adapt their behavior to the norms or rules relevant to the particular setting, and display an awareness of identity which sustains face-to-face communication. The action framework, in other words, feeds into the 'impression' which individuals seek to convey to others as well as what actually unfolds in public areas of social life. A crucial distinction advanced by Goffman for understanding what goes on in social interaction is that of "front" and "back" regions.[9] Front region action and behavior generally requires of individuals that they engage in strictly controlled self-monitoring, both the monitoring of their own conduct as well as that of others. This can involve particular attention to social cues and the responses of others, as well as strong emphasis on the professional impressions that individuals are seeking to cultivate. A back region, by contrast, often involves action and behavior which might well discredit the impressions that a person is seeking to project in front region encounters. In back regions, individuals tend to 'lower their guard' and act in ways which are free of the stresses and strains of front region impression management.

In most areas of everyday life, the front region behavior of individuals in companies and organizations contrasts with back region behavior, where individuals do not have to be overly concerned about the impression they seek to cultivate. In some sectors of commercial life – for example, in restaurants – the distinction between front and back regions is reasonably well-defined and fixed. Where individuals work in restaurant kitchens, there are often swinging doors or glass partitions to separate staff and diners, and the passage between these areas is usually strictly regulated. This is equally true of the reception areas of many organizations, which serve effectively as a transition point for the management of front and back region behavior. Goffman identified such regional demarcations as essential to social interaction and the impression management of the self. The question of how communication media might reshape processes of social interaction is something that Goffman touched on throughout his own writings, but for the most part only in a provisional and partial fashion. This is hardly surprising, given that Goffman developed his sociological approach at the historical moment in which the rise of mass media was only coming to redefine the twentieth century. Nonetheless, the profusion of electronically mediated materials into the social interactions of daily life is addressed, at least in part, in some of Goffman's writings. The contrast between, say, a TV newsreader's formal presentation of self (with front region props of jacket and tie) whilst wearing jeans (below the news desk, beyond the reach of the camera and thus 'sealed off' as a back region) is illustrative.

Since Goffman's time, the utter centrality of communication media to the reshaping of the process of self-formation and the changing character of social relations has been well documented in various studies, especially in the fields of media and cultural studies. Consider, for example, John B. Thompson's work on the social impact of global communication networks and information diffusion.[10] Thompson argues that the development of communication media, together with the changing dynamics of power and visibility in the public sphere, created the conditions for the emergence of new forms of action and interaction which are fundamentally different to traditional forms of face-to-face interaction characteristic of premodern societies. In accounting for the emergence of new forms of social interaction, Thompson attributes particular importance to communication media, from the rise of print media across the towns and cities of early modern Europe to the advent of mass communication and the growth of media industries. Mass communication, commodification and the growth of the media industries went hand in hand with the rise of new types of mediated social interaction. The consequences of these institutional changes in communication were of very broad social and political significance for modern societies, with lasting impacts all the way from personal life and intimate relationships to large-scale shifts in the nature of publicness and democratic politics.

Part of Thompson's argument is that, with the spread of various types of electronic media during the twentieth and early twenty-first centuries, face-to-face interaction has come to be supplemented by forms of mediated interaction. In developing this argument, Thompson draws extensively on Goffman and analyzes the quite profound impact of communication media on the nature of front and back regions and the relation between them in social life. In the case of technically mediated interaction, according to Thompson, there is a multiplication of regions which impacts upon social interaction; this is a multiplying of regions which must be responded to, and coped with, by participants. This is how Thompson describes these specific changes in social interaction:

> Since mediated interaction generally involves a separation of the contexts within which the participants are situated, it establishes an interactive framework that consists of two or more front regions which are separated in space and perhaps also in time. Each of these front regions has its own back regions, and each participant in the mediated interaction must seek to manage the boundary between them. In the course of a telephone conversation, for example, an individual may seek to suppress noises which arise from the physical locale in which he or she is speaking – the sound of a television, the comments or laughter of a friend or colleague, etc. – as such noises may be regarded as back-region behavior relative to the mediated interaction.[11]

Thompson invokes Goffman to underscore that individuals engaged in interaction, whether talking face-to-face or filtered through communication media, are always deploying skills and accumulated resources of various kinds to produce their joint performances. A central dimension of Thompson's argument, however, is that social interaction structured by communication media acquires an additional complexity compared to face-to-face interaction as a result of complex multiple regions and regional demarcations. In the case of an employee responding to a telephone enquiry whilst working on the front reception desk of a company, for example, a high level of reflexivity is demanded to cope with two (or possibly more) front regions and to manage these interactions in the context of the back region relative to this framework.

Thompson's argument, sketched only briefly here, has the substantial merit of underscoring the broader social and political significance of the development of communication media as regards the changing character of social interaction. The development of communication media is treated not only as an institutional transformation, but one that reshapes self-formation and the very fabric of social relations. But there are limitations here as well. Thompson's work on communication media and social interaction was undertaken in the 1990s – prior to the digital revolution and the rise of the Internet. With the launch of a new global narrative of digital technologies, along with the AI and robotics revolution, social scientists are presented with a fresh challenge. My conjecture is that Goffman's sociological insights remain of considerable value for grasping the changing character of social interaction, but that equally we need to explore newly emerging forms of digital action and virtual interaction in order to understand the transformed dynamics of communication and power in contemporary societies.

How to explain the seeming paradox of sophisticated digital participants in global networks that continue to employ (whilst transforming) established rules of social interaction and forms of impression management? Karin Knorr Cetina and Urs Bruegger convincingly show that information technologies in global financial markets function as "objects of attachment" for traders, who continue to deploy a range of action frameworks in the microconstruction of the global economy at the level of the trading room.[12] Knorr Cetina and Bruegger draw from Goffman's account of the action framework to study global financial systems, but argue that traders' sets of practices, communications, and deployment of computational market infrastructures need not require physical co-presence as a necessary condition. The complexity of digital systems lies in the non-linear relationships between the virtual and the actual, imagining "the global market" in and through informational systems and alongside the production and performance of interactional trading in the space of the local. For Knorr Cetina and Bruegger, digital information technologies, especially the speed of transmission signals, draw together geographically distant domains as if they were in the same place: it is on the computer screen that "the market" is constituted through the gathering together of otherwise dispersed participants – in a complex bridging of distant economies and economic sectors, economic policies and complex financial instruments. This raises some fascinating questions about digital transformations in social interaction. Ultimately, Knorr Cetina and Bruegger help us to understand that digitalization involves "distantiated spatial configurations" in which interactional frameworks are "mutually represented to individuals participating in a global situation".[13] This, in turn, is where issues of AI, smart algorithms and machine learning enter and where questions about the criss-crossing of online and actual, virtual and communicative interaction need to be posed in a new light in the broader context of the digital revolution.

At this point we have to rethink the orthodox critique of how digital technologies are transforming our lives in an innovative way. Does the ubiquity of new technology mean a digital apocalypse is coming? Do we need to switch off our devices in order to reconnect with each other again? Surely not. The distinction between face-to-face interaction and digitally mediated interaction is not simply one in which a prioritization of the former over the latter will put everything right in modern societies, or return us to some by-gone, and allegedly harmonious, age. The distinction is instead institutional, involving complex and wide-ranging action frameworks which constantly involve people adapting their behavior to shifting boundaries. Today's widespread and ever-growing tendency to supplement human interaction with simultaneous digital communication might be experienced by some as socially alienating or fragmenting; but many equally enter routinely into communicational multitasking. Unlike face-to-face interaction, in which the coordinates of space and time match for conversational participants, digitally mediated communication involves differential time-space coordinates which are spliced or fused together by participants deploying digital technologies. These communicational splicings or fusings express orderings of a transformed space-time environment in which the significance of place has rapidly altered, and oftentimes largely diminished. Characteristic of the interaction mix of contemporary times is the space-time interweaving of physical, communicative, digital and virtual communication. Common in many households in developed countries today, for example, is engagement with multiple tasks on multiple screens – and often undertaken alongside of periodic face-to-face interaction.[14] Whether using a smartphone, tablet, notebook or laptop, more and more people divide their attention across multiple tasks and multiple screens as they exchange conversational gambits. These communications can be at once online and offline, with others physically present and those at-a-distance.

Also increasingly characteristic of digital technologies in modern times is a related feature: the intrusion of back region events into front regions as well as everyday consciousness. The distinction between front and back regions, as indicated previously, is seldom definite; Goffman's work brilliantly chronicles the many ways in which back region behavior can 'leak into' the self-presentation individuals seek to project in front regions. In conditions of digital life, however, there has been a multiplication of the interactive frameworks which redistribute relations between front and back regions. The injection of people's mobile phone use into public space is illustrative of this. Many conventional methods of impression management have largely declined in significance as a result of mobile phone use in the public realm, such as when queuing for retail shopping purchases or waiting in airport terminals. Such situations involve a blurring of boundaries between front and back regions and thus confrontation with the collision of physical and digital interactive frameworks. This blurring refers to the changing character of the line between public and private life, as often intimate and occasionally embarrassingly personal phone conversations enter into the fabric of common cultural life. But it is not just that digital technologies promote a merging of older and newer techniques of impression management, or the resorting of front and back region behavior. Rather, much front region behavior does not conform either to social expectation or cultural convention. Experimentation, and oftentimes improvisation, is actually the key to the character of contemporary digital life. In some cases the back regions of digitally mediated interaction may simply be located around the edges of front region encounters. A woman applying make-up whilst travelling on a train, preparing for an impromptu video conference call, is illustrative of this crossing of front regions and back regions.[15] Moreover, such criss-crossings of interactive frameworks are not only less and less rare in day-to-day life but promote direct confrontation with actual phenomenon which previously was sealed off as inappropriate for public display, or, in Goffman's idiom, appropriate only for back region behavior.

Bots, talk and co-presence

In the previous section, I have shown that professional and private life have each become more digitalized and networked. The growth of new digital technologies and multiple extended networks carries major consequences for face-to-face interactions, which are today increasingly distributed across and dispersed between ongoing digitally mediated communications. Such revisions to professional and personal life stem from the rise of communications at a distance and extensive use of new technologies in order to supplement, and sometimes supplant, face-to-face co-presence. Indeed, as John Urry pithily summarizes this, the organizational structure of modern institutions has been "blown to bits" by new digital technologies.[16]

I now turn to consider the increasingly significant pattern of automated actions that take place in digital life today. Several recent analysts estimate that over 60% of all Internet traffic is now generated by machines, including bots, scrapers, hacking tools and spammers. In much analysis of communications it is presumed that automated services and platforms are of limited social consequence beyond the functional transmission of information. Automated actions, such as software services and dial-in automated phone interfaces, have been understood as largely separate from the flow of daily communication between social actors. However, it now seems that time spent using mobile apps, automated messaging systems and bots is not simply functional in outcome; these are automated activities (usually conducted at a distance) which increasingly overlap with face-to-face encounters, and which underpin new possibilities for activities which occur across communicative, digital and virtual fields.

One of the most significant developments concerning automated actions in digital life is the rise of messaging bots. Powered by AI, bots or chatbots represent the new apps of the Internet. Bots are a form of messaging interface, or bundles of code. A chatbot performs tasks and interacts with users through the basic interface of either texting or talking. There are already a stunning variety of different sorts of bots, capable of automating conversations, transactions or workflows. Content bots collect and share selected content with users, such as news or sports updates. Food bots order and arrange the delivery of dinner. E-commerce bots facilitate the purchasing of goods and services. Trading bots provide financial services. Workflow bots automate business workflows and transaction reports in sales, operations, finance and administration. Bots geared to the Internet of Things connect people to their devices, cars and smart homes. There are other professional and personal benefits of chatbots too, as summarized well by Beerud Sheth:

> Bots de-clutter our mobile experience. Bots send us a message when we need to know or respond to something, but stay invisible otherwise. Bots reside in the cloud and upgrade themselves with new functionality – without any user action. Bots can interact with one other and can be chained together to perform a series of actions in sequence. Bots can supervise other bots, leading to bot hierarchies. Your personal bot will supervise other bots on your behalf, per your personal preferences. You may choose to delegate authority to bots that act autonomously on your behalf. Your shopping, scheduling, tracking, monitoring and messaging can be automated according to personal preferences.[17]

A substantial proportion of app developers have moved (or are moving) into the bot market. Yet whilst bots can help people to manage, or declutter, the vast information flows of life lived in conditions of intensive digitalization, they are hardly neutral or benign. David Beer has written of the power of algorithms to shape processes of social ordering; he notes that smart algorithms – precisely as a result of their functionality, their ability to classify, sort, order, rank and select – promote certain visions of calculative objectivity.[18] Some of the less desirable aspects of bot technologies, particularly in relation to civil society and democracy, are discussed further in Chapter 6.

A central question for artificial intelligence, information science and indeed the social sciences as a whole is the extent to which these automated interactional programs can be thought of as creative in a generative sense. Traditional notions of creation imply some kind of interiority; but while creativity may be solitary and individualistic more recent research has underscored that human creation is in practice a function of its circumstances. On this view, creativity is less an autonomous entity than a relational one. Other people, resources, processes and social networks are essential constituents in the production and reproduction of creativity, innovation and imagination. And if by 'others' we refer to both the human and non-human, then this raises the thorny issue of the creativity of chatbots for the *doing* of everyday social activities. Arguably, no form of life in history has been held more in thrall to creativity and innovation, more enamored of imagination and ingenuity, than our hi-tech society. Technological society, especially that version of it advanced through AI, seeks women and men who are infinitely pliable, adaptable and creative. Chatbots might be thought of as a kind of break out point between traditional and post-traditional understandings of creativity. Douglas Hofstader contends that creativity is the capacity to make variations on themes.[19] Chatbots, for the most part, follow a set of relatively fixed codes. But variation is increasingly possible, and one might plausibly argue that automated services will become a vital interactional resource in social life.

We should also consider here that whilst text-based bots are most common, the rise of bots via voice are well underway. Central to the chatbot ecosphere has been Amazon Echo, Apple Siri, Facebook Messenger's M as well as the Google Assistant. These conversational assistants, whilst quite basic in operation, conduct dialogue which is somewhat similar to human conversation. More advanced, human-like chatbots are expected to represent the future of our digital lives. For example, Ray Kurzweil – Director of Engineering at Google, and founder of the Singularity movement – has developed a chatbot ("Danielle") which demonstrates high-level human conversational characteristics. Especially significant is the promise that Google will assist in turning your own identity into a bot. This individual customization of bots is the result of recent advances in AI, which is based on the feeding of data directly into software. As Kurzweil argues, "You can actually create one with your own personality if you feed in your blog, that expresses your style and personality and ideas, and (the bot) will adopt those".[20]

Central to many hyperbolic claims about the social impacts of chatbots is the ideology of techno-optimism.[21] A powerful discourse has assembled across many sciences and the public sphere which projects how AI in general and chatbots in particular will develop comprehensive knowledge regarding everything we do. The techno-optimist claim, in effect, is that chatbots will know us better than we know ourselves. Kurzweil is more cautionary, noting that chatbots are not yet capable of achieving the normal patterns of sociality realized in face-to-face talk. But he does argue that society is not far away from such a transformation, identifying 2029 as the year which will witness AI powered human-quality machine talk.

The possibility of AI, software-driven chatbots demonstrating fully human-quality talk raises the questions of multiple complex futures, new kinds of social and system interdependence, as well as long-term and large-scale shifts in the nature of conversations and the links of those conversing – not only person-to-person but person-to-machine. Perhaps the clearest example of an emergent transformation in communication concerns the uses of talk in order to sustain social life itself. Sociality is made and remade, as Diedre Boden writes, through "talk, talk, talk and more talk".[22] Talking face-to-face is not only how we exchange information but also how we carry out many tasks, such as agreeing to contracts or arranging meetings. With face-to-face talk there is the expectation of mutual attentiveness – one of the core norms of co-presence. Such norms, today and in the future, might become more or less completely deconstructed. In other words, chatbots – or machine-based talk – inaugurate "new rules of sociality". For one thing, a good deal of talk itself may be directed towards machines. Utterances aimed at chatbots, for example, will be enacted to do things: ordering pizza, booking tickets, confirming reservations and so on. That is to say, machine-talk may replace the need for face-to-face talk in specific situations and, along with that, the conversational burden of mutual attentiveness is likely to decline.

For another thing, chatbots can be linked with the increased significance in impersonal trust and the taken-for-granted way in which everyday actions are geared into complex, abstract systems elaborated by Giddens and others. "With the development of abstract systems", Giddens argues, "trust in impersonal principles, as well as anonymous others, becomes indispensable to social existence".[23] It may transpire that one of the most significant kinds of abstract systems, looking forward to the future, will be that of chatbots. Indeed trust in abstract systems such as chatbots provides for a new form of security as regards the day-to-day reliability of social organization. Every time a person asks a chatbot to make a reservation, book tickets, send automated email replies or rearrange a scheduled meeting, there is an implicit acceptance that large tracts of daily life can now be coordinated and managed through digital systems. Unlike face-to-face talk, chatbots do not require the routine "working at conversing" of joint performances. The production of trust is, as a result, less about mutuality of response, involvement and attentiveness; mediated interactions via digital devices, such as abstract systems like chatbots, rely on impersonal, functional mechanisms for generating confidence and trust. There is an implicit faith in impersonal principles, which can of course be disrupted when automated actions go astray and hence the complex, contingent and fragile patterns of social life come starkly into focus. Producing trust with others (acquaintances, colleagues, friends, family) through digital systems becomes especially significant as relationships become increasingly networked and at-a-distance. Chatbots might thus be thought of as a form of reembedding the personalized, less structured self within digital systems, involving various impersonal mechanisms to effect trust. An early accompaniment to this transition was e-Bay, which established various impersonal mechanisms of seller-ratings and associated customer feedback loops to effect trust. Chatbots are today extending such impersonal principles, and this becomes a prime means whereby social relations of a networked and at-a-distance kind are further sedimented and layered in society at large.

What happens to the contextuality of talk – the *doing* of talk in situations of co-presence – in a world of intensive AI? How far does machine talk (chatbots, virtual personal assistants) itself contribute to the reengineering of conversations? Should a theory of talk and conversation now essentially be a theory of machine language? These are all questions that have to be confronted in the wake of AI and technological advancements in natural language processing, and which compel us to look at the relation between human conversation and machine language in a new way.

We can best grasp the differences between day-to-day talk and automated machine conversation when something goes awry or there is a breakdown in technical functioning of the latter. As an instance of this phenomenon, glitches generated by Amazon's Alexa in accidentally recording and relaying human conversations can be mentioned. In 2018, it was widely reported that a family in Portland, Oregon, had received a phone call from an acquaintance advising them to disconnect their Amazon Alexa device. The reason? The device had recorded private conversations in the family home and forwarded these, apparently randomly, to a person in the family's contact list. The conversation recorded, it transpired, was of a mundane nature – though commentators were quick to forecast the arrival of a dystopic world where chatbots spy on us. Rather than focus on the relation between AI and privacy, however, I want to reflect on this instance of a device recording a conversation and sending it to a random contact in terms of some of the notions analyzed in this chapter. These notions assist in the reinterpretation of the interconnections between day-to-day talk among people on the one hand and machine language on AI devices on the other.

Let us return to Goffman. Because Goffman has so comprehensively analyzed the routines of social interaction, his writings offer significant illuminations about the character of day-to-day talk. Goffman's most powerful contributions to understanding the sustaining and reproduction of talk are to do with the immense skill which human agents display in communicative dialogue and the mutual coordination of social interaction. This constant connecting of talk with the forms of day-to-day experience rarely happens in a technically smooth or ordered way. There is a plethora of contingencies and hesitations which infuse daily talk: people break into (and often disrupt) conversational flows; turn-taking is not perfectly ordered; and, in general, the talk which makes up conversations is of a fragmented nature. Hence, the skill of human agents in traversing the complexities of ordinary day-to-day talk.

Now compare this to machine-generated language. AI devices deploying natural language processing programs are quite divergent from the ordinary conversations of people. Their talk occurs as part of pre-programed sequences, from which they can rarely respond to conversational contingencies save in minor ways. These devices are designed to convey an impression of "immediate talk" geared to the needs of the interlocutor, but the production of machine talk is, in fact, drawn from an enormous database of code, scripted utterances and network conversation. For example, the database of chatbots and virtual personal assistants consist of programmed "appropriate replies" to even the most obscure conversations. Brian Christian, in *The Most Human Human: What Artificial Intelligence Teaches Us About Being Alive*, says of such machine talk: "What you get, the cobbling together of hundreds of thousands of prior conversations, is a kind of conversational purée. Made of human parts, but less than a human sum. Users *are*, in effect, chatting with a kind of purée of real people – the *ghosts* of real people, at any rate: the echoes of conversations past".[24]

It is only when we recognize how distinctive this relatively perfect speech mode of chatbots and virtual personal assistants is that we can begin to appreciate just how removed such technologies are from the complexities of ordinary day-to-day talk. Notwithstanding the immense technological advancements of natural language processing software such as Google's *Duplex*, everyday talk is, by contrast, much less ordered or perfected than that which is realized through these AI-powered technologies. The managing of turn-taking in conversations rarely happens in such a way that people finish the sentences they are speaking, but this in itself indicates the immense skill and practiced learning that participants demonstrate in talking and listening to each other in situations of co-presence. And, again, it is a key reason why machine language, which is linear and pre-programmed, so often falls short of the overall character of ordinary communicative exchange. Consider, for example, this statement which Amazon gave as an explanation of how snippets of the Portland family's private conversation were recorded by Amazon's Alexa and forwarded to a contact in their address book:

> Echo woke up due to a word in background conversation sounding like "Alexa". Then, the subsequent conversation was heard as a "send message" request. At which point, Alexa said out loud "To whom?" At which point, the background conversation was interpreted as a name in the customer's contact list. Alexa then asked out loud, "[contact name], right?" Alexa then interpreted background conversation as "right".[25]

Many commentators have argued that meeting the asymmetrical, inconsistent and spontaneous requirements of ordinary talk in a technologically error-free way is the next major challenge for AI natural language processing. But whether or not this is technologically feasible is not the point I am making. My argument is that what gives ordinary language its precision, as Wittgenstein showed, is its use in context – and this is something which, for the moment at least, sharply differentiates day-to-day talk and machine language. As Christian writes, chatbots appear "so impressive on basic factual questions ('What's the capital of France?' 'Paris is the capital of France') and pop culture (trivia, jokes, and song lyric sing-alongs) – the things to which there is a right answer independent of the speaker. No number of cooks can spoil the broth. But ask it about the city it lives in, and you get a pastiche of thousands of people talking about thousands of places. You find it out not so much by realizing that you aren't talking with a *human* as by realizing that you aren't talking with *a* human".[26]

Dimensions of the digital revolution: portals, desynchronization, instantaneity

These transformations in the action frameworks of talking face-to-face and digitally mediated interaction underlie and propel broader social changes. There are three such changes I seek to identify here. The first is that digitally mediated relationships, both professional and personal, are more mobile in form than face-to-face interactions. The second is that digital life is both desynchronized and individualized. The third is that the time horizon of digitally mediated interaction is shorter. Let us look at these developments here in more detail.

"Mobile" means the removal or transfer of the individual from fixed places or locations and a recasting of identity as dispersed, adrift, flowing. Throughout history, it can be said that the construction of a person's sense of identity has occurred more or less through face-to-face social interactions with co-present others. Social relations unfolded with geographically propinquities communities. In the previous section of this chapter, I have underscored that what has changed today is that digital technologies usher into existence forms of engagement with others at-a-distance based upon network connections that cross into multiple other social spaces. This does not mean, absurdly, that face-to-face social interactions decline in significance. But what it does mean is that talking face-to face is increasingly supplemented by digitally mediated interactions. Today social life is a complex, contradictory mix between being present with others – at home or in the office, for example – and digitally engaged with others through online screen encounters using information, images, communications, virtual objects and the like.

"Mobile" means equally that the person is recast as the portal. The change is exemplified by mobile devices. On digital platforms such as Facebook, LinkedIn and Twitter, individuals forge social relationships in and through networked connections. The spread of mobile devices – from smartphones to tablets – has meant a shift from fixed locations (such as the office landline telephone) to more mobile socialities (based on wireless technology and international roaming). "Mobile phones", writes Barry Wellman, "afford a fundamental liberation from place".[27] As more and more individuals use their smartphones whilst "on the move" for voicecalls, texts, emails and social media, social relations become increasingly fluid, flexible and blended. Smartphones have, in effect, liquefied the social world. It is estimated that not only do mobile phones outstrip landline telephones, but that over two-thirds of the world's population today enjoy mobile connectivity. It is perhaps difficult to overestimate the extent to which the ubiquity of digitally based, software operated, mobile communications have transformed contemporary societies and their associated patterns of social relationships.

"Desynchronization" means replacing certain traditional ways of organizing social relations with more impromptu, temporary measures. Across digital societies, today's pluralization of lifestyles and diversity of communication contexts means that the *continuous coordination and scheduling of activities* becomes central to the basic organization of social relations. A universe of social activity in which digital technologies have a central and constitutive role is one in which women and men construct their lives "on the move", fashioned on the ever-shifting ground of instant communications and information updates. The result is to change the organization of social relations away from "punctual time" and towards "negotiated time". The new way of working, and indeed of living, emphasizes ongoing "revisions to clock-time" – as we text, phone, or email colleagues and friends to readjust (and often at the last moment) previously agreed times for meetings or appointments. Making social life "work" today involves such scheduling and rescheduling of meetings, events, dates, appointments, videoconferences, trips and holidays. Desynchronization is, in short, the living of just-in-time lives – as people negotiate anew the temporal and spatial patterning of their social relations in the age of digital technologies.[28]

"Desynchronization" also refers to do-it-yourself, individualized ways of developing and deepening social relations – through the ongoing making and remaking of connections. Several years ago I wrote a book with the American sociologist Charles Lemert about identity, *The New Individualism: The Emotional Costs of Globalization*.[29] Our argument was that globalization – with its stunning technological innovations, inauguration of "global real time", and synchronization of communications, digital technologies and financial flows across the world – ushered into existence a new individualism geared to instant change, immediate gratification and the logic of the quick-fix. This new individualism which we described connects directly with the life-scheduling and do-it-yourself event-building of desynchronized social relations I am outlining here. Digital life is one in which social relations are networked, and in which the networked self must undertake regular, routine and repetitive actions of connecting and disconnecting, logging on and logging off. Another way of putting this point is that people today face the complexities of social life knowing – sometimes explicitly, but more often implicitly – that they must find ways to connect their own digital lifestyles to the networked worlds of significant others – family, friends, work colleagues.

"Short" means the logic of the instant, which seeps into social life at ever greater speed. Milan Kundera wrote that the technological revolution has bestowed on our world a fascination with "pure speed, speed itself, ecstasy speed".[30] In place of the solidity of face-to-face social interaction, and the waiting-times which accompany them, the online world of "pure speed" permits fast connections and even faster disconnections. This increasing social acceleration is not just a product of new cultural values; it derives from the very structure of contemporary social institutions and organizational life. Globalization has afforded high-speed patterns of digital interconnectedness, lightning-fast information technology and just-in-time global production processes. These affordances have infiltrated the ways we now live, resulting in shorter credible social interactions. In the shift away from jobs-for-life of traditional bureaucratic institutions analyzed by Max Weber and towards the short-term contract of globally networked organizations analyzed by Zygmunt Bauman, the unleashing of short-termism is a world of people who are rushed, squeezed, time-poor, hurried and harried.[31]

"Short" also refers to the short-term multiplication of options, rather than long-term spans of commitment. This is, in sum, the world of digital multitasking. This new way of working, living and socially interacting emphasizes multiple connections, episodic encounters, social networking, adaptable assemblages and flexible friendships. Multi-device usage has given rise to individuals who appear relatively comfortable watching Netflix, surfing the web, texting, and instructing their digital butlers to control their central air-conditioning, book restaurants and sort through options for upcoming holiday trips – and all simultaneously. "We live now", Paul Virilio writes, "in an era of no delays".[32] To which, we might add, we live in an era of limitless multiplication. That is to say, digital life is intricately interwoven with the multiplying of experiences, events and experiments. Email, messaging, mapping, apps and bots: individuals are active participants in conversations across multiple devices, seeking to stimulate life projects, business innovation, digital intimacies, and all kinds of experience which have relatively (and declining) short time spans.

Digital noise: silence is golden?

In an age of digital noise and constant communications connections, what price silence? In *The End of Absence: Reclaiming What We've Lost in a World of Constant Connection*,[33] Canadian journalist Michael Harris contends that people today have become distracted and disrupted by the continual buzz of their digital devices. The digital revolution, says Harris, has inaugurated the end of solitude, the eclipse of absence, the loss of lack. With solitude extinguished and daydreaming reveries cancelled out, our encounters with the world are now digital through and through. Very soon, Harris laments, women and men will not remember what life was like before digital connectivity. In a culture where digitalization is dominant, culture for Harris presents largely as a synthetic surface – a world of endless self-tracking, in which we are more eager to monitor software counting calories than enjoy the food we eat; and where the posting of updates on social networking sites means we are more focused on uploading photos of our social engagements than engaging in genuine dialogue with others. For Harris, the upshot is that we lose the possibilities for cultural creativity and personal innovation; we become disconnected, he writes, from "the kinds of thoughts that present themselves in our emptiest moments – the moments when we stare out the train's windows or hover on a lawn to monitor the sky".[34]

Is there anything that can be done to reverse this situation? Harris is nostalgic for the sociality we have lost in our lives, but remains optimistic that people can act otherwise. In a call for the virtues of digital monasticism, Harris recommends the full digital detox. He speaks up for the benefits of periodic digital disconnection, with no Facebook, Skype, Twitter, texts, email or Google searches. He writes of his own month-long 'sabbatical' from online life, where he turned away from digital distractions to instead concentrate on what he presents as weightier tasks. Free of endless digital distractions, he is able to read Leo Tolstoy's *War and Peace*! Interestingly, Harris acknowledges that his retreat from the domain of the digital was not always successful, and he often found himself sneaking the occasional look at his smartphone in order to check on what was happening across his digital network. Ultimately, however, the retreat was rewarding. We need, says Harris, to find ways to replace text messages with person-to-person engagement, to shift back from the world of posting status updates to talking with others about our lives and our lives in these times.

Harris's lament about the consequences of digitalization for our lives and our encounters with the world reenacts the influential view that technology produces a fragmentation of, and disengagement from, public life. As the spheres of public life shrink, and daily life becomes composed of ever-expanding digital networks and platforms, the self retreats inwards and as such cannot successfully engage with others and interpersonal communication. Such a view of communication media can be traced back as far as the second half of the fifteenth century, when Johannes Gutenberg began experimenting with new techniques of printing. It was during this time that Gutenberg's innovations in printing spread throughout towns and cities in Europe, and publishing presses came to be established in Germany, Italy, England, Spain, France and elsewhere.[35] These early presses produced proliferating volumes of the scriptures, but also books of classical theology and medieval philosophy. Many critics, including most famously Johannes Trithemius, were deeply concerned about these mass-produced volumes and their undermining of religious scribes. Whilst both Church and state sought to engage the early presses for their own ends, their control over these nascent publishing industries was limited. At risk was religious authority and the hold of the Church on political power.

Worries about the corrupting of religious belief through the advent of printing has, in our own time, metamorphosized into anxieties about the fracturing of human cognition and thought itself. Harris contends that we are living in our own Gutenberg crisis, where once sacred subjectivity is fragmented by constant communicational buzzing. In previous chapters, I have already expressed disagreement with the view that digital technology hollows out the public sphere, leaving the individual self distracted by devices and overwhelming communication demands. Harris is mistaken to believe that what passes from digital technology to our daily lives must inevitably be publicly retrograde or corrosive. It may indeed be the case that there is much about our digital lives which is passive, constrained and distracting. But this equally can be a source of social reflexivity, not an obstacle to it. Recent research shows that many individuals are actively reinventing new forms of identity and social relation out of the interplay of digital and pre-established forms of social interaction. Such reinvention is particularly pronounced in young people who have grown up with digital devices and who use digitalization in their interactions with others, communications and institutions; but digital reinvention is also a source of power for older generations as well. This can be illustrated with reference to one of Harris's central themes – the eclipse of silence. On the one hand, digital noise is undoubtedly characteristic of large areas of contemporary urban life, from unplugged Skype conversations on crowded trains to the ringing of mobile devices in cinemas and theaters. On the other hand, digital technology permits the novel development of public, cosmopolitan life – and often in ways which engage contemplation and solitude which were not available in more traditional forms of social interaction. This is evident, for example, in galleries and museums around the world, where the direct provision of digital devices serves the cultivation of a diversity of interests – including the promotion of silent reflection itself.

5
MODERN SOCIETIES, MOBILITY AND ARTIFICIAL INTELLIGENCE

The global spread of complex digital systems, such as AI and advanced automation, ushers into existence new challenges of coping with uncertainty and risk. Autonomous or self-driving cars, for example, are beset with such challenges – which involve multiple feedback loops. In early 2018, two road fatalities created worldwide attention. On March 18, 2018, a woman was knocked down and killed by an Uber test vehicle operating in self-driving mode in Tempe, Arizona. Later that week, on March 23, 2018, a Tesla Model X crashed in Mountain View, killing the driver instantly, who, it transpired, had activated the driver-assistance system. Faced with a vast array of information about these fatalities in particular and the complexity of self-driving technology in general, critics raised various concerns over hardware and software systemic capacities.[1] Some critics pointed to failings in regulations governing human monitoring procedures. The systems complexity, algorithms and travel indicators which self-driving vehicles offer are seductive. But risk does not disappear, and consequently people are wrong to place excessive trust in self-driving systems. Other critics raised important questions about the testing programs for self-driving vehicles, arguing that regulators and manufacturers must do more to make tests more effective.[2] Richard Priding argued, for example, that "the public should put pressure on regulators to set manufacturers appropriate standards for autonomous cars, so the manufacturers can then shape their tests around them and provide the necessary evidence that their technology is safe enough for use on public roads".[3] Complex systems of self-driving technology are not enough, according to some critics. What matters are the kinds of questions asked by the public, and equally relevant is the place assigned to the individual (read: passenger) in the complex digital system of autonomous cars.

What holds for self-driving technology also holds for other complex automation systems. Take, for example, air travel and the risk of flight disasters. In *The Glass Cage: Automation and Us*, Nicholas Carr – former editor of the Harvard Business Review – argues that automated technology can and often does produce shocking accidents.[4] Aviation is a signal example. Carr focuses on the Air France Airbus 447 that crashed into the Atlantic off South America in 2009, killing everyone on board. The flight was operating on autopilot when, upon entering a storm, the plane's air-speed sensors iced up and the automated system shut off. The pilots were surprised, and struggled – unsuccessfully – to regain control of the plane. For Carr, Air France 447 exemplifies the disabling contradiction that automation promises freedom yet impairs human expertise and skills. The apparently miraculous benefit of smart algorithms, says Carr, dulls human reflexes and can lead to deskilling.[5] In a related vein, Sydney J. Freedberg Jr writes of "artificial stupidity".[6] Human subjective judgment, he says, fades in the face of AI. The confidence to challenge smart algorithms atrophies. Freedberg Jr argues that the technocratic response has been to engineer the minimization of human input into complex automated systems. But what is actually needed, he suggests, is the deepening of human–machine interfaces, to reinforce the strengths of each.

Social and political engagement with technological innovation has to be a core part of any successful AI strategy and the same is true of robotics and advanced automation. The government and policymakers must have a significant role in formulating appropriate regulation and oversight of such innovation, including public accountability – which needs to be posed anew in the context of complex digital systems. In this chapter, I address the embedding of complex systems integrating AI and machine learning in dynamic social organizations – with special reference to issues of movement, mobility and immobility. I shall focus on automated mobilities and specifically self-driving cars in the first half of the chapter, and on military drones and killer robots in the second half of the chapter. Complex digital systems, I shall argue, cannot be left to themselves. How we adapt and respond to new technology that is already occurring is vital, as is human judgment in assessing and evaluating our culture of increasingly automated technology.

Automated automobility: the Google car

Current worldwide interest in the possibilities, pleasures and perils of inhabiting cars and roads through autonomous vehicle technology represents a powerful rupture in the growth of the car system. From the period of the car's development in the early 1900s, and from the inception of extensive paved roads which appeared during the 1930s, the car was deemed a self-driven vehicle.[7] As part of an emerging culture of modern technology, the car rapidly became a consumer item to be purchased and prized. A vehicle which did not require a professional driver, the car initially developed (aptly described by John Urry) as a "system of automobility", in which self-driven subjects came to traverse the (ever-widening) distances of home, work, business and leisure. Innovations in automated driving systems threaten to decisively break this connection between the car as a system of automobility and self-driving subjects. Speculation about self-driving cars is not new, and has been extensively explored through science fiction, artistic images and symbols, as well as trade exhibitions. The 1939 World's Fair in New York was one of the earliest to depict an automated highway system, at the General Motors *Futurama* exhibit. By the 1950s, various popular mechanics magazines speculated about technology-embedded highways to support driverless cars. And in 1968 the Cornell Aeronautical laboratory invented the Urbmobile, an electric car that utilized roadside magnetometers and mainframe computers.[8]

The major technological breakthrough was not to arrive, however, until 2010 with the announcement of the Google Car. Google symbolizes the advanced edges of digital technology that grew so rapidly in the early decades of the twenty-first century. With the arrival of the Google Car, this Internet giant was powerfully transformed into almost the global center for autonomous cars. The Google Car illustrated well what Jitendra N. Bajpai maintained, that whilst it "may sound like fiction the reality of traveling on robots is here now".[9] As Bajpai developed the point:

> A driverless vehicle, called autonomous vehicle, equipped with radars, cameras, sensors and equipment for communication, algorithm computations and mapping are able to steer, keep the vehicle within its lane, maintain safe distance from vehicles ahead, automatically use breaks, facilitate parking, read the road signs and talk to other vehicles.[10]

The Google model was in fact based on a sophisticated mix of software and hardware, comprising video cameras, radar sensors, lasers and the use of Google Maps to facilitate navigation between destinations. The result was a hi-tech vehicle which automatically adjusted to dynamic traffic environments without the intervention of a driver, and which could instantly take into account local traffic laws and environmental obstacles.[11]

Our present car system, based as it is upon various experiments with driverless technology, has fast reached a tipping point. Google's self-driving car reached over 2 million miles trialled on public roads across four states of the USA. This is roughly the equivalent of 300 years of road experience. But such innovation does not end with Alphabet Inc.'s car program. Many traditional car manufacturers are also investing resources in, and trialling, driverless technology. Numerous trials are ongoing in many US and European cities, including Tesla's semi-autonomous Auto-pilot Feature and Mercedes driver-assisted technologies. Other companies such as Daimler, Volvo, GM, Ford and Jaguar have developed driver-assisted technologies such as parking, cruise control, collision avoidance and lane keeping. Companies such as BMW have indicated that driver-assisted prototypes will shift to full-scale self-driving technology in the next decade. Meanwhile, it is estimated by some analysts that the Google Car will be commercially available by 2020.[12]

Thus the system of automobility inaugurated through steel and petroleum cars is undergoing extensive and multiple reorganizations, and looks increasingly likely to be supplanted by self-driving cars in the coming decades. In what follows, I briefly examine some features of this emergent system of automated automobility, concentrating on its remaking of core temporal and spatial dimensions that influence both social and personal life. There are five central points which must be underscored.

First, self-driving cars are not only a means of transport designed to get the passenger from point A to point B, but are crucially part of very many technical and system interlinkages with other advanced technologies. Self-driving cars, embedded with computing and communication technologies, are interlinked with smart road systems and hi-tech highway infrastructure which are increasingly computer-controlled through wireless network technology. Automated vehicle platooning is a good example. Recent research indicates that platooning of computer-controlled cars on smart transport grids may improve road capacity by almost 500%.[13] With self-driving cars positioned something akin to a bumper-to-bumper train, as they whizz along smart grid highways, there will be a dramatic increase in the load capacity of existing roads. Since distances between cars will be computer-controlled, it is likely that many road signs and signals will be eliminated. The implications for road transport are massive. Smart transport intersections, with vehicle technologies communicating with each other, will significantly limit both acceleration and deceleration "shock waves" which amplify along roads and highways. The gains to roadway systems will include smoother traffic flow, elimination of blocked freeway exits, reduced congestion and associated efficiency improvements for transport fleets and logistics services.[14] In short, the system of automated automobility sees a remaking of the relation between cars and roads, with a dramatic increase in the throughput of highways and motorways.

Second, the new system of automated automobility is set to deliver dramatically improved road safety. That is to say, the social benefits of these technologies will encompass not only an improved functional efficiency for transport systems and thus economic productivity, but, crucially, the well-being of people and their safety. It was estimated in 2017 that nearly 1.3 million people die worldwide in road crashes, on average 3,287 deaths a day.[15] Almost 90% of traffic accidents are caused by driver errors, and vulnerable road users such as pedestrians and bicyclists account for more than half of traffic deaths.[16] In the car system of automation, where people take the back seat to technology, there is consequently the potential to eliminate millions of road accidents. Self-driving technologies do not come under the influence of alcohol, nor do such technologies fall asleep or suffer distractions. According to Nidhi Kalra and Susan M. Paddock, automated vehicles perform better than human drivers because of improved perception (for example, there are no blind spots to visualization), enhanced decision-making (such as better planning of complex driving maneuvers like parallel parking), and better driving execution (including faster and more-precise control of steering, brakes, and acceleration).[17] Collision avoidance technologies have already significantly lowered road fatalities, estimated at a 30% reduction in the EU over recent years. Self-driving technologies thus have the potential to significantly improve public health by eradicating many of the errors that human drivers routinely make.[18]

Third, automated automobility is a disruptive innovation which threatens many industries. This point follows directly from the preceding ones. That is, an increase in road safety arising from automated vehicles does not just happen in a social vacuum; there are, again, various unanticipated consequences and system linkages. It is likely that current and future increases in road safety generated by self-driving vehicles will lead to significant reductions in insurance premiums, emergency hospitalization, car crash repairs, and traffic enforcement and policing. Car insurance companies are especially vulnerable to disruption.[19] Over $200 billion is paid in personal automotive premiums in the USA annually, a figure which will dramatically decrease as a result of the improved safety of semi-autonomous and autonomous vehicles. In addition to likely significant change to insurance and healthcare, automated vehicles are interlinked with licensing authorities and – as a result of computer-controlled driving devoid of human error- will largely eliminate the need for traffic police, infringement tickets and associated fines. Furthermore, self-driving cars will decrease pressures on urban parking, with automated vehicles self-parking in remote location when not required.[20] In short, huge disruptions to the previous locked-in interlinkages of the car system are underway, with newly emergent 'lock-ins' arising from how the system of automated automobility will develop with connected industries in the decades ahead.

Fourth, self-driving vehicles are set to powerfully transform how people spend their time 'on the road', as well as what it is they do whilst being auto-driven.[21] Mainstream transport research has, by and large, assumed that travel time (whether by car, bus, train or plane) is coterminous with wasted time.[22] Such research failed to identify the myriad of connected activities that passengers undertake whilst travelling. Recent research had highlighted that people undertake multiple forms of activity related to both work and leisure whilst 'on the move'.[23] Working, reading, studying, talking with others and communicating via mobile phone are prevalent among those travelling for both business and leisure. Moreover, such travel-related activities are often planned in advance, sometimes in great detail, by passengers before setting off for their journey.[24] With the arrival of automated vehicles, where driving does not depend on a human driver, how might these trends develop and deepen? Some early studies of automated automobility have found that – with the driver released from driving and thus able to become a passenger – the driverless car promises to become a new mode of both private and professional dwelling.[25] Passengers in automated vehicles will be able to undertake, with limited distraction, insular activities such as work, reading, or computing. So too, driverless vehicles will open up new possibilities for social interaction. The interior cabin of cars, subsequent to the eclipse of a human driver, will be significantly reconfigured in design and layout, providing greater flexibility for work, leisure and related social activities. Other studies which have addressed what we shall do whilst being driven by automated vehicles highlight that the car will now become, first and foremost, a "dwelling space".[26] Automated vehicles thus might be said to foster a new kind of 'dwelling-ness',[27] a hi-tech cocoon in which passengers are cushioned from the external environment by smart grids and informational road systems on the one hand and surrounded by micro-electronics and digital technology, including the Web, email, messaging and social media on the other. The future fully autonomous vehicle may represent a sanctuary, a zone of privatism, however minimal, between points of departure and arrival and between an uncertain present and the promises of safer futures.

Fifth, the emergent system of automated automobility promises to reduce carbon emissions and thus generate significant environmental benefits.[28] Transport is responsible for approximately one-third of CO_2 emissions, but semi-autonomous and autonomous vehicles will potentially reduce fuel consumption as well as transport and ozone pollutions.[29] Today's semi-automated systems of driver-assistance – such as cruise control – have averaged 25% in fuel savings. Moreover, innovations in car engines – for example, those that inject low GHG emission alternatives such as biofuels, liquefied petroleum gas or compressed natural gas – have resulted in considerable transport efficiencies. Vehicles with hybrid drive-train technology, which generate electricity from start-and-stop actions, have produced energy efficiencies of up to 90% compared to 37% realized in gasoline engines. Beyond the potentials of electric vehicles, EVs (such as e-scooters and e-buses) and E-mobility, self-driving cars also produce significant de-carbonization through increased overall throughput of roads, tunnels and bridges thanks to automated platooning, as well as improved efficiency as a result of projected weight reductions in future automated cars.

New wars, drones and killer robots

Advances in AI are not only about self-driving cars, smart grid cities and informational road systems. Such advances are also about war, terrorism, and the routine management of organized violence that underpins and shapes modern societies. The technological advances which have given us the Google self-driving car have also given us the Packbot, a military robot used extensively in global counter-terrorist and military operations.[30] The Packbot has been largely used to collect sensory data on dangerous military locations, and more than 2,000 of these track-wheeled robots were deployed in the recent wars in Iraq and Afghanistan. Powered by remote control, and able to climb stairs, shift over rocks or squeeze along twisting tunnels, the Packbot has been used to sift through debris following the destruction of the World Trade Center on 9/11, and was also sent to assess the damage at the Fukushima nuclear plant following the 2011 earthquake and tsunami in Japan. But on the face of things, the Packbot's military appeal has been largely as a robot war-tank, fitted with USB platforms for connecting various sensors, cameras, special weapons and other military tools for everything from remote-controlled bomb disposal to dangerous surveillance missions. The newest, updated version of the Packbot is a semi-autonomous killing machine called the Warrior, a mobile robot platform which can be fitted with lethal weaponry. The Warrior has been dubbed "a Packbot on steroids",[31] and various national defence agencies have sought the advantages of armed robotics to supplement existing weapons, chemical, biological, and nuclear systems.

The company that makes the Packbot and the Warrior is iRobot, an advanced technology group in the USA. iRobot has produced over 5,000 military robots such as the Packbot, and use of this technology has also been growing for non-military purposes such as security operations at sporting events. But if iRobot is internationally known for its production of robots to fight wars, it is equally well-known for making robots which clean floors. The Roomba, iRobot's hoovering robot, can vacuum an entire house without constant human direction. Many people throughout the world have heard about this compact hoovering robot, such has been the high level of media and public interest.[32] Global sales figures of the Roomba as of 2014 exceeded 10 million units.[33] Driven by an algorithm which sends the robot from room to room across the house, the robot vacuum is fitted with sensors which enable it to perform cleaning tasks and then return to its docking station for recharging. Other iRobot consumer products includes Scooba, a mopping robot which washes floors, and Dirt Dog, a heavy duty cleaning robot which scoops up nuts and bolts from factory floors.

As a corporation, iRobot operates a consumer division focused on household markets and an industrial division focused on sales to governments and the military. The history of technology has seen the integration of various commercial and military processes and pursuits, and iRobot is a company that has taken this convergence to a new level. According to the geographer Nigel Thrift, we witness today "society in thrall to a *security-entertainment complex*, an era of permanent and pervasive war and permanent and pervasive entertainment".[34] Thrift calls these sectors "coextensive":

> The first sector, boosted by the replacement of the binary of war and peace by a generalised state of conflict, now takes in a vast array of activities from prisons and myriad private security forces and new forms of predictive policing to the multiple kinds of surveillance that populate everyday life, which rely on vast material infrastructures. Increasingly,

after events like 9/11 and the generalised response to the war on terrorism and drugs around the world, defence has been recast as a part of this sector rather than vice versa. Equally, the entertainment sector has grown in size and influence, becoming a pervasive element of the world. From the base of consumer electronics, through the constant innovations in the spatial customisation of pleasure found in mass leisure industries like toys or pornography, through branding, gaming, and other spatial practices to the intricate design of experience spaces, entertainment has become a quotidian element of life, found in all of its interstices amongst all age groups.[35]

The parallels between the military and entertainment sectors are today not difficult to spot. Thrift argues that war and entertainment are, in a sense, becoming synonymous. Thanks to global media systems, video gaming, 24/7 surveillance and "information targeting", the military and entertainment industries have become more closely integrated in terms of their aims, procedures, protocols and operational principles.[36] Thrift calls attention to the striking juxtaposition that the iconic TV series *Law and Order* was a product of the defence giant General Electric. In the wake of the robotics revolution and advances in AI, we certainly have to consider afresh the interconnections between technology, the military and the commercial or private sector and their association with the means of waging war.

Much public understanding about new technology and warfare is either scant or imprisoned in concepts and theories that owe more to the twentieth century, and often the nineteenth century, than to today. At a time when technological advances in warfare are of signal importance to transformations in military affairs, political conflicts and escalating world violence, developing a cogent analysis of the complex terrain of technological warfare is a matter of rather more than scholarly interest. The main parameters of modern social science, following the account set out by Max Weber, holds that the nation-state has to be understood against the background of military power.[37] The nation-state, according to this standpoint, is a national community that successfully claims the monopoly on physical coercion within a given territory. This notion of the nation-state was largely based on the developing complexity of the world military order in the late nineteenth century and early twentieth century, where high-intensity political conflicts meant that states resorted to the threat or deployment of organized violence in a more-or-less chronic fashion in the management of international relations. The twentieth century witnessed a system of nation-states develop in which two World Wars unleashed the deadliest violence in history, and in which states exerted a monopoly on the legitimate use of physical force over members of their "imagined communities", to invoke Benedict Anderson.[38] The World Wars introduced factory-scale killing, in which millions of young men perished in a remarkably short space of time.

Today, the interconnections between nation-states and military society look remarkably different. There are three key institutional dimensions which have substantially transformed the international military order today: globalization; the communications and digital revolution (including the rise of the entertainment society); and systems of robotics. These institutional transformations have powerfully subverted the capacity of national societies to possess a monopoly over the means of physical violence. First, and against the backdrop of the rise of globalization, traditional ideas of a nation-state exerting a monopoly on the legitimate use of military violence are plainly dated. Not only does globalization disrupt national governments in terms of their control of economic processes such as trade and financial markets, but globalism also reshapes the very way that nation-states approach military affairs. The impact of the transnationalization of military forces is especially consequential in this regard, as soldiers and military professionals now work with and compete against many other transnational agencies and bodies. These transnational agencies include the European Union, the United Nations High Commission for Refugees (UNHCR), the United

Nations, Oxfam, Medicins Sans Frontiers, the International Red Cross and many more.[39]

At the same time, the monopoly of violence at the level of the nation-state is eroded from below as much routine military and security activity becomes outsourced to private security agencies. This privatization of security agencies needs to be contextualized in terms of growing organized crime and the spread of paramilitary groups, involving massive violations of human rights. War recast as comprising actors both public and private, global and local, has been further transformed by the discounting of the means of violence in recent decades. A dramatic fall in the cost of the means of violence has gone hand-in-hand with the communications revolution and cultures of rampant consumerism. Weapons such as knives, guns and pistols have been rendered more affordable and accessible through the Internet, and many basic weapons can now be purchased at supermarkets and hardware stores in various countries. Weapons have been individualized, stylized, and indeed sometimes rendered as 'fashion accessories'.

In recent decades, there have been many ways in which war has been recast as a hi-tech affair. Digitalization has been a crucial part of this more general process by which technology has become militarized and contested by many different kinds of intelligent machines powered by AI.[40] The widespread deployment of satellite technology to underpin real-time communications throughout the 1990s marked a significant turning point in the United States and its "Revolution in Military Affairs". New forms of network-centric technology (guided missiles, smart bombs) increasingly became a tool of war, and were initially applied in the Gulf War of 1991, the latter phases of the war in Bosnia-Herzegovina and in Kosovo, as well as more recent wars in Afghanistan and Iraq. Satellites were at once deployed as sophisticated systems of surveillance and systems of killing-at-a-distance.[41] Reflecting on the deployment of computerized weapons systems in the systematic destruction of Iraq in the Persian Gulf War, the philosopher Manuel De Landa anticipated as early as 1991 the transfer of cognitive structures from humans to machines in *War in the Age of Intelligent Machines*. According to De Landa, "it is precisely the distinction between advisory and executive capabilities that is being blurred in other military applications of artificial intelligence".[42] War becomes informationalized as never before, overlapping and intersecting with surveillance technology, artificial perception and cybernetic battle-management systems. De Landa, with an astute sense of anticipation, noted:

> robotic intelligence will find its way into military technology in different ways and at different speeds. Traditional computer applications to warfare . . . will become 'smarter' following each breakthrough in AI. Mechanical intelligence will once again 'migrate' into offensive and defensive weaponry as AI creates new ways for machines to 'learn' from experience, to plan problem-solving strategies at different levels of complexity and even to acquire some 'common sense' in order to eliminate irrelevant details from consideration.[43]

Against the backdrop of these global transformations from above and below of military power, and in terms of assessing the significance of digital technology to warfare today, several key questions can be posed. To what extent are modern-states increasingly dominated by AI imperatives in terms of their military organization? Are patterns of the techno-industrialization of war likely to become more, rather than less, prevalent as the twenty-first century advances? On a global level, what are the interconnections between warfare, robotics and mobility and how might these interconnections relate with other characteristics of AI? These questions, whilst crucial to both the current paths of development of contemporary societies and the social sciences, are too complex to be analyzed in detail here. Instead, I shall concentrate in what follows on offering some schematic answers to these questions, focusing mainly upon current and future intersections between warfare, robotics and AI.

To begin with, the stupendous scale of military expenditures in the global economy on unmanned ground vehicles, autonomous weapons systems and weaponized drones provides an important insight into the political and social changes fostered by AI imperatives. As indexed by officially published statistics in the US alone, the Department of Defense possesses nearly 11,000 unmanned aerial systems of many different types and capabilities, including unmanned surface vessels and unmanned underwater vehicles.[44] So, how many unmanned aerial systems do other countries now possess? The answer is nuanced, depending on what exactly constitutes a "weaponized system", and what figures there are should be considered estimates at best. In 2012, *The Guardian* identified 56 different types of UAVs used in 11 different countries.[45] Taken on their own, such figures might serve only as a snapshot of the influence of AI in the current global military order. It is perhaps of greater use to consider armed drones, on which there are some more comparative figures. According to an influential 2015 report, there are over 10 countries now deploying armed drones, including the US, the UK, China, Israel, Pakistan, Iran, Iraq, Nigeria, Somalia, and South Africa, as well as two non-state organizations – Hamas and Hezbollah.[46] The weaponized drone club, according to the report, reached double-digit membership primarily as a result of easy access to Chinese technology, which is less expensive than US drone technology. In 2017, it was estimated that UAVs for the military market will reach $13.9 billion by 2026, and will increase 39% from 2016 to 2022. By contrast, military drone markets at $3 billion in 2014 are anticipated to reach $11 billion by 2021.[47] Such figures at once dazzle and depress. But, again, to understand how AI imperatives have become one of the main organizing axes in global military affairs, these figures need to be contextualized in wider social, cultural and political terms.

The political character of the global flow of surveillance and killing at a distance which is carried out by armed drones is the outcome of various technological and informational factors. A central feature of the militarization of drones is the fact that the capture and organization of information by algorithms is now a direct means of waging war. In addition to analyzing the patterns of "targeted killings" through distributed forms of computation and computer-controlled "smart bombs", it is essential to consider new systems of warfare which the uptake of artificial intelligence has unleashed and which is now transmitted through global informational networks. Much of the research on new military technologies has been based on investigations of drone operating teams,[48] from computer technician's programming of code to automated software programs and algorithms used to ensure that target combatants are accurately identified on "kill lists". Quite apart from the difficulties of access that researchers encounter when investigating computer-mediated warfare, what emerges from these studies is that a vast array of military personnel and technical specialists work together on drone operating teams targeting enemies through screens, satellites, software programs and big data. Derek Gregory argues that drone warfare has inaugurated "a militarized regime of hypervisibility", one in which the extraction and archiving of data underpins the identification, targeting and execution of combatants.[49] This AI, data-driven mode of war, rich in visualization through an array of cameras, screens and surveillance, is one in which computer programmers, sensor operators, mission intelligence coordinators and drone pilots (based at their desk behind a computer) work together on "precision targeting" as part of team "kill-chain". This process of global restructuring of military warfare in terms of AI and algorithms institutes a fundamental shift in the social and political character of organized violence. In terms of how AI impacts the means of waging war, Neal Curtis has suggested that this is a shift from the age of multilateral international relations and industrial warfare to the age of unilateral transnational pre-emptive defence and algorithmic warfare.[50] Another way of putting this is that, in the shift from the Industrial Age to the Information Age, the fields of the digital and AI profoundly reshape the development of sophisticated weaponry and the means of waging war.

A further consequence of automated militaristic decision-making is that advances in new technologies and AI are able to produce potentially enormous consequences in the present and the future. Algorithms and the programming of code has recast the relationship between determinism and chance in military affairs, with the strategic and operational language of "precision bombing", "focused logistics", "predictive analysis", "battlespace awareness" and indeed the emergence of a "system of systems" defining the institutional parameters of war since the US defence establishment launched the Information Technology Revolution in Military Affairs. The classic example is the use of algorithms in the military to determine which individuals display the "signature of a terrorist" and, via software programs, the setting of the "kill target" through the deployment of killer robots or Lethal Autonomous Weapons Systems (LAWS). Such large-scale AI patterns or properties, when applied to military systems on a global scale, indicates that war in our own time has come to mean technological innovation, automation, software, data read-outs, information system architectures, speed, mobility and precision strike. Military power in the sense of big data, informational capabilities and lethal high-technology weapons are today key to the global connections stretching across the borders of nation-states and the means of organized violence.

However, what in the rhetoric of military affairs should result in "precision strikes" and "targeted killings" has, in actuality, often resulted in lethal unintended consequences. The application of AI and big data for the predictive targeted killing in war has routinely failed to produce a single or confined effect, and, for example, many drones have killed innocent civilians. I will turn to consider the claims and counter-claims regarding the accuracy of AI guiding "precise strikes" shortly. What I want to underscore here is that, when software programs, big data and AI are used to target specific individuals in settings of war and terrorism, the reason more people have been killed than the planned targets is that technological interventions in military affairs tend to produce an array of possible side effects right across the war-zone system. These unintended consequences are sometimes labelled "side effects" or "collateral damage", and one influential commentator describes them as generating "a world of irregular, chaotic motions". Colleen McCue has argued that in the deployment of predictive analytics to determine likely terrorists or suicide bombers a "significant increase in false alarms is a common problem associated with the challenge of modelling infrequent events".[51] To express this point in terms of the complexity turn in the social sciences, there is a kind of "orderly disorder" present within AI and high-tech military systems. Military officials describe war in the Informational Age using words such as "clinical" and "precise", and the technocratic imaginary promises the delivery of certainty, but the very complexity of dynamic systems means that unexpected effects with abrupt switches often occur.

Even so, unmanned drones unleash an unparalleled killing at a distance where "desk pilots" can undertake their fatal work without being physically present on the battlefield. Some critics of drone warfare argue that such technology renders invisible the human consequences of military-industrial killing. Simon Jenkins contends that drones are "fool's gold", offering the lure of killing-at-a-distance with supposed surgical precision whilst heralding unprecedented counter-productive military outcomes.[52] Drones, he says, displace and screen enemies from view – thus ushering in the "no-hands war of the future, safe, easy, clean, 'precision targeted'. No one on our side need get hurt". But the problem with this promise of technology is that it does not easily fit the contemporary realities of human suffering on the ground. Drawing from several studies of recent drone wars in Afghanistan, Pakistan and the horn of Africa, Jenkins argues that drones have in many cases killed thousands of innocent civilians and children, and largely failed to reverse or seriously impact Taliban or al-Qaeda activities. Along with Jenkins, critics have highlighted that drones remain illegal in many jurisdictions, largely because of the shocking "collateral damage" killing of non-combatant civilians and children.

One significant impact of drone warfare is the growing disconnect between contemporary societies and mediated publics on the one side and the victims of warfare on the other side. Drones epitomize war as a new kind of videogame: both the surveillance of suspects and targeted killings occur in and through an array of screens, satellites, software programs and big data. Drones are routinely operated by desk pilots killing-at-a-distance. In *Drone Theory*, Gregoire Chamayou contends that unmanned aerial vehicles, in delivering long-distance remote-controlled warfare, cancels out "any immediate relation to reciprocity".[53] Drone pilots, often dressed in "flight suits", might be located at a home base but form part of a complex "kill-chain" which is highly technically administered. A combination of desk pilots, sensor operators and strategic intelligence operators work in conjunction with superior military offices, creating a phenomenon Ian Shaw has called the "lethal bureaucrat".[54]

Unmanned aircraft systems will be crucial to the future of war because they straddle three core dimensions – digitalization, mobility and miniaturization. The 2010s has witnessed an explosion in the miniaturization of unmanned drones, some as tiny as bugs. The role of technology in promoting the shrinkage, variety and sophistication of drones means that their impact on organized violence is bound to be considerable. One of the most popular smaller drones is the Raven, a remote-controlled three-foot-long plane designed for the US military. Used extensively in battlefields across Afghanistan, the Raven has been widely adopted by defence departments throughout the world. Newer micro-drones have become so small that they resemble children's toys, and the names of such aerial vehicles – MicroBat, SLADF, and Black Widow – might have come straight from science fiction. One particularly intriguing development has been the compression of drones to such tiny sizes that their functioning can now mimic insect flight. Drones recast in the shadow of a dragonfly or wasp, with the aim of getting up close and personal to enemies with tiny sensors and video cameras, has guided the direction of recent research developments. The arrival of various "parasite UAVs", such as the Wasp and Wing-store UAV, are creating "the most sensitive installations for processing, exploiting and disseminating a tsunami of information from a global network of flying sensors". It is a tsunami of data because, whilst automatically operating algorithms process this information, there is simply too much big data – with defence and security forces now overloaded.

The advent of miniaturized, semi-autonomous weapons systems also becomes increasingly treated as the automated instrument of warfare. The result is a complex series of technologically based transmutations of the military parameters of modernity far beyond anything previously witnessed. In early 2017, for example, it was widely reported that the US military had successfully tested micro-drones as part of the future development of intelligent, autonomous weapons systems. Approximately 100 Perdix micro-drones were dropped from three F/A-18 Super Hornet fighter jets over California, and these remarkably small 16cm machines were able to swarm. According to a statement released by the Pentagon: "The micro-drones demonstrated advanced swarm behaviours such as collective decision-making, adaptive formation flying and self-healing".[55] Once constituted in this way, with each micro-drone able to communicate with the other micro-drones, the UAVs operate as a kind of collective organism, swarming throughout designated environments without being monitored or attacked. These developments are in various ways quite decisively influenced by the expansion of AI, and the strategic military objective is to overwhelm the defence capabilities of opponents with the sheer numbers of micro-drones.

It is surely evident that today's dynamic processes of technological change effected by the combination of AI, industry and sophisticated weapons development are revolutionizing the institutional parameters of organized violence and the means of waging war. The proliferation of drones in warfare, and advances in the integration of micro-drones and modes of conducting war, must have a primary position in any analysis of military power in the age of AI. Most disturbingly, the spread of AI technology has led to the further expansion of weapons development in the form of "killer robots", or Lethal Autonomous Weapons Systems (LAWS). These are weapons mediated by AI which can autonomously select, target and strike (potential) enemies without any human intervention. As we will see in the final chapter of this book, there has been a massive global debate on weaponized AI and deadly autonomous weapons, with many scientists, industry leaders and agencies demanding a pre-emptive ban on such technology. Whilst this has been a crucial debate pertaining to global futures and the techno-industrialization of war, it is vital to underscore that such killing machines already proliferate the developed arms industries. Examples of current use include the MARCbot, Pakbot, Talon and Gladiator Tactical Unmanned Ground Vehicle. The US military has invested heavily in research and testing of increasingly automated weapons systems, including the development of autonomous fighter jets and bombers.

The development of the means of waging war in the age of AI thus involves the *literal outsourcing of killing to machines*. This is a development which directly connects the control of the means of organized violence to algorithm, software and computer code. But whilst there have been very significant levels of investment in the research and development of killer robots in the main centers of the arms industry (most notably in the USA and Europe), this has also been a development which has affected a growing number of nation-states as well as non-state actors. Russia, Israel and other advanced militaries are pursuing killer robot technology for weapons development. China, according to various reports, is exploring the use of AI weaponry for the production of its next generation of cruise missiles.[56] In South Korea, an arms manufacturer has designed and built a gun turret which can identify, track and shoot targets, theoretically without the need for human intervention. Automatic military defensive systems, such as the German AMAP-ADS, the Russian Arena, and the Israeli Tropy, can autonomously identify and strike oncoming missiles, rockets, artillery fire, aircraft and surface vessels. The diffusion of automated weaponry from the advanced societies to a growing number of other states has unfolded more recently, with many countries seeking to join the LAWS race. At the World Economic Forum in 2016, Sir Roger Carr, the chairman of British weapons manufacturer BAE, stated that 40 countries are currently working on killer robot technology.[57] Whilst the application of the technological development of autonomous systems to the delivery of military weapons is only one aspect of a battery of technical advances in this area, the crucial point is that there is no agreed international relations framework specifying how these weapons might be used in times of armed conflict, and nor are there global governance mechanisms for the regulation and control of autonomous killer bots.[58]

We should be clear about what is at stake here. The automated techno-industrialization of war, and especially the application of AI and advanced robotics to the militarized world, creates high-consequence risks not previously encountered by humanity. Warnings issued about the existential threat to humanity as a result of the intensive development of AI sophisticated weaponry are many and varied. Elon Musk has spoken of people becoming second-class citizens in a Terminator world of robot wars.[59] Oxford philosopher Nick Bostrom has commented of AI threats: "We're like children playing with a bomb".[60] The late Stephen Hawking remarked: "The development of full artificial intelligence could spell the end of the human race".[61] Prophets of AI doom abound. Certainly, the global impact of lethal autonomous warfare would be instantaneous and could well be catastrophic. The social, political, economic and environmental consequences would be equally calamitous. Only time will tell whether the risks of AI warfare can be tamed, but there is plenty of action occurring aimed at countering or limiting these trends. In 2017, more than 100 signatories of AI specialists from across 26 countries called for an UN-led ban of lethal autonomous weapons. Most recently, many of the world's leading AI experts have signed a pledge refusing to work on the development of lethal autonomous weapons.[62] These are important developments. But if it is so that AI warfare presents humanity with a radical challenge, it is equally clear that today's global situation demands fresh thinking. A social theory alert to the high-consequence risks of AI warfare cannot be reduced to a concern with countertrends of resistance to military developments – however important such collective action might be – but has to investigate the possible trajectories of AI social futures. This provides a convenient transition to the final chapter.

6

AI AND SOCIAL FUTURES

Thinking about the culture of AI is essential for all societies and our potential social futures. There have been many technological transformations of the fabric of society previously, from the industrial revolution and the advent of manufacturing to the shockwaves of post-industrialization and the rise of global outsourcing and electronic offshoring. Today's breakthrough technologies, with the advent of Industry 4.0 and truly automated industries, promise stunning opportunities and new personal freedoms, on the one hand, and threaten soaring technological unemployment and global inequalities, on the other. What is happening in the digital universe is truly double-edged, split between new opportunities and threatening risks. Whilst today's technological transformations are intricately interconnected with previous historical shifts, such as the impacts of modernization and post-industrialization, this time around the global shocks induced by new digital technology look very different and the stakes of the AI revolution are arguably unlike anything previous generations have ever faced. Consider, for example, what is happening in the digital universe. The World Economic Forum's "Global Agenda Council on the Future of Software and Society", which in 2015 identified various "tipping points" with leading experts and executives from the information and communications technology sector, underscored the likely future shocks to the global economy in the next 10 to 15 years. According to the World Economic Forum, the advanced societies in the coming period will have to deal with not only mobile device body implants and widespread blockchain technology but, much more threateningly, big data government and the management of corporate boards through advanced AI algorithms.

Today we live in a world where robots move boxes in factories as well as conduct shelf-auditing in supermarkets, and where complex algorithms complete tax returns and trade on financial markets. But the consequences of our increasingly automated global world are not, as I have argued in this book, straightforward. The culture of artificial intelligence is not a one-dimensional world. In preceding chapters, I have demonstrated that advanced robotics and accelerating automation are far from simply economic in impact. It is essential to understand that AI, robotics and digital technologies must be situated within analyses of multiple everyday practices, social institutions and the forces of globalization. The contemporary phase of artificial intelligence and robotics is radically transforming the world order, shifting societies away from a world largely organized around employee-based industrial manufacture to new and future industries of biomaterial engineering, nanomedicine, advanced manufacturing, optical and electrochemical biosensors, microfluidic devices, and many more. Fundamental changes in organizational structures, social practices, interpersonal relationships and individual outlooks are accordingly unavoidable. As these technologies develop, deepen and accelerate, more and more people will be affected. But if new technologies have powerful social consequences, it is equally important to examine how the people these technologies impact deal with these changes. That is to say, it is crucial to focus on how people actually respond to, and cope with, AI, machine intelligence and robotics. My aim throughout this book has been to develop analyses of the culture of artificial intelligence, particularly as contrasted with the more technologically determinist or economistic critiques which are prevalent in the existing literature.

One of the most public advocates for the positive role that new technologies and AI will play in our very long-term futures is Kurzweil. As discussed in previous chapters, he has written at some length about "the law of accelerating returns" arising from enhanced computing power, and in particular regarding the technological enhancement of societies stemming from AI.[1] According to Kurzweil, today's exponential rates of technological change will produce a "singularity", the historical point where nonbiological intelligence outstrips biological intelligence.[2] Kurzweil is very precise about this looming global shift, and predicts the singularity will occur in 2045. The singularity will erase distinctions between humans and machines, and computer-based intelligence and AI will go into overdrive, exceeding the capacities of collective human brainpower. Clearly, Kurzweil is supremely optimistic about our AI long-term futures. Possibly utopic? Many critics argue so, dismissing Kurzweil as simply another utopian futurist.[3] His notion of the singularity, so the critics say, is simply pie in the sky. My own viewpoint is that the notion of the singularity is logically possible, though I doubt it. Whether likely or not, however, my central point is that such a scenario is far from preordained. The central argument I have developed in this book has concerned the utter centrality of complex systems to global transformations affecting relations between self, society and technology. Complex systems such as robotics and technological innovations such as AI and machine learning are characterized by unpredictability, uncertainty, zigzags and reversals. Cultural attempts at instigating new technologies, and coping with complex systems at the level of the everyday, often produce unintended consequences, revealing or generating other issues or problems, and other solutions or synergies in turn emerge in response to such interdependencies between adaptive systems.[4] I think one of the primary takeaways from complex systems thinking, when conceptualized in relation to an adequate theory of identity and everyday social practices, is that technological innovation sits cheek-by-jowl with unpredictability as well as various global shifts, convergent social developments, cultural reversals and contested futures. We have seen this in previous chapters when analyzing transformations in the dynamics of urban mobility and the possibilities for self-driving cars; multiple AI systems and the possibilities and perils of global surveillance; and the implications of advanced robotics for global manufacturing and employment and unemployment.

This book has sought to analyze and explain the big cultural changes of the digital revolution – the shifts, synergies and shocks at the levels of society and economy associated with artificial intelligence, advanced robotics and accelerating automation. In previous chapters, I have raised but not explored in any detail the various kinds of social futures unlocked by the culture of artificial intelligence. In this final chapter of the book, I shall attempt to pull some key remaining issues together and look into the future. We have seen that AI has been a central driving force for the reshaping and reconfiguring of employment and professional life, but what of our likely futures in respect of personal life, intimacy and sexuality? What kinds of future opportunities and risks might AI pose for health and medicine in the coming decades? And what contribution might AI make to public and political life? Can the renewal of democratic politics reconcile automation with autonomy, participatory democracy with AI-generated inequalities? How might a sense of cosmopolitan belonging be realigned with big data? And might an ethics of reciprocity and social responsibility be fostered in the age of advanced robotics? These are some of the questions I shall pursue here. In doing so, I shall draw on the growing number of proposals to conceptualize, visualize and elaborate AI social futures, as well as a wide range of ideas from the world of academia, social policy and think tanks. The chapter will be necessarily partial and provisional in places. It aims to contribute to the emerging academic and public debate across borders and regions about potential AI futures and alternative technological scenarios characterized by complex problems and system interdependence within this new century.

Robot intimacy

In April 2017, a Californian sex-tech company – Abyss Creations – announced it was about to unveil the world's first sex robot. The company had risen to prominence some years earlier as a result of innovations in silicon sex toys. The migration of leading-edge AI into the sex industry was to facilitate the application of machine learning to sex dolls, and as a result the sex robot *Harmony* was born. Jenny Kleeman reported on the arrival of this AI sex robot in the following terms:

> Harmony smiles, blinks and frowns. She can hold a conversation, tell jokes and quote Shakespeare. She'll remember your birthday . . . what you like to eat, and the names of your brothers and sisters. She can hold a conversation about music, movies and books. And of course, Harmony will have sex with you whenever you want.[5]

Harmony's appearance, perhaps unsurprisingly as a creation of the $US30 billion sex-tech industry, was one constructed in the image of a silicon sex doll. A sex robot with large breasts, a tiny waist, impossibly slim thighs and French-manicured fingernails, *Harmony* was marketed as "the girl you always dreamed of". A passive, pliable mechanical sex toy, Harmony can be purchased with various customized options, including a selection from 14 different labias and 42 nipple color options. These customizable features were advertised to prospective customers against the mantra of consumer choice, with different female body types presented as "prototypes".

In one sense, *Harmony* is the stain of masculinist, hyper-pornographic fantasy, which the sex-tech industry has fully colonized in its raiding of AI and robotics through a relentless search for profit. In another sense, however, *Harmony* is an invention closely allied with groundbreaking AI technologies. For this sex robot is the result of innovative convergent technologies, including facial recognition software, voice activation coding, animatronic engineering and motion-sensing technology. In the case of Abyss Creations, the deployment of AI which powers *Harmony* offers customers a machine learning system with 18 different personality traits – from kind, shy and naïve to sexual, jealous and thrill-seeking. These traits are effectively robotic platforms which can be leveraged by consumers in various ways to foster new forms of self and machine interactions. The entry level cost for this kind of robotic experimentation, bridging as it does sexuality and commercial eroticism, is approximately $US10,000.

How much can we glean about generic social changes affecting intimacy from the case of *Harmony*? Does the arrival of *Harmony* indicate that social relations are poised for dramatic transformation as a result of new artificial intelligence capabilities deployed in sexual and intimate life? It is surely clear that, broadly speaking, developments of the kind indicated by the arrival of *Harmony* are occurring across many Western societies and beyond. Dozens of firms around the world have committed research and development funding to the advancement of sex robots. Perhaps the more poignant question, then, is this: in what ways do advances in AI technologies intersect with transformations in sexuality and intimate life more generally? We can discern, I think, that robotics, smart algorithms and machine learning not only are on the frontier of intimate life today, but are opening up self-identity and personal life to new kinds of experience and technologically mediated frameworks of social and intimate relationships. This does not necessarily mean, thankfully, that men and women will be trading engagement with other people for sex assistant robots in the near future. But it does mean that the field of advanced robotics – from chatbots to telepresence robots to sex robots – is pushing new frontiers in gender, sexuality and personal life. As a result, AI is likely to become increasingly prevalent as a technological connecting point between the body, self-identity and intimate relations.

What is the significance of AI to changing conceptions of intimacy today?" Above all, it is that new cultural ideas have arisen in a world of accelerated technology for which digital transformation has become more and more important. These new cultural ideas have their roots deep in the age of information technology, the rise of robotics, cloud computing, 3D printing and the spread of artificial intelligence. The whole sensibility of intimacy has consequently undergone a radical mutation. In various traditions of social thought, from actor-network theory to post-humanism, the very word "intimacy" commingles the animate and inanimate, man and machine, subject and object. If intimacy was once about interpersonal relationships rather than impersonal objects, the affective rather than the material, this is no longer the case. Intimacy now is not just a question of erotic bonds, but crucially the cultivation of our connection to technology itself. Intimacy is the space where the erotic and *technics* meet, opening the very passions of the self to complex technological forces without. If intimacy celebrates the self in relation with others, it also cultivates technology as self-realization and not just a bundle of impersonal tools.

Intimacy has thus acquired an inescapably technological imprint. Beyond the cultivation of personal and erotic bonds, intimacy today has also come to mean dating apps, sexting, virtual reality eroticism, AI sex toys, webcam sex and other sensory devices. If the concept of intimacy has mutated in order to accommodate new digital technologies, however, this shift of cultural sensibility has not been without its problems. The trouble begins with a conflict between interpersonal and material forms of the intimate. New AI technologies, from advanced robotics to complex self-learning machine systems, open the question of an intimate bond which is no longer based on reciprocity, intersubjectivity, or communality.[6] Instead, the intimate now denotes how social life is conducted under the promptings of software code, in which formulaic statements and stereotypical expressions reign supreme.

All of this needs to be cast in terms of the wider debate over sex robots, a debate which has been conducted in the academy certainly but also the wider public sphere. This debate divides, broadly speaking, between those who consider that sex robots are a transformative force in the realm of intimacy – the boosters – and those who consider that this assessment is not only erroneous but dangerous in social and political terms – the fatalists. Dividing the debate over sex robots between boosters and fatalists is, of course, an oversimplification – as there have been various competing accounts and perspectives on the consequences of human-robot sexual relationships. But I use these terms – boosters and fatalists – to highlight some of the main lines of contention in what follows, and as a foil to try to clarify both the possible impact and future of robot sex in terms of making sense of transformations of intimacy.

Robot sex comes with a strong booster literature to support it. The British author David Levy is often cast with the boosters. His book *Love and Sex With Robots* advances the thesis that by 2050 "love with robots will be as normal as love with other humans", and indeed the study is subtitled *The Evaluation of Human-Robot Relationships.*[7] Levy says that robots are developing beyond rudimentary forms of sociability, and that we are now entering a transition phase of significant technological innovation. With AI and robotics technology advancing faster than ever before, robots are becoming more human-like, which in turn creates the possibility of new modes of human-robot configurations – including, for instance, robo-friendships and AI intimacies.

Central to Levy's argument is a conception of robots involving a significant transformation of both human sexuality and social relations. Three aspects of this tend to permeate Levy's primary lines of argument: namely, the transformation of traditional patterns of falling in love, of sexuality and sexual activity, and of relationships. By extending the field of objects with which people fall in love (from teddy bears in childhood to computer games in adolescence), robots generate new possibilities for emotional identification and sympathy, further widening the terrain for individuals to impute emotions onto inanimate objects. Simultaneously, robotics also involves a reordering of human sexuality and particularly impacts sexual activity. Put simply, as the sexual activities of people increasingly become intertwined with technological innovation – incorporating shifts, for example, from telephone sex to the remote-controlled sex devices of "teledildonics" – robots disrupt the traditional correspondence between self, sexuality and human sexual partners.[8] In transforming both the social context of falling in love and the conditions for sexual activity itself, robots reconfigure the very definition of intimate relationships. Indeed, Levy goes as far as predicting that humans will marry robots, with the additional claim that marriages between *Homo* and *Robo* will be commonplace by 2050.[9]

Enter the fatalists. For the fatalists, the whole discourse of human-robot relationships is not simply unsatisfactory but erroneous. What, they ask, could possibly be 'intimate' about robotics? Robots may be increasingly engineered as emotionally responsive to people, but this is not the same thing as emotional literacy, nor does it come close to the relational depth of human relationships. Given that both the scientific and public debate on sex, love and digital technologies has largely sidelined identity and gender, it is hardly surprising, then, that the much-heralded arrival of sex robots brings with it the death of intimacy.

Kathleen Richardson, head of the *Campaign Against Sex Robots* and a specialist in the ethics of robotics, is one of the most influential authors to contend that the risks from sex robots have been dramatically underestimated.[10] In *Sex Robots: The End of Love*, Richardson argues – *pace* Levy's boosterism – that sex robots are dehumanizing and isolating, generating new dangers especially to women and children.[11] Instead of providing new possibilities for the development of sociability, the commercialization of sex robots, argues Richardson, performs a very different function. For Richardson, sex robots help to justify and legitimize growing links between hyper-capitalist societies and neo-liberal ideologies centered on property relations. In this respect, the discourse of sex robots operates as a kind of 'intimacy myth', offering the promise of simulated human connection and communication whilst people are, in fact, increasingly distant and disconnected from each other.

To situate sex robots in terms of property relations and advanced capitalism is to see it as an intricately woven texture of unequal power relations and gender hierarchy. Richardson identifies the social relations that appear to be fostered by sex robots as modelled on sex work – though, tellingly, she deploys the value-laden language of "prostitute-John relationship" rather than "sex worker-client relationship". Enjoyment of sex robots, according to Richardson, replicates the master-slave relation. She casts robots as passive, purchased, the 'female slave'; the active, human male, by contrast, is full of agency and power – though devoid of emotion. If this makes human-robot connections sound dangerous, the risks in Richardson's interpretation prove catastrophic. The catastrophe is that sex robots unleash the darkness of human hearts, with people ruinously yielding to sexual gratification disconnected from any human reciprocity. In the face of such disconnection and distraction, with people suffering intense personal disenchantment and a callow hedonism, the only course of action remaining – says Richardson in high fatalist mode – is to abolish sex robots.

It would, presumably, be difficult to make sex robots sound more thoroughly nasty or violent. If this really is the future of sex, it is then hardly surprising that Richardson calls for a ban on sex robots. But as various critics have argued, the actuality and future of human-robot relationships need not be understood in such monolithic terms. One important criticism of Richardson's work is that developed by Danaher, Earp and Sandberg, who point out that Richardson's highly negative assessment of sex robots depends, in turn, on a very selective conceptualization of prostitution as coercive or objectifying.[12] These critics argue that Richardson ignores a vast literature highlighting that many sex worker-client relationships entail mutual respect and interpersonal understanding, especially with regular clients, and that many clients are searching for intimacy. Related objections to Richardson's call for a ban on sex robots have been developed. "Surely rather than calling for a ban on [sex robots], to forlornly try stalling technology", as Eva Wiseman questions Richardson's standpoint, "the pressure should be to change the narrative. To use this new market to explore the questions we have about sex, about intimacy, about gender".[13]

Discussions of social robots (including sex robots) often insist on the dangers of cultural self-undoing. The more actual robots appear debased and predatory, the more society is cast in the throes of a debilitating and painful change. The trouble begins with mass unemployment stemming from advanced automation, shifts to scoop up novel intrusions into privacy and data security breaches, and then spirals all the way to a full-blown death of intimacy through the replacement of human sexual relations by intelligent machines. The open question, however, is why we should necessarily view sex robots as the intensification of patriarchal ideology by other technological means. Many of the standpoints mentioned rightly dwell on disturbing trends indicating that human-robot sex can degrade respect for women in general, but tellingly remain silent on how robots might transform human needs for intimacy, possibly beneficially. It is as if the gloomy outlook developed by certain contributors to this debate can be represented only as some universal truth, as opposed to a conflict between robots and rationality, or automation and autonomy, which has come to shape our lives in these times.

Another starting point is that intimacy should be distinguished from sexuality in general and eroticism in particular. On this view, intimacy means not some grand, sweeping intersection of sexual relationships and erotic ties, but a diversity of non-sexual friendships, relationships and life-forms, each with its own modalities. In an increasingly secular age, where sexual relations are all too often reduced to the purely commercial or instrumental, it is human connection, emotional experience and the realm of the affections that sustain and multiply the intimate. In short, sexual activity is often an intrinsic aspect of achieving intimacy – but it is not coterminous with it, as the enduring importance of friendship in personal and social life testifies. To pluralize the concept of intimacy in this way is to re-open the question of how self-actualization, autonomy and other facets of emotional life could be enhanced through human-robot interaction.

As an illustration, take the changes now occurring in elderly care, associated with a raft of AI technologies and sensor-equipped environments that automatically collect data on aged users without requiring the direct involvement of such individuals. Experts in the preventative medicine and health-promotion literatures have emphasized the gains of smart digital technologies and social robots, and referred to the importance of automated health data and indicators as a means of aged patients avoiding disease and illness. But in matters of health for the elderly, robots and automated digital technologies may offer much more than simply enhanced personal health information. The work of Maartje de Graaf on elderly people's acceptance of companion robots provides a source of evidence here.[14] As de Graaf and colleagues demonstrated, in experiencing relationship-building with social robots in elderly domestic environments, with all the challenges that human-robot interactions entail, individuals are constructing innovative forms of emotional attachment with robots. The work of de Graaf was set against the background of an EU Social Engagement with Robots project, and involved elderly participants welcoming a companion robot "Karotz" (which resembled a rabbit) into their homes over two month period. There were, needless to say, negatives as well as positives for these elderly people in their engagements with the companion robot, Karotz. Significantly, the connections established with the social robot were not simply functional or utilitarian, but often appeared to involve enjoyment, care and companionship.

The work of de Graaf concerns two key modes of human-robot interaction. Individuals, she points out, "seem to respond to robots in one of two ways: either humans love and nurture social robots and build relationships with them, or humans see social robots as artificial, as machines". The ability to build a relationship with a companion robot, as de Graaf shows, depends on imagination and empathy. Constructing new forms of companionship and emotional relation to robots depends on an individual's capacity to "anthropomorphize" technical objects. Participants in the study described human-like attributes of the robot in the following ways: Karotz "gives you a few funny looks"; the robot "went into a coma with its lights still on"; or, Karotz "would sort of start to wake up and have its ears up and down". The study by de Graaf shows how individuals actively "anthropomorphize" robots and construct new forms of sociality. Yet certainly many individuals reported a sense of feeling beleaguered or ashamed. A concern that other people might think them odd for spending time and interacting with robots was prevalent. However, at the same time, it is strikingly evident from the study that individuals did share stories and confide secrets, promoting a psychological attachment to these robots.

These findings chime strongly with research I've been conducting with a team in Japan and Australia, investigating how robot developers conceive robots as possible companions in elderly care.[15] My colleagues on the team call the application of robotic technologies to the aged care sector an "imagining out" of connections with social robots. "Imagining out" involves the mobilization of imagination, fantasy and empathy as a resource to create connections, drawing together social robots and related socially assistive digital technologies to actively restructure relations between the self and the object-world, as well as new forms of sociality. Like de Graaf, Mark Coeckelbergh wants to speak up for the potential positives of social robots, or at least help us to think about digital developments in this area in less constraining ways. As Coeckelbergh writes:

> Just as we are used to living with fiction and non-fiction, we are also increasingly used to living simultaneously online and offline, or at least we are used to switching between them. The future of elderly care is a future which may or may not have robots in it, but it will certainly have us in it: care receivers and care givers who are used to dealing with ICTs or who are even digital natives: people who have never known a world without ICTs. If robots are going to swarm elderly care and health care at all (it may not happen), it is very likely that they will meet "robotic natives" who are used to having all kinds of ICTs around in their lives, including

robots. In that scenario, they will not experience living with robots as deception; they will see it as part of what it is to live with technology: part of what it is to work and to entertain, part of what it is to connect and communicate with others. New technologies might even influence what we mean by dignity, autonomy, reality, and social relations.[16]

Acceptance of social robots is in some ways even more generative than this characterization suggests. With the conjoining of AI and advanced robotics, faith or trust in impersonal technological systems, as well as in non-human others such as social robots, becomes paramount to social life. But this is not simply a reordering of relations between human actors and non-human technical objects, with robots recast as social actors; it is a fundamental transformation of the nature of personal identity itself. Personal life is increasingly intertwined with networked technological systems and objects. Both the external and internal characteristics of human-machine configurations, including relations with social robots, are shot through with personalized connections.

So, how should we assess these possible scenarios in which robots play different future roles in intimate relationships? To begin with, none of these scenarios is simply probable or preferable. Overall, the future imagined by Levy – in which human-robot marriages will be commonplace by 2050 – is relatively unlikely and obviously controversial on a range of grounds. But nor is the alternative sketched by Richardson – the banning of sex robots – the most likely AI scenario of future intimacies. The problem of ownership of the body is undoubtedly complex and one which feminist scholarship has powerfully addressed; it is also one which involves a range of problems of defining a 'person' on which Richardson is largely silent. As was mentioned before, however, an overemphasis on property relations and sex work as a model for understanding human-robot relations has had a constraining impact on this debate. In the sphere of intimacy, understood as an 'opening out' of the self to both external and internal affairs, AI and advanced robotics are evidently becoming more immediately relevant to the lifestyles, choices and identities that individuals choose. The clear risk of sex robots is that of reducing sexuality to commercialized sex, intimacy to the instrumental, and individuals themselves to isolated monads. It is as if the move to install sexuality in robots is just what risks undermining erotic intimacy itself. But, thankfully, the futures of sexuality, intimacy and technology are hugely contested. It is essential to reclaim the terrain of intimate technology futures, and to underscore the plurality of choice which is likely to prevail as women and men navigate their personal and private lives. In this section of the chapter, I have tried to underscore the importance of affection, empathy, care, concern, inwardness and imagination in human-robot relations in the field of aged care as a means to rethink intimate futures. Further research which looks at the significance of robotic technologies in childhood, friendship, long-distance relationships and many other transformations in personal life is also needed.

Healthcare after AI

Advances in information technology, artificial intelligence and robotics have to date made uneven inroads into welfare systems and the healthcare sector. In the early years of the rise of the Internet, many commentators emphasized the important benefits of the growing digitalization in medicine and healthcare. The 1990s and early 2000s witnessed the rapid development and adoption of computers that changed the way people accessed healthcare information. More and more, people became proactive in accessing medical research about healthy lifestyles and their health conditions. Others experimented with peer-to-peer support networks in care and health, sharing their learning and interests with others across the globe. The General Practitioner (GP) as the principal medical expert-system, it was widely thought, would become yesterday's model of healthcare practice. Some online GP connect programs enjoyed a period of rapid success before subsequently entering into a period of decline. Women and men, it transpired, still felt the need to consult GPs to help manage the state of their health and achieve desired medical outcomes.

During the 2010s, digital technology accelerated dramatically and more and more users of various health technologies are today navigating the novel blending of traditional medical consultations in specific institutions with online healthcare services and new virtual forms of data collection and medical imaging. Indeed, we might be on the verge today of a dramatic transformation of medicine and healthcare systems as a result of the AI revolution. One recent UK industry estimate indicates that AI health technologies will be worth £5 billion globally by 2021, which represents a 40% growth on current AI healthcare markets.[17] A raft of changes account for this rapid expansion in AI healthcare. The smartphone is hardly new, but it has taken over from where the personal computer left off, with people using increasingly sophisticated health apps to monitor the state of their bodies, track sleep patterns, monitor energy levels, map fertility statistics and other diagnostic data. The fad of Fitbit, for example, operates at both the diagnostic and normative levels; it is the continual reminder to strive for 10,000 steps each day as well a technological mapping underscoring the importance of lifestyle choices for healthy futures. Smart assistive technology, including hospital-level diagnostic and treatment technologies such as portable x-ray machines and blood-testing devices, has considerably empowered patients, allowing them more control over the medical activities or tasks associated with their disability or condition. Machine learning algorithms can recognize data and issue predictions, from reminders to schedule an appointment with a medical specialist to identifying suspect melanomas.

Mathew Honeyman, Phoebe Dunn and Helen McKenna have provided a convincing overview of innovations to the UK healthcare system – specifically, the National Health Service (NHS) – which digital technology makes possible. In their report "A Digital NHS",[18] Honeyman and colleagues cogently argue that the digital revolution represents a "step change" in how the NHS can deliver healthcare, coordinate medical services and support wellbeing. New technologies, the authors contend, offer the possibilities for far-reaching changes in the relationship between patients and health professionals in medical diagnosis, treatment, aftercare, storage of health records and data monitoring, and the advancement of healthy lifestyles. "IT, data systems and information sharing", the report concludes, "are critical to delivering integrated care and can help to coordinate care delivered by professionals across different organizations and even across patients' wider support networks". Elsewhere, Honeyman has identified the technologies most likely to transform health and care over the coming decades on a global scale. This ranges from new sensor technologies such as smart pills and implantable drug delivery to digital therapeutics and computerized cognitive behavioral therapy to blockchain technology and decentralized health records.

Honeyman and his colleagues have their eyes on near-term future transformations in healthcare. But longer-term futures are also important. Many suggestions have recently been developed to engender future automated healthcare and especially future surgical robotics. During the 2010s, a growing number of surgeons and other medical practitioners became increasingly self-conscious about the new technologies of the operating theater. By that decade, a growing divide had come to distinguish the "technological" from the "traditional" surgeon; medics who dealt with dexterous surgical robots from medics who dealt with scalpels and syringes. In this new technology terrain, the traditional tools of surgery were fast replaced by location sensors, micro-cameras and surgical bots. Abdominal surgical robotics is illustrative of this, with very significant adoption and commercialization worldwide. Surgeon Michael Stifelman, former Director of the Longone's Robotic Surgery Center in New York and one of the world's leading experts on the uses of increased automation in healthcare, has been a strong advocate of robots as providing greater accuracy and precision to surgeons in the operating theater. As Stifelman notes, more and more surgeons now sit in front of a bank of computer display screens, with their work ranging from guiding robotic arms to best position open surgery to determining the optimal exit point for machine-guided stitching. This robotic approach to surgery represents man and machine working side-by-side, and some have even suggested that these technological developments mark the arrival of the "supersurgeon". But there remains considerable debate over robot-assisted surgeries and the possible benefits of robot surgery compared to laparoscopic operations. Again, Stifelman offers an interesting perspective on the arrival of this semi-automated surgical assemblage when commenting of his own surgical practice: "The robot is one with me".[19]

Stifelman is supremely positive about the potential for artificial intelligence to transform healthcare on a global scale. Certainly, the worldwide numbers of surgical robots handling basic, as well as increasingly advanced, procedures at the surgeon's command supports this standpoint. Focusing specifically on abdominal surgical robots, which has been the fastest growing segment of the hi-tech medical device industry, market research predicts worldwide growth from $2.7 billion in 2016 to $15.8 billion by 2023. Robotic-assisted surgery has witnessed significant growth not only in the treatment of abdominal disease conditions, but also benign and malignant urological and gynecological diseases. There are several major technologies for these robotic surgery applications, and one of the most significant is the da Vinci robot manufactured by Intuitive Surgical in California. The da Vinci robot costs in excess of $2.5 million, and there are now more than 3,600 of these surgical robots installed in hospitals worldwide.

"The robot is at one with me". Stifelman's reflection is interesting, and it is worth considering its implications a little further. Does this mean, for instance, that surgical robots are always under the control of the medical practitioner? Or, alternatively, might it mean that surgical robots handle routine medical tasks in relatively autonomous ways? The answer to the last conjecture at present is no, though as the divide widens in medicine and healthcare between "technologists" and "traditionalists" the role of automated surgical bots is likely to remain a flashpoint. For the most part, surgical robots operate under a surgeon's command. The promise of the technological sciences may be great, with implications far beyond current models of healthcare and medicine, but for the moment surgical robots remain under direct human control and medical supervision. Yet it is interesting to note that this is not always so in other areas of medicine and healthcare. In corrective eye surgery, robotic automated systems make incisions into the patient's cornea. In arthroplasty, or knee replacement surgery, semi-autonomous robots cut through bone with the kind of precision that many leading specialists are unable to attain. In hair transplant surgery, robotic systems are used for identifying healthy hair follicles, harvesting them, and making minuscule incisions in the scalp of the patient in preparation for hair transplantation.

Thus a shift from automated to autonomous robotic surgeries might take place sooner than anticipated by many experts. As one analyst writes: "If robotic surgeons become commonplace in operating rooms, it seems only natural that we'll trust them with increasingly complicated tasks. And if the robots prove themselves reliable, the role of human surgeons may change dramatically. One day, surgeons may meet with patients and decide on the course of treatment, then merely supervise as robots carry out their commands."[20] Developing transition to autonomous robotic surgery would involve very significant changes to healthcare and medical systems, and there are a host of complex issues, problems and possibilities arising that will require informed public policy responses now and in the future. Digital technology continues to promote an unprecedented level of dynamism, however, and the speed of technological innovation is such that the dilemmas of autonomous robotic surgery are already being eclipsed by new and advanced micro-robotics in the medical and healthcare fields. Smart or implantable drug delivery technologies have been under development for some period, but it is the arrival of miniaturized robotic surgical devices and edible robots which has taken the AI revolution in healthcare to an altogether different level. Soft micro-robots now can perform medical procedures once thought purely the province of medical practitioners. Recent examples include the following:

- Rani Therapeutics have developed an ingestible robot, designed with a carbohydrate-based syringe, which can deliver medicines to designated locations of the body – such as the intestinal tract.
- Researchers at the Max Planck Institute in Germany have pioneered an ingestible endoscope, a kind of micro-bot which medics can operate from outside of the patient's body. This microscopic bot can pass through the human gut and deliver a fine-needle biopsy.
- Researchers at the Swiss Federal Polytechnic School in Lausanne have tested concepts in soft robotics, designing softbots made out of edible gelatin and glycerin materials. These softbots are biodegradable, and will breakdown and be digested by the patient's body. One possible future use of this research is that of food transportation, where the micro-bot effectively functions as food.

The overall level of scientific and technological innovation here is stunning. Yet we have no easy way to determine whether edible bots are set to transform people into cyborgs and revolutionize healthcare, or whether many of these innovations in robotic medicine and automated drug delivery are simply the latest form of society's hankering for technological utopia. What does appear plain is that many of these shifts in healthcare and medical technologies have no precedent in history, and consequently presents society, culture and politics with fresh opportunities and risks in equal measure.

So the prospect of robot physicians replacing surgeons is not as futuristic as it may sound. Virtual and augmented reality within operating theaters is already used to train medical students, and is transforming medicine in countries where there is limited access to training facilities. Future medical teaching is likely to deploy haptic technology, where student surgeons will be able to use "virtual blades" and experience the sensation of the medical operation through virtual simulation.[21] In addition, thanks to miniaturization and cost-reduction trends in technology, robots will not only assist surgeons with routine tasks, but look set to take over entire fields in medicine and healthcare. That is to say, there is an emergent shift from automatic to autonomous robotics occurring in the healthcare environment. Over the past decade, robotics and AI technology has become the subject of lively discussion in biomedicine, especially among authors with an interest in social futures. One influential author in this field, mentioned throughout this book, is Kurzweil. In *The Singularity Is Near* and some other studies, Kurzweil has sought to elaborate in some considerable detail upon the implications of contemporary biomedicine, and the possible augmentation or optimization of the human body arising from AI and nanobot technology. According to Kurzweil, "accelerating progress in biotechnology will enable us to reprogram our genes and metabolic processes to turn off disease and aging processes. . . . As we move toward a nonbiological existence, we will gain the means of 'backing ourselves up' (storing the key patterns underlying our knowledge, skills, and personality), thereby eliminating most causes of death as we know it".[22]

There appears no occasion here for the predictable biologically determinist or culturally historicist riposte that aging is always genetically sealed or contextually specific. For the point that Kurtzweil is making is not that biology and aging are noncontextual, but that they will be altogether outflanked with alarming speed by nonbiological information technology, erasing distinctions between human and machine or between the physical and virtual worlds. The most significant feature of Kurtzweil's analysis, for my concerns in this chapter at any rate, bears upon the *life consequences* of nanobot technology, established as a generative form of nonbiological redesigning of the biological realm in the late twenty-first century. Kurtzweil argues that artificial intelligence and nanomedical interventions into biological health will radically transform "frail version 1.0 human bodies" into "more durable and capable 2.0 counterparts", based upon reverse engineering and superintelligence. In some places Kurtzweil speaks as if AI were the direct instrument of immortality, sweeping away once and for all the constraints of biology imposed by the human body and the aging process. There is a passage, for example, where Kurtzweil predicts that in the near-future: "Billions of nanobots will travel through the bloodstream in our bodies and brains. In our bodies, they will destroy pathogens, correct DNA errors, eliminate toxins, and perform many other tasks to enhance our physical well-being. As a result, we will be able to live indefinitely".[23] One might be forgiven for thinking that such utopic forecasting is easily lampooned, and indeed there have been many criticisms levelled against Kurzweil's futuristic claims. But it would, I think, be a mistake to see this analysis as portraying an unrealistically utopian view of AI societies. Kurzweil has a remarkably impressive track-record in predicting social futures, and much of his analysis is grounded in medical research on nanobot technology. Kurzweil invokes, for example, the research of amongst others Robert A. Freitas Jr. on nanomedicine, and specifically his reengineering of biological systems on a molecular scale. Nanobots designed by Freitas can remove unwanted chemicals and debris (from prions and protofibrils to malformed proteins) from human cells; such medical micro-robots, says Kurzweil, will function as "cleaners" of the human body.

These points being noted, however, it still seems important to develop a critical perspective capable of addressing contemporary biomedicine and technologies of optimization in such a way as to show what form biotechnology will take within the overall society in both the near and long-term future. Medical sociologist Nikolas Rose's formulation of what he calls "the politics of life itself" is an endeavor to do just this. Rose's ideas were worked out against the theoretical backcloth of the late French historian Michel Foucault's brand of post-structuralism as an attempt to provide a more sophisticated account of developments in the life sciences, biomedicine and biotechnology. Like Kurzweil, Rose emphasizes that biotechnology is fundamentally geared to an optimization of the human body and self-identity. Contemporary biomedicine, says Rose, enables intervention into vital biological systems in ways previously unimaginable. He writes, for example:

> Once one has witnessed the effects of psychiatric drugs in reconfiguring the thresholds, norms, volatilities of the affects, of cognition, of the will, it is difficult to imagine a self that is not open to modification in this way. Once one has seen the norms of female reproduction reshaped by assisted conception, the nature and limits of procreation and the space of hopes and fears around it are irrevocably changed. Once one has seen the norms of female aging reshaped by hormone replacement therapy, or the norms of aging male sexuality reshaped by Viagra, the "normal" process of growing old seems only one possibility in a field of choices, at least for those in the wealthy West.[24]

Rose thus contends, in strikingly Foucaultian vein, that contemporary biomedicine and biotechnology inaugurates a new order of social relations by marking the limits of the organic realm, and thus refiguring the contours of human life itself. "The new molecular enhancement technologies", writes Rose, "do not attempt to hybridize the body with mechanical equipment but to transform it at the organic level, to reshape vitality from the inside".[25] New biotechnologies of enhancement, says Rose with a neo-Foucaultian emphasis on containment and regulation, redraw the boundaries between the biological and the nonbiological through processes of isolation, mobilization, accumulation, storage, delimitation and exchange.

Rose's writings at this point serve as an apt counterweight to Kurtzweil's accentuations. According to Kurtzweil, contemporary biotechnology is engaged with the biological reengineering of human life. Future trends in medicine and healthcare are almost certain to realize the surpassing of biological constraint, says Kurzweil. It is no doubt for this reason that Kurzweil gave his book, *The Singularity Is Near*, the subtitle: *When Humans Transcend Biology*. But things may not be as cut and dried as Kurzweil postulates. According to Rose, the future of biomedicine and biotechnology represents not so much a transcendence of biology as a lifting of biology to the second power. In the age of biotechnology and artificial intelligence, says Rose, "the human becomes not less biological, but *all the more* biological".[26] According to Rose, AI and new biotechnologies do not just enhance health, reverse aging or transform self-identity, but fundamentally alter the realm of the biological. While Rose's claim that "biotechnology changes what it is to be human" should be preceded by the dictum that "biotechnology changes what it is to be biological" is a useful corrective to Kurzweil's thesis of transcendence, it is arguable that it also illuminates important aspects of AI and the digital transformation of medicine and healthcare. Perhaps we can best express this, however, by saying that the advent of AI societies promote a transformed mixture of the biological and nonbiological at the level of both individuals and social organization radically different to that prevailing in late 20th-century post-industrial societies.

Even so, and not withstanding these theoretical differences of interpretation, there remain significant practical limitations to the influence of nanorobotics on medicine at the current juncture. One key challenge concerns getting nanoparticle robot approval from the US food and drug administration (FDA). The FDA requires that both nanoparticle robots and the relevant pharmacological drugs are proven safe in combination, which has resulted in a complex approval process with many retests in laboratories, on animals, and on people in clinical trials. FDA approval rates of nanorobots tell an interesting story. The first nanoparticle robot was approved by the FDA in 1995. In the time elapsing since then, it is estimated that only 30 or so nanoparticle drugs have been marketed. In making this point, I do not mean to suggest that current administrative hurdles will blunt the most stunning technological developments in nanomedicine. Yet it is hard to resist the conclusion that Kurtzweil's prediction that nanorobotics and intelligent computation will soon restructure entirely our bodies and brains, destroying pathogens such as viruses, bacteria and cancer cells before they can even strike the individual, is somewhat blindly optimistic. The point is that we do not know when, and with what consequences, advances in nanorobotics might generate new practices, habits, dispositions and values to re-organize the molecular level on which human life is understood in medicine and on a global scale. So there are no guarantees that Kurzweil's future of "nanobots in the bloodstream" will be automatically realized anytime soon. And yet nanorobotic advances in medicine involving the building of micro packages which sense metabolic chemical imbalances, check hormone levels, repair cell membranes, deliver drugs and potentially correct DNA errors suggest that we are at a profound turning point in many areas of the life sciences and biomedicine, as well as the management of healthcare and human life.

Democracy beyond AI

The digital revolution creates daunting challenges for democracy and democratic politics. Among these challenges are to be counted the new benefits and burdens to democracy resulting from the coming of AI, smart algorithms and chatbots; the dynamics of the immediacy of communication (Facebook, Twitter, Tumblr, YouTube and the rest) which produce advantages and difficulties in equal measure within polities and between nation-states; the development of natural language processing and advancement of machine learning which has transformed the service industries, customer sales as well as political elections and novel techniques to influence voters; and, the rapid growth of big data which, combined with advances in computing technology, has generated new government surveillance systems and surveillance-based business models throughout modern societies.

Against this backdrop, the sociologist Manuel Castells has argued that democracy today is negotiated on two battlefronts.[27] The first battlefront is that of representative democracy – entrenched in territorial politics and the machinery of government. The fundamental institutional features of representative democracy are the nation-state, local or regional politics, and industrialized economies. As a system, the pace of representative democracy is unhurried: political deliberation and negotiation happen slowly. The second battlefront is that of digital tech, or data-driven politics. The fundamental features of this model are the Internet, the extra-territorial, globalization, decentralization and data networks. Politics in this model is instantaneous in nature. According to Castells, the two models are at odds with each other, and it is not self-evident that democracy can survive the challenges of the digital revolution.

What are the implications of this argument for democracy, and for the current fortunes of democratic politics? In earlier chapters we have considered how, with the advent of the digital revolution in general and the diffusion of artificial intelligence in particular, public life and politics – in everything from employment, unemployment and the future of jobs to mobility and transport policy – have come to confront new challenges and risks. One central development is the growing amount of data which underpins institutional and state activities today. As we have seen, data production is now roughly doubling every year, and with the emergent Internet of Things the world's production of data is set to skyrocket. This explosion in data is generated by smartphones and social media to be sure, but increasingly by smart homes, smart factories and smart cities too. This raises the vexed question of whether, in the aftermath of the automation of industry and the digitalization of mobility, the automation of politics and public life might be next? That is to say, might artificial intelligence – parallel with a programming of the economy and industry – usher in a world of the programming of citizens? Such an Orwellian scenario requires us to confront the issue of how democracy can survive the unleashing of AI, advanced automation, and big data. There is a widespread feeling of threat to democracy today, triggered by foreign influence campaigns and election crises, but also by growing signs of governmental and corporate intrusions to privacy and private life. This section of the chapter seeks to address these threats and challenges by exploring the meaning of democracy in the context of the progressive enmeshment today of polities and societies in complex systems of AI, mass-surveillance networks and automated phenomena.

Few notions have been as fiercely contested – both inside the academy and on the streets – as that of democracy.[28] I shall not seek here to trace the trajectory of those debates, nor shall I attempt to sketch an outline of the development of modern democracy in relation to the media age and the digital revolution. But I do want to underscore the importance of liberal representative democracy for understanding some aspects of the structure of modern states, economies and societies, even though I will go on to argue that (1) the tradition of liberal democratic thought is unable to adequately comprehend dimensions of contemporary large-scale social organization; and that (2) there are today various global and technological developments occurring which put considerable pressure on democratic polities and stretch liberal democratic theory, in effect, to breaking point. David Held has eloquently explored the distinctive liberal traditions which embody quite different understandings of the foundations and structure of liberal democracy, examining different conceptions of the individual person, of freedom, and of the rights and responsibilities of citizens in the wider context of political communities.[29] One particular thread of the liberal tradition – as developed in the writings of Jeremy Bentham, James Mill and John Stuart Mill – emphasizes the free expression of opinion as essential to the democratic flowering of a diversity of viewpoints across society at large. This is the familiar liberal account which seeks to explain the origins of democratic participation in terms of individualism and the freedom of the individual. Although this liberal account has been developed with varying degrees of subtlety, its basic outline emphasizes that the freedom to express personal thoughts and individual opinions in public, however troubling such viewpoints might be for government authorities, is a constitutive feature of modern democratic life.[30]

What role have individual human rights played in the formation of modern democracies? In a world of conflicting values, how should we understand the social impact of the freedom of expression in the cultivation of democratic public life? As noted, early liberal political theorists saw the main transformative power impacting the spread of democratic politics in terms of individual liberties, freedom of expression and it's empowering of citizens to engage in democratic debates over civil and political rights. Other authors who have articulated contrasting interpretations of the development of modern democracy have also emphasized the cultivation of forms of "public opinion" to the spread of democracy. Writing from a more critical perspective, Jürgen Habermas – in his much celebrated volume *The Structural Transformation of the Public Sphere* – traced the emergence of forms of "public opinion" in early eighteenth-century Europe across literary salons, coffee houses and 'table societies', where a diversity of groups met to exchange opinions on a dizzying array of ideas and ideologies. In this work, Habermas confronted more recent social developments, including the rise of mass media (newspapers, radio, TV), and argued that the public sphere during the twentieth century entered into a period of sharp decline. The global expansion of capitalism, and associated commodification of media, spelt major problems for the democratic vitality of the public sphere. The public sphere became shrunken, according to Habermas, as the corrosive bureaucratic logic of capitalist society came to eat away at the practical and civic agencies of everyday life as well as eroding the influence of broader democratic norms; in one passage of the book, Habermas writes of "a great mass of consumers whose receptiveness is public but uncritical".

Notwithstanding the ongoing significance of these conceptual accounts of democracy and public life, today's world is clearly a very different one to that of the nineteenth and twentieth centuries. As the Cambridge sociologist John B. Thompson has previously argued, the transformation of media industries into large-scale corporate entities and the rapid globalization of communication have profoundly altered the conditions and contours of public life and democracy. As Thompson writes:

> early liberal thinkers did not anticipate the extent to which the autonomy and sovereignty of particular nation-states would be limited by the development of transnational networks of power and by the activities and policies of institutions which operate increasingly on a global scale. . . . [T]he degree of interconnectedness has increased significantly. This is true in the sphere of information and communication just as it is in other sectors of commodity production. In an age when global communication conglomerates are key actors in the production and distribution of symbolic goods, a reflection on the conditions of the freedom of expression cannot be restricted to the territorial framework of the nation-state.[31]

Thompson is undoubtedly correct, in my opinion, to emphasize the transmutation in democracy as a result of the interacting forces of economic globalization, the globalization of communication and of large-scale media conglomerates. Freedom of expression has been significantly impacted in both positive and negative forms, as a consequence of the changing nature of global communication networks. But the idea of the free individual as the foundational core for freedom of expression in modern democratic society can no longer be taken for granted as a result of other, more recent, technological transformations and scientific advances too. Vast increases in computational power, advances in artificial intelligence, innovations in natural language processing, and super-fast data which facilitates social bots to pass as flash-and-blood agents on social media: these are just some of the recent technological developments which might reasonably make us pause and question liberal, individualist conceptions of democracy.[32]

The boundary between the institutions of representative democracy and the digitalization of public life and politics is becoming blurred, an historic development in the advancement of technology. There has come into existence a generalized digital world which is restructuring global power and the modern democratic state. Social bots routinely perform automated social media manipulation, influencing consumer trends and swaying political opinions in equal measure. Predictive AI targets consumers according to their personal preferences, device usage and social networks. Automated software ramps up political communications during elections, spreading 'fake news' with ever-more sophisticated Twitter and Facebook bots. Governments, and on a massive scale, deploy AI to 'nudge' citizens towards social policies, whether in the spheres of health, education, the labor market or the environment; the shift to governmental "big nudging" – the blending of big data with nudging – also promises the coordination of citizens without participation in democratic processes.[33] There is an even darker side to the development of AI which is predictive too. Governments in Asia, including India and China, have created social media labs to monitor online social media and create massive centralized databases to conduct mass surveillance. Predictive AI, smart algorithms and big data, in other words, have been deployed as technological tools by the state to gather information on what citizens do, what they think and, increasingly, to monitor how they feel. This new digitalized order is one of multiple risks, threatening to tip the balance of power in favor of the state, and reshape the contours of the sovereign political subject.

An exemplary instance of the threat to democracy posed by artificial intelligence is that of Russiagate, and the associated raft of investigations into Russia's interference in the 2016 US election.[34] The complexities of these investigations are many and varied, but the core elements of this political scandal (at least for our purposes) can be summarized as follows. In January 2017, when Donald Trump was sworn in as President of the United States, the Federal Bureau of Investigation, the Central Intelligence Agency and the National Security Agency concluded a report "with high confidence" that the Russian government had conducted a covert operation to influence the 2016 US election by damaging Democrat Hillary Clinton's campaign and promoting Republican Donald Trump's bid for the Presidency.[35] Whilst President Trump questioned the accuracy of these claims, the report by the FBI, CIA and NSA set off shockwaves around the world. Now there is, of course, nothing new about foreign influence operations, which have long been exercised by security agencies throughout the world.[36] In Russiagate, however, the influence operations were exercised not only by Russian intelligence employees but paid hackers or "trolls" in Eastern Europe and a vast network of social media bots, powered by AI. Former Director of National Intelligence James Clapper wrote of the scale of this influence operation: "Facebook has said Russian content reached 126 million of its American users – an astonishing number, considering that only 139 million Americans voted".[37]

In May 2017, Robert Mueller – the former Director of the FBI between 2001 and 2013 – was appointed Special Counsel to conduct the US Justice Department's investigation into "any links and/or coordination between the Russian government and individuals associated with the campaign of President Donald Trump, and any matters that arose or may arise directly from the investigation". At the time of writing, the Special Counsel investigation had resulted in dozens of indictments for federal crimes, including five guilty pleas from former Trump administration and campaign officials.[38] One of the most damning assessments of the Trump Administration's handling of Russiagate was delivered by former FBI Director James Comey. In his book *A Higher Loyalty*, Comey writes that, upon learning the intelligence community's findings on Russian election meddling, Trump's team "had no questions about what the future Russian threat might be".[39] Instead, Trump and colleagues concentrated on how to "spin what we'd just told them" for media dispatch. Specifically in respect of Russian interference in the US election, Special Counsel Mueller brought charges in 2018 against 26 Russian nationals and 3 Russian companies. A first set of indictments was issued in February 2018 against the Internet Research Agency, sometimes labelled a "Russian troll farm", relating to propaganda designed to interfere with the 2016 US election campaign. In July 2018, a second set of indictments was issued against Russia's military intelligence service, in which Russian GRU officers were charged with hacking and leaking emails from the Democratic National Congress.[40]

A series of investigative reports by *The New York Times* uncovered some of the key processes used in this influence operation, with a strong focus on the role of AI and social media bots. US intelligence agencies had identified the website DCLeaks.com as the products of the Russian military agency G.R.U. Uploaded onto DCLeaks.com was a diverse collection of hacked emails from the Democratic National Committee, which in turn was picked up and promoted by some users (both human and non-human) on Facebook, Twitter and Reddit. In time, WikiLeaks were to publish thousands of these Democratic emails – filtered from Russian intelligence hackers. Perhaps the most notable feature of this foreign influence operation was the informational operations conducted on social media, where a range of users deploying fake accounts would draw attention to, and comment on, the email leaks. These thousands of fake accounts, routinely posting anti-Clinton messages, were in fact bots – firing off automated responses to influence voters.

Clinton Watts, who had worked as a cyber intelligence officer mapping Russian influence activities for the FBI, concluded that social media – including Twitter and Facebook – incurred a "bot cancer eroding trust on their platforms".[41] Whilst some analysts have argued that bots can advance the democratic process, through, for example, disseminating policy information, this deployment of social media bots to sway political opinion in the US amounted to major subversion of the democratic process. As investigative reporter Scott Shane for the *New York Times*, examining an in-depth study of how this Russian 'bot attack' unfolded, wrote:

> The researchers discovered long lists of bot accounts that sent out identical messages within seconds or minutes of one

another, firing in alphabetical order. The researchers coined the term "warlist" for them. On Election Day, one such list cited leaks from Anonymous Poland in more than 1,700 tweets. Snippets of them provide a sample of the sequence:

@edanur01 #WarAgainstDemocrats 17:54
@efekinoks #WarAgainstDemocrats 17:54
@elyashayk #WarAgainstDemocrats 17:54
@emrecanbalc #WarAgainstDemocrats 17:55
@emrullahtac #WarAgainstDemocrats 17:55

During the US election campaign, in short, Twitter accounts (and other social media accounts too) were taken over by bots, with the large bulk of these accounts suspected of links to Russia.

The development of softbots, combined with the rise of artificial intelligence, has created the conditions where the security, freedoms and democratic processes of advanced societies have come under pressure as never before. But sustained critical analysis of these pressures on democratic politics has been thin on the ground. In some instances, critics have dismissed the political significance of data mining incursions into the functioning of democracy as over-reactions generated by liberal elites or the media. In a related vein, some critics have preferred to focus on the eccentricities or idiosyncrasies of President Trump – making the point that it is hardly surprising that the former reality TV star should seek to transform the White House into reality TV – rather than seriously consider the political consequences of the corrupted 2016 US election as a result of the malicious deployment of social media and AI to spread disinformation. There are many difficult questions surrounding AI and democracy, and it is important to understand that the uncertainties over softbots and social media trolls pushing misinformation on voters must be situated in wider social and political terms than the 2016 US election alone. For one thing, and as various commentators have pointed out, data mining was first used in the 2008 US election campaign by President Obama.[42] Another important point is that signs of the corruption of democracy through the malicious use of AI have impacted upon electoral processes around the world, from the UK's vote to leave the EU to the Catalonia independence vote in Spain. Indeed, the University of Oxford's Computational Propaganda Project estimates that, in 2015, more than 40 countries used political bots or automated algorithms to influence public opinion.[43] A whole range of broader questions need to be asked and answered here. But still the 2016 US election and the impact of Russian interference in American politics remain a focal point when it comes to considering whether democracy is threatened by AI, algorithms, automation and machine learning. Russiagate stands out as of key global importance because US security agencies agreed that Russian deployments of AI and social media bots had secretly swayed political opinions in America, thereby delegitimizing democratic political processes. But Russiagate is also important because it highlights not only that the digital revolution is undermining democratic politics, but also that such processes of corruption operate through largely *invisible* means, with the hard-to-detect work of softbots and below-the-radar impact of smart algorithms deployed by foreign governments to subvert the procedures, rules and laws of liberal democracies.

It seems self-evident that the problems confronting democratic politics in the face of AI and big data are enormous.[44] There can be little doubt that the intrusion of AI and big data into modern politics and election practices pose new questions about how processes of democratization can be protected, let alone advanced, in our new information age. What is perhaps less clear is why AI and big data create such breeding grounds for the undermining of the institutions of representative democracy. Certainly, the trend towards micro-targeting risks moving nation-states further away from the democracy of the public sphere, towards a digitized, disillusioned democracy in which "cynical voters" are targeted based on narrow issues inflaming fear, deploying false claims or misinformation that are not subjected to public scrutiny. The scandal of Russiagate (and the associated scandal surrounding the data mining of Cambridge Analytica, discussed in Chapter 1) raise huge challenges to democracy in an age of big data, where sophisticated AI and machine learning are increasingly targeted towards persuasive computing, and a systemic online environment in which there are substantial financial incentives to promote misinformation, with advertising revenue flowing most rapidly to those achieving 'resonance' and 'shareability' rather than factual accuracy. These are clearly massive challenges for policymakers, and in early 2018 the European Commission responded by appointing experts – comprising representatives from civil society, news media organizations, social media platforms, journalists and academics – to formulate recommendations on countering the spread of fake news and online disinformation.[45] I will return to such policy developments in the next section of this chapter.

Reconciling new technology and democracy is a deeply contentious issue, and hence it is important to underscore the massive impact across democratic polities that the digital revolution has had in terms of threatening the democratic involvement of citizens. Those that live in liberal societies today might be said not just to inhabit representative democracies but digital ones too. The Internet, social media, fake news, bots and trending algorithms: digital technologies and other technological innovations are transforming established connections between the nation-state and democracy. At the core of social anxiety about deceiving trending algorithms and the spreading of fake news in political elections lies concern over the participation of individuals in democratic decision-making and the collective will-formation of the democratic polity. Now democracy, in its broadest sense, has long been regarded as equivalent to 'polyarchy' – meaning rule by the many, involving polyarchic systems and procedures promoting debates and other expressions of preference to counter the arbitrary use of power.[46] Many theorists of democracy have emphasized that freedom of expression and the formation of debate between citizens to influence policy decisions are fundamental to democratic norms. But if we stop and pause to relate the discussion of democracy back to that of digitalization, we can see that the growing influence of AI is highly problematic for democratic politics. With data-politics, the aggregation of multiple streams of data and the growing reach of digital surveillance, some of the core rights and prerogatives of liberal democracy are profoundly threatened. Dialogue with the opinions, and consideration of the preferences, of other citizens considered as political equals is important to the democratic process, but in our own time where softbots can influence citizens on social media platforms this can no longer be assumed to operate unproblematically. The sociological trend, in short, may be that of a shift from the *programming of computers* to the *programming of people*.[47]

Over recent years, AI has become associated with the conquering of democracy as machine learning has influenced people's emotions and bots have spread misinformation during general elections. Some critics have spoken of the erosion, diminution or undermining of democratic politics, while some people – politicians, political activists and public intellectuals – have insisted that what is needed today is nothing less than a full reboot of democracy in the face of the new digital age. Whilst it is certainly evident that AI has heralded new limits to traditional politics and presented radical challenges to democracy, the argument I set out here is sharply critical of such political resignation. Simplistic formulations about the death of democracy in the aftermath of AI misrepresents the nature of today's challenges and risks. While AI is undoubtedly reconfiguring the terrain in which democratic institutions support and sustain public debate, it remains the case that political parties, public authorities, intelligence agencies and citizens more generally are deeply involved in this very process of realignment (for example, through public scrutiny and parliamentary investigation of instances of systematic misuse of AI-driven technologies to manipulate elections). In other areas, such as media and the creative industries, innovators have advocated an activist approach to deploying new technologies to enhance democracy, while in the scientific domain the advancement of prevention strategies to counter the malicious use of AI by dictators, criminals and terrorists has moved center-stage in recent times.[48] These are not developments which can be apprehended convincingly from the standpoint of the erosion of the public sphere and decline of democracy. Rather, these developments are better understood as the expansion of arenas of contestation and conflict, each linked to the culture of AI. Not all disputes over AI are, of course, either clear-cut or resolvable: such an outlook would be to misrepresent the high degrees of technological innovation and scientific experimentation which are driving social changes across the world.[49] But it is valid to say, I think, that democratic contestation has been at the core of public engagement with AI, rather than to say that the advancement of AI has blunted democracy *in toto*.

It is important to be clear about what is at stake here. On the face of it, the advent of advanced AI softbots, machine learning, big data, psychographic profiling and social media propaganda trolls lies at the core of all this turmoil spreading throughout democratic societies. Unfortunately, the conceptual and practical resources for confronting these social ills are not easily found in the traditions of either liberal democratic thought or classical political theory. Nor do I think that such resources can be drawn from critical social theory and Habermas's account of transformations of the public sphere. Habermas's pioneering contributions to this area date from the early 1960s, and subsequently played a significant role in the German student revolts of 1968. But in those cultural conflicts it was persons, protagonists and public figures which featured prominently; today, by contrast, the frontlines of political contestation are more opaque, suffused with chatbots and related new technology.[50] At this point we have to rethink the relationship between democracy and the digital revolution, and in an innovative way. To begin with, democracy and digitalization are not simply antithetical, but are profoundly linked and interrelated. No matter how far-reaching AI might be, a politics of resistance that reasserts privacy or individual rights to counter the alleged incursions of automated bots and other machine learning trends poorly misconceives the present-day situation of technological innovation. In this connection, there are important insights to be gleaned from a range of scholars rethinking the relation of humans to intelligent machines.[51] "Today's information and communication machines", wrote Felix Guattari in an early anticipation of the extraordinary global transformation that is AI, "do not merely convey representational contents, but also contribute to the fabrication of new *assemblages* of enunciation, individual and collective".[52] This is an important insight, and appropriately extended can be used to grasp the reordering today of identities, organizations and intelligent machines. Since social identities – ethnicity, gender, sexuality, and politics – are hooked into AI, the platforms of automated algorithms and advanced machine learning, those very identities cannot provide a refuge from disinformation or miscommunication, nor a privileged point of resistance from which to launch a nostalgic reassertion of the rights of the "autonomous individual". For the global interconnectedness promoted by the digital revolution has already constituted a dense web of relations linking identities, socialities, sub-cultures and political affinities.

To counter the threats to democracy by AI, some commentators have suggested a new emancipatory politics based on accessible access to big data or random spot-checks of smart algorithms, at once governmental and corporate. Such ideas amount, in effect, to a proposed 'freedom of data act' to meet the challenges of AI. But as a strategy of resistance, such a politics is hardly knew. In the late 1970s, for example, the celebrated French philosopher Jean-François Lyotard, in *The Postmodern Condition*, concluded: "give the public free access to the memory and data banks".[53] Today, discussions of "data access", "data freedom" and "data play" that engage the politics of AI are increasingly shaping academic and public forums. But such discussions often fail to acknowledge the profound consequences of the discourse of AI on individuals and social relations, and especially the reordering of relations between self, society and intelligent machines which is underway. Instead, an either/or logic often prevails. In *The People Vs Tech*, for example, Jamie Bartlett writes: "In the coming few years either tech will destroy democracy and the social order as we know it, or politics will stamp its authority over the digital world".[54] For Bartlett, it is self-evident that today's "grand struggle between two incompatible systems can result in only one winner". Bruce Schneier, in *Data and Goliath*, makes an urgent political call for less secrecy, and more transparency to deal with mass-data surveillance. "Data", writes Schneier, "is the pollution problem of the information age, and protecting privacy is the environmental problem".[55] But will the protection of privacy, in fact, actually serve to democratize AI? The implication of some recent calls to democratize AI is that individuals can readily reclaim the knowledge or power inherent in algorithms or big data, enabling an alternative politics to emerge. However, the degree to which people actually grasp how AI impacts and transforms their lives, as well as the proliferating ways in which AI reconfigures identities and produces new articulations of social relations, surely requires further analysis and critical examination.

For many political analysts, the arrival of the digital revolution signals the end of privacy – AI is now ubiquitous, and every person's digital experiences can be monitored, manipulated or censored. Yet rather than an erosion of privacy, I am suggesting that the 'private' in our age of intensive AI might in fact be reinforced in its privacy. The possibility of conversation or translation between private and public worlds becomes increasingly detached from politics, subject to behind the scenes government surveillance programs, or direct AI-driven business models of profit. The logical consequence in a political context would seem to be that the future of democracy is profoundly threatened by the escalating impotence of representative public institutions in the face of digital transformation, accompanied by a failure of politics to harness common social issues from private insecurities, worries and concerns. As Zygmunt Bauman writes: "the most haunting of political mysteries is nowadays not so much '*what* to do', as '*who* would do it, if we knew'".[56] The basic implication of Bauman's position is that people today are highly attuned to their limited freedom to maneuver in a world of bewildering global transformation. There is also a more positive side, however. The culture of AI reconfigures multiple positions of identity and novel articulations of both social relations and technologies mingling humans and intelligent machines. The consequences of a world of extensive and intensive AI are not so much the institutionalization of surveillance power structures against the individual, but rather a radical reconfiguration of the nature of the individual and personal life. These are the new stakes of democracy, as reconfigured in and through AI.

AI futures and public policy

So how should we think about the future of governance in a world increasingly mediated by AI, machine learning and big data? Is there a normative dimension to the new kind of problems confronted by democratic politics in the age of AI? It is possible to identify several policy strategies (no doubt, more could be found) which have received serious consideration over recent years, although the full sociological impact for modern societies of each approach will require further critical examination. *Digital tooling up of an active and engaged citizenry* is the first possible AI future. Digital citizenship is at the core of this approach. Governments, civil society and industry have sought to create the social and political conditions for the safe and responsible use of online technology, and those that argue for this approach stress that digital skills are fundamental in an advanced technological age for learning, for employment, for interacting with others, for buying and selling online, for entertainment, and for cultural, political and civic participation.[57] At stake is the development of *digital literacy*. Measures undertaken in various countries to promote digital literacy include the teaching of critical media literacies in schools, basic computer skills, e-safety, enabling responsible online environments, management of digital information, combating e-bullying, and grasping how digital technology impacts on the lives of people in terms of their democratic rights and responsibilities. Reducing digital exclusion is fundamental in this connection, as is the bridging of the digital skills gap. This is what Rachel Coldicutt has termed "digital transformation for all, not just a few". But many have suggested that the core challenge, especially in the age of AI and advanced robotics, extends well beyond digital literacy. At issue here is what Baroness Lane-Fox has eloquently called "digital understanding".[58] Beyond basic digital literacy, Lane-Fox contends that digital understanding encompasses the "ability to both use technology and to comprehend, in real terms, the impact that it has on our lives".[59]

The second is that of *public policy addressing what governments should do about AI*. In the UK Parliament, for example, there have been several Select Committees looking at digital transformations through interviewing experts from industry, academia and think-tanks. The House of Lords established a Select Committee on Artificial Intelligence, which recommended a Charter that AI should: (1) advance the common good; (2) operate on principles of fairness and intelligibility; (3) respect rights to privacy; (4) link to thorough-going changes in education, especially the advancement of digital skills; and (5) not be granted autonomous power to deceive, injure or destroy human beings. The German government passed a law in 2017 imposing penalties of up to €50 million on social media companies that do not remove fake news or hate messages within 24 hours.[60] In Italy, legislation has been proposed criminalizing the posting or sharing online of 'false, exaggerated or tendentious news'. The European Commission, as noted, has launched a committee investigating the spread of fake news and online disinformation, and is working to promote counter-measures across Europe. Moreover, the EU Parliament in 2018 introduced the General Data Protection Regulation, which expands previous data protection rules to require greater consent with respect of the use of personal data, and allows for consent to be revoked at any stage. Penalties are set at 4% of a company's global turnover.

Public policy responses to the challenges of AI and big data vary considerably, and are often uneven in terms of their approach to what public life should be or the protection of democratic norms.[61] In the United States, for example, the Honest Ads Act was proposed to widen the legislative definition of "electioneering communications" from traditional media to all public forms of digital communication. The bill was an attempt to promote regulation of companies such as Facebook and Twitter in the aftermath of Russiagate, although critics were quick to highlight the many technical flaws of this attempt at digital governance.[62] By contrast, the Chinese government has developed arguably the most restrictive regulations governing the digital universe, imposing penalties (including jail terms of up to three years) on the operators of social media networks who allow 'online rumours' to circulate. Some governments have raised the question of whether their administrations now require a separate ministry and standalone strategy on AI. This matter was addressed by the UK's House of Lords Select Committee on Artificial Intelligence. Some governments have gone one step further. In late 2017, the United Arab Emirates appointed Omar Bin Sultan Al Olama as the country's first Minister of State for Artificial Intelligence.

The third strategy focuses upon economic markets but develops a different approach: of *systemic corrections*. The claim is that the age of AI and its major new phase of technological innovation should be managed through developing and implementing market solutions, especially around systemic self-correction of the market which presents opportunities for policy responses whilst avoiding restrictive regulation that might endanger freedom of expression and media autonomy. This necessitates structural change focused on greater transparency and accountability of social media and associated digital organizations by way of instruments such as industry codes of conduct and measures to facilitate third-party fact-checking and verification projects.

Sometimes advocates of 'systemic corrections' or 'market adjustments' point to companies and large-scale conglomerates that are engaged in efforts to remake the relations between business and the digital universe.[63] There are some interesting examples of how such a restructuring can be achieved. Unilever as well as Proctor and Gamble – two of the largest advertisers internationally – announced significant cuts to their advertising budgets in 2017, especially for digital advertising (by 60% and 40% respectively). Senior executives at Proctor and Gamble indicated that this decision was based upon concerns that algorithmic micro-targeting was resulting in the company losing control over their digital advertising targets; too often, it was felt, the company's advertising content became associated with controversial issues on social media platforms, the result being that the company was inadvertently financing the circulation of 'objectionable material'. Such a development amongst companies has led to some social media platforms and digital providers adopting new standards of transparency and enhanced reporting procedures, with a focus on algorithms to identify and rank authentic content, the implementation of anti-tracking and ad-blocking capacities, and renewed engagement with independent fact-checking organizations.[64] So too, there has certainly been a wave of activist groups pressuring advertisers to distance themselves from targeted media sites and social media platforms.[65] The Twitter account *Sleeping Giants*, for example, has achieved considerable success through posting screenshots of advertisements on Breitbart News. Whether developments such as these represent a substitute for the power of legislative regulation and media governance, however, is a more vexed question.

All of the above strategies have, to date, informed public policy addressing the challenges which AI and big data pose to democratic politics. Some authors confronting the current realities and future possibilities of AI and democracy are more positive, however. Certainly the dangers posed by the advent of automated social media bots to the public sphere and the democratic process are considerable, but it is important to also grasp the potential gains to democracy as a result of AI – or so some contend. John Cook has argued, for instance, that the same enabling technologies underpinning the spread of fake news can be used to counter it, as super-fast evaluative algorithms are now far superior to human fact-checkers.[66] The notion that AI might be the solution to the problem of fake news is interesting, with some critics noting that misinformation detection systems have achieved an accuracy rate of 90% in unearthing fraudulent stories.[67] Other authors have developed arguments in favor of algorithmic decision-making tools to *upgrade democracy*. Some of the strategies that have been suggested include deploying AI to provide decision-making support to public authorities with respect to tackling complex social problems. It is argued that AI can enhance both the efficiency as well as the fairness of decisions, and hence better determine resource allocations.[68] The assumption here is that AI is unaffected by political or ideological bias, and other human failings. This would entail an extension of already existing uses of data-driven human behavior analysis in areas such as credit evaluation, recruitment and healthcare.

Whilst these arguments capture some important aspects regarding the possible contributions of AI to the development and deepening of democratic politics, much of this thinking is too functional and too technologically deterministic, ignoring the complex social and emotional bases of changing social practices. One signal problem, nowhere satisfactorily addressed in this literature, is that AI has, in fact, been shown to reproduce and amplify the biases and other human failings to which some critics argue it is ostensibly resistant.[69] Consider, for example, the increasing number of US jurisdictions where automated risk-assessment reports are prepared for the criminal justice system, where prisoners are scored on their potential for recidivism, which in turn directly influences parole determinations. A recent report has revealed a strong racial bias to these algorithms: reoffending risk scores for black prisoners were assessed very highly, while white prisoners – some of whom would go on to commit more crimes – were evaluated as considerably lower-risk.[70] Similar problems have been revealed with "predictive policing" algorithms used to generate models of future crime predictions, deploying data on the times and locations of past crimes, leading to the targeting of certain neighborhoods or profiling of certain demographics.[71] From one angle, the 'benefits' of new digital technologies are clearly more ambivalent than advocates recognize. AI advocates often hype the transformative potential of complex algorithms, failing to recognize that machine learning relies on masses of data which itself contains bias, is incomplete or lacking in diversity. Advocates of the socially transformative qualities of AI also sometimes exhibit an exorbitant faith in the idea that mathematical procedures are neutral, or immune to bias.[72] The embedding of AI technologies in social institutions is often more complex and more contested than technology optimists admit.[73]

A range of strategies will be required to confront the opportunities and challenges of AI and big data, rather than a single approach, and much will depend on getting the right mix of global governance, local regulatory mechanisms, civic society participation, industry support and business compliance, and the development and deepening of digital understanding throughout populations will be of key importance. Governments the world over will face increasing dilemmas in balancing technological innovation and scientific advancement with popular support, especially in terms of employment policies. Embracing the uncertain terrain of AI and advanced robotics remains an open-ended political process. When it comes to the grand challenges like jobs in the age of AI and how machine learning affects education and the development of digital skills, uncertainty and risk are likely to remain pervasive features of the public policy landscape.

Our present global order is based upon a vast spread of intelligent machines intersecting with everyday social life. With the advent of a new global narrative of artificial intelligence, along with Industry 4.0 and the Internet of Things, it may well transpire that our traditional theoretical frameworks for understanding social life are now approaching an end. If the social, cultural and political debates sparked off by current digital transformations teach us anything, it is that the scope, intensity, speed and long-term consequences of technological innovation are so profound that we might have, as it were, simply run out of styles of thinking or frameworks for understanding the impact of such changes. Perhaps we are now living, as Anthony Giddens has argued, "off the edge of history".[74] Certainly what we need today is not new terminology of a new technological age – such as talk of post-humanism – but rather critical thinking on how the spread of intelligent machines transforms our lives. This, in effect, presents social theory with a fresh challenge. "The rise of powerful AI", commented the late Stephen Hawking, "will be either the best or the worst thing ever to happen to humanity".[75] But perhaps it is not an either/or scenario, but rather both/and instead. If so, confronting ambivalence, and coping with uncertainty, are key factors of the AI revolution. We need fresh thinking to confront this breathtaking challenge, to break out of stifling theoretical orthodoxy, in order to explore new issues. Examples proliferate. Research in cross-linguistics and the possibility that AI might spawn a universal translator. Copying the human brain in order to build more emotionally sensitive AI.[76] Crafting algorithms that can process medical images, such as CT scans and x-rays, in order to confront shortages in medical experts around the world. Designing self-piloting air taxis to transcend the urban gridlock of major cities. And on it goes. Much will depend not only on how these technological innovations are operationalized from a scientific perspective over the coming years, but crucially also the grounding or embedding of such scientific advances in large-scale social systems. Advances in AI, machine learning and robotics are not simply the terrain of discovery, but fundamentally the ambivalent realm of lived experience, human experimentation and alternative social futures.

NOTES

Preface

1 Rachel is a fictionalized character, which I develop here to capture the culture of feeling embedded in everyday life in conditions of AI. For further discussion on how global processes can be 'read off' from the production and performance of the self, see Anthony Elliott, *Concepts of the Self*, 3rd edition, Cambridge: Polity Press, 2014.

2 See www.mensjournal.com/gear/quip-review-toothbrush-dental-hygiene-brushing-teeth/ Regarding the cyber-security evidence to the House of Lords Inquiry into Artificial Intelligence see: http://data.parliament.uk/writtenevidence/committeeevidence.svc/evidencedocument/artificial-intelligence-committee/artificial-intelligence/written/75825.html

3 See https://venturebeat.com/2018/06/14/ziprecruiter-announces-ai-tool-that-matches-businesses-with-ideal-job-candidates/

4 See www.wsj.com/articles/cutting-edge-cat-toys-your-pet-wont-immediately-destroy-1520361361

5 See www.howtogeek.com/347408/why-smart-fridges-are-the-future/

6 See https://venturebeat.com/2017/07/09/how-ai-will-help-you-sleep-better-at-night/

7 In Australia, CSIRO's Data61 – which has been appointed by the government to lead the development of a national AI road map that

will guide future national investments, AI and machine learning – is leading these initiatives. See Adrian Turner, 'We Need to Drop the Robots-Are-Taking our Jobs Mindset.' *Australian Financial Review*, July 13, 2018, www.afr.com/technology/perfect-examples-of-why-our-ai-conversation-is-all-wrong-20180710-h12i3t

8 IBM is leading this AI initiative. See: www.ibm.com/blogs/research/2018/03/microscopic-reality-ai-microscopes/

9 See Nick Bostrom, *Superintelligence: Paths, Dangers, Strategies*, Oxford: Oxford University Press, 2014. See also Toby Walsh, *It's Alive: Artificial Intelligence from the Logic Piano to Killer Robots*, Carlton, Vic.: La Trobe University Press, 2017.

10 Bratton calls this megastructure "The Stack", which is a concept I find lacking in analytic precision, and which can be criticized for a failure to adequately theorize the space/time dimensions of embedding and re-embedding of everyday life in global conditions of advanced AI. See Benjamin H. Bratton, *The Stack: On Software and Sovereignty*, Cambridge, MA: MIT Press, 2015.

11 McKinsey & Co., 'Artificial Intelligence: Implications for China.' *McKinsey Global Institute*, April 2017.

12 Dr. Arnand S. Rao, Gerard Verweij and et al., 'Sizing the Prize: What's the Real Value of AI For Your Business and How Can You Capitalize?' *PwC Global Artificial Intelligence Study, Exploiting the AI Revolution*, June 27, 2017.

13 The importance of AI to geopolitics has not been adequately analyzed, but see Kai-Fu Lee, *AI Superpowers: China, Silicon Valley, and the New World Order*, San Diego, CA: Houghton Mifflin Harcourt, 2018; and James Bridle, *New Dark Age: Technology and the End of the Future*, New York: Verso, 2018.

Introduction

1 On the pre-history of artificial intelligence, see Jessica Riskin (ed.), *Genesis Redux: Essays in the History and Philosophy of Artificial Life*, Chicago: University of Chicago Press, 2007; John Cohen, *Human Robots in Myth and Science*, A.S. Barnes, 1967 and Eric Wilson, *Melancholy Android: On the Psychology of Sacred Machines*, Albany, NY: SUNY Press, 2006.

2 The comment is attributed to Pamela McCorduck: http://expedite-consulting.com/invention-artificial-intelligence-means-world-work/

3 See Nils J. Nilsson, *The Quest for Artificial Intelligence: A History of Ideas and Achievements*, Cambridge: Cambridge University Press, 2010.

4 Ibn al-Razzaz Al-Jazari, *The Book of Knowledge of Ingenious Mechanical Devices*. Trans. Donald Hill, Dordrecht: D. Reidel Publishing Company, 1979

5 See Kevin LaGrandeur, 'The Persistent Peril of the Artificial Slave.' *Science Fiction Studies*, (38), 2011, pp. 232–251.

6 Gaby Woods, *Edison's Eve: A Magical History of the Quest for Mechanical Life*, New York: Anchor, 2003.

7 Ian Bogost, ' "Artificial Intelligence" Has Become Meaningless: It's Often Just a Fancy Name for a Computer Program.' *The Atlantic*, March 4, 2017, www.theatlantic.com/technology/archive/2017/03/what-is-artificial-intelligence/518547/

8 In a review of the first 50 years of AI research, for example, Hamid Ekbia identified eight major science and engineering approaches to AI, each centered on very different characterizations of what 'intelligence' is. See Hamid Ekbia, 'Fifty Years of Research in Artificial Intelligence.' *Annual Review of Information Science and Technology*, 44(1), 2010, pp. 201–247.

9 Department for Business, 'Energy and Industrial Strategy, Industrial Strategy: Building a Britain Fit for the Future.' (November 2017), p. 37, www.gov.uk/government/uploads/system/uploads/attachment_data/file/664563/industrial-strategy-white-paper-web-ready-version.pdf (accessed May 23, 2018)

10 PwC, 'Sizing the Prize: PwC's Global Artificial Intelligence Study.' 2017 www.pwc.com/gx/en/issues/data-and-analytics/publications/artificial-intelligence-study.html

11 More recently, there has been considerable academic and public discussion over a new Captcha-breaking algorithm. A variant of the Turing test, the Completely Automated Turing Test to Tell Computers and Humans Apart, or CAPTCHA, has been deployed on websites to differentiate human users from potentially malicious bots. Whilst humans typically humans find these questions easy to solve, they have proven difficult for algorithmic classifiers. Advanced neural network based CAPTCHA-cracking algorithms require, for example, a minimum of 50,000 training images. Researchers at the AI start-up Vicarious published in 2018 new research on algorithms that use a recursive cortical network (a

generative vision model) which can break text-based CAPTCHAs with very little training data. New generation CAPTCHAs are now being developed using contextual understanding in addition to deciphering, or which look for signs of human behavior. An example of this is Google's 'Invisible reCAPTCHA', which looks at the way a mouse is moving and the time it takes to click on a page. See Dileep George et al., 'A Generative Vision Model that Trains with High Data Efficiency and Breaks Text-based CAPTCHAs.' *Science*, 358, 2017, http://science.sciencemag. org/content/358/6368/eaag2612/tab-pdf; also see Matt Burgess, 'Captcha Is Dying. This Is How it's Being Reinvented for the AI Age.' *Wired*, October 26, 2017, www.wired.co.uk/article/captcha-automation-broken-history-fix

12 John Searle, 'The Chinese Room,' in R.A. Wilson and F. Keil (eds.), *The MIT Encyclopedia of the Cognitive Sciences*, Cambridge, MA: MIT Press, 1999.

13 Next to the Turing Test, Searle's Chinese Room Argument has been the most widely debated philosophical argument in cognitive science. See, for example, M. Shaffer, 'A Logical Hole in the Chinese Room.' *Minds and Machines*, 19(2), 2009, pp. 229–235; and G. Rey, 'What's Really Going on in Searle's "Chinese Room".' *Philosophical Studies*, 50, 1986, pp. 169–185; G. Rey, 'Searle's Misunderstandings of Functionalism and Strong AI,' in Preston and Bishop (eds.), 2002, pp. 201–225.

14 Futures have become big business, not only in private enterprise but also in higher education. A good recent example is the establishment of the Institute of Social Futures at Lancaster University, UK. There are of course also well-established academic forums of the future, most notably the Hawaii Research Center for Futures Studies at the University of Hawaii.

15 While some wearable devices such as FitBit and the Apple watch are mainstream, their primary role is information gathering and feedback on specific parameters. Apple watches currently provide some access to AI-supported services such as Siri, yet this is actually performed on a nearby iPhone.

16 www.vtpi.org/avip.pdf

17 For a more in-depth account of driverless cars, it is useful to consult H. Lipson and M. Kurman, *Driverless: Intelligent Cars and the Road Ahead*, Cambridge: MIT Press, 2016.

18 See Malene Freudendal-Pedersen and Sven Kesselring (eds), *Exploring Networked Urban Mobilities: Theories, Concepts, Ideas*, London: Routledge, 2018.

19 www.newscientist.com/article/mg23030732-600-london-to-see-fleet-of-driverless-cars-on-public-roads-this-year/

20 See Gwyn Topham, 'Driverless Pods Plot New Course to Overtake Humans.' *The Guardian*, April 25, 2017, www.theguardian.com/technology/2017/apr/25/autonomous-car-projects-plot-course-uk-driverless-futur

21 www.businessinsider.com.au/why-driverless-cars-will-be-safer-than-human-drivers-2016-11?r=US&IR=T

22 H. Claypool, A. Bin-Nun, and J. Gerlach, *Self-Driving Cars: The Impact on People with Disabilities*, Boston: Ruderman Foundation, 2017.

23 See Daisuke Wakabayashi, 'Self-Driving Uber Car Kills Pedestrian in Arizona.' *New York Times*, March 19, 2018, www.nytimes.com/2018/03/19/technology/uber-driverless-fatality.html

24 See Hod Lipson and Melba Kurman, *Fabricated: The New World of 3D Printing*, Hoboken, New Jersey: John Wiley & Sons, 2013.

25 Thomas Birtchnell and John Urry, *A New Industrial Future?: 3D Printing and the Reconfiguring of Production, Distribution, and Consumption*, London: Routledge, 2016.

26 www.domain.com.au/news/3dprinted-house-built-in-just-three-hours-in-chinas-xian-20150729-gim4e9/

27 www.dailymail.co.uk/sciencetech/article-3322801/Will-humanoid-Mars-Nasa-gives-superhero-robots-universities-train-deep-space-missions.html

28 The field of Science and Technology Studies (STS) has done much to develop this view. For an informative account of the 'social shaping of technology' approach, consult: D. MacKenzie and J. Wajcman, *The Social Shaping of Technology*, Buckingham, UK: Open University Press, 1999. In this book, I take a very different tack to STS as detailed in Chapter 1. See also Anthony Elliott, *Identity Troubles*, London and New York: Routledge, 2016.

29 Nigel Thrift, 'The "Sentient" City and What It May Portend.' *Big Data & Society*, 1(1), 2014, p. 9

30 www.images-et-reseaux.com/sites/default/files/medias/blog/2011/12/the-2nd-economy.pdf

31 www.itu.int/net/pressoffice/press_releases/2015/17.aspx#.VWSF32Bjq-Q

32 www.bcg.com/documents/file100409.pdf

33 Some industry figures have adjusted their predictions downwards to 30 billion interconnected machines and devices according to this report: https://spectrum.ieee.org/tech-talk/telecom/internet/popular-internet-of-things-forecast-of-50-billion-devices-by-2020-is-outdated

34 Erik Brynjolfsson and Andrew McAfee, *The Second Machine Age: Work, Progress, and Prosperity in a Time of Brilliant Technologies*, New York and London: WW Norton & Company, 2014; M. Ford, *Rise of the Robots: Technology and the Threat of a Jobless Future*, New York: Basic Books, 2015; J. Rifkin, *The Third Industrial Revolution: How Lateral Power Is Transforming Energy, the Economy, and the World*, Basingstoke: Palgrave Macmillan, 2011; Nicholas G. Carr, *The Big Switch: Rewiring the World, From Edison to Google*, New York and London: WW Norton & Company, 2008.

The digital universe

1 Zoe Flood, 'From Killing Machines to Agents of Hope: The Future of Drones in Africa.' *The Guardian*, July 27, 2016, www.theguardian.com/world/2016/jul/27/africas-drone-rwanda-zipline-kenya-kruger.

2 Some accounts have predicted that UAVs will transform aspects of the agricultural industry, wildlife management and disaster monitoring systems. See, Ivan H. Beloev, 'A Review on Current and Emerging Application Possibilities for Unmanned Aerial Vehicles.' *Acta Technologica Agriculturae*, 19(3), 2016, pp. 70–76.

3 See Sherisse Pham, 'Drone Hits Passenger Plane in Canada.' *CNN News*, October 16, 2017, http://money.cnn.com/2017/10/16/technology/drone-passenger-plane-canada/index.html

4 UAVs have the potential to be used to deliver medical care and medicines. See, Cornelius A. Thiels, Johnathon M. Aho, Scott P. Zietlow, and Donald H. Jenkins, 'Use of Unmanned Aerial Vehicles for Medical Product Transport.' *Air Medical Journal*, 34(2), 2015, pp. 104–108. UAVs can also be used to map infectious disease landscapes. See Kimberly M. Fornace, Chris J. Drakeley, Timothy William, Fe Espino, and Jonathan Cox, 'Mapping Infectious Disease Landscapes: Unmanned Aerial Vehicles and Epidemiology.' *Trends in Parasitology*, 30(11), 2014, pp. 514–519.

5 Clement Uwiringiyimana, 'Rwanda to Start Using Drones to Supply Vaccines, Blood in August.' *Reuters*, May 14, 2016, www.reuters.com/article/us-africa-economy-rwanda-drones-idUSKCN0Y426D.

6 Madhumita Murgia, 'Lord Norman Foster to Build World's First Droneport in Rwanda.' *The Telegraph*, September 21, 2015, www.telegraph.co.uk/technology/news/11879956/Lord-Norman-Foster-to-build-worlds-first-droneport-in-Rwanda.html.

7 For a useful overview and discussion of how United States drone policy in the early years of the 21st century has involved the death of civilians, despite there being controversy about how 'innocence' is defined by various parties, consult Ian G.R. Shaw, 'Predator Empire: The Geopolitics of US Drone Warfare.' *Geopolitics*, 18(3), 2013, pp. 536–559.

8 Chantal Grut explores how autonomous lethal robotics presents a serious problem for international humanitarian law. While some legal mechanisms currently exist to regulate autonomous warfare, they are by no means adequate to address all of the issues that autonomous weapon systems raise. Chantal Grut, 'The Challenge of Autonomous Lethal Robotics to International Humanitarian Law.' *Journal of Conflict and Security Law*, 18(1), 2013, pp. 5–23.

9 See John Urry, *Global Complexity*, Cambridge: Polity Press, 2003.

10 See 'Digital Skills Crisis.' House of Commons Science and Technology Committee, UK Parliament, Second Report of Session 2016–17, https://publications.parliament.uk/pa/cm201617/cmselect/cmsctech/270/270.pdf

11 Karin Knorr Cetina, 'From Pipes to Scopes: The Flow Architecture of Financial Markets.' *Distinktion*, (7), 2003, pp. 7–23.

12 Ayres and Miller, 'The Impacts of Industrial Robots,' 1981, p. 3; V. Sujan and M. Meggiolaro, *Mobile Robots: New Research*, New York: Nova Science Publishers, 2005, p. 42.

13 John Urry, *What is the Future?* Cambridge: Polity Press, 2016.

14 John B. Thompson, *The Media and Modernity: A Social Theory of the Media*, Stanford: Stanford University Press, 1995, p. 153.

15 Manuel Castells, *The Collapse of Soviet Communism: A View from the Information Society*, Los Angeles: Figueroa Press, 2003.

16 Adam Greenfield, *Everyware: The Dawning Age of Ubiquitous Computing*, Berkeley: New Riders, 2006.

17 Ibid.

18 Semiconductor Transistor Association, *International Technology Roadmap for Semiconductors*, 2015, www.semiconductors.org/main/2015_international_technology_roadmap_for_semiconductors_itrs/ (accessed August 31, 2016)

19 There are numerous works which express a sceptical view about the quickening pace of technological advances. Bob Seidensticker's work, *FutureHype*, offers one such sceptical account, but there are of course others. Bob Seidensticker, *FutureHype: The Myths of Technological Change*, San Francisco: Berrett-Koehler Publishers, 2006.

20 www.theverge.com/2015/6/8/8739611/apple-wwdc-2015-stats-update

21 Numerous authors writing on the theme of surveillance in society, such as Christian Fuchs, have been highly influenced by the work of Michel Foucault. However, it should be noted that there have been numerous calls to recognize the limits of Foucault's theories, especially on the theme of panopticism. See for example Kevin Haggerty, 'Tear Down the Walls: On Demolishing the Panopticon,' in D. Lyon (ed.), *Theorising Surveillance: The Panopticon and Beyond*, pp. 23–45. Uffculme, Devon: Willan Publishing, 2006.

22 See David Lyon, *Surveillance Studies*, Cambridge: Polity Press, 2007.

23 See Rob Kitchin, *The Data Revolution*, New York: SAGE Publications, 2014.

24 For further discussion see Christian Fuchs, 'New Media, Web 2.0 and Surveillance.' *Sociology Compass*, 5(2), 2011, pp. 134–147. See also Samantha Adams, 'Post-Panoptic Surveillance Through Healthcare Rating Sites.' *Information, Communication and Society*, 16(2), 2013.

25 Cambridge Analytica had been established in 2013 as a subsidiary of Strategic Communications Laboratories, an entity which was partly owned by Robert Mercer – an American hedge-fund manager who has strongly backed various conservative political causes. Steve Bannon, then publisher of the alt-right Breitbart News and subsequent advisor to Donald Trump, was Vice-President of Cambridge Analytica. See Matthew Rosenberg, Nicholas Confessore, and Carole Cardwalladr, 'How Trump Consultants Exploited the Facebook Data of Millions.' *New York Times*, March 17, 2018, www.nytimes.com/2018/03/17/us/politics/cambridge-analytica-trump-campaign.html

26 In a UK TV investigative report, Cambridge Analytica's then CEO, Alexander Nix – who was subsequently suspended by the company – boasted to an undercover reporter about the 2016 Trump campaign: "We did all the research, all the data, all the analytics, all the

targeting, we ran all the digital campaign, the television campaign, and our data informed all the strategy". See ABC News, 'Cambridge Analytica Bosses Claimed they Invented "Crooked Hillary" Campaign, Won Donald Trump the Presidency.' March 21, 2018, www.abc.net.au/news/2018-03-21/cambridge-analytica-claimed-it-secured-donald-trump-presidentia/9570690

27 Bruce Schneier, *Data and Goliath: The Hidden Battles to Collect Your Data and Control Your World*, New York: Norton, 2015, p. 7.
28 Louise Amoore, 'Algorithmic War: Everyday Geographies of the War on Terror.' *Antipode*, 41, 2009, pp. 49–69.
29 Schneier, *Data and Goliath*, p. 91.
30 For an informative account of 'the posthuman', consult Nicholas Gane, 'Posthuman.' *Theory, Culture & Society*, 23(2–3), 2006, pp. 431–434. One of the most well-known articulations of the 'transhumanist' position is Steve Fuller and Veronika Lipinska, *The Proactionary Imperative: A Foundation for Transhumanism*, New York: Palgrave Macmillan, 2014.
31 The best overview arguably is Hubert L. Dreyfus, 'Why Heideggerian AI Failed and How Fixing it Would Require Making it More Heideggerian.' *Artificial Intelligence*, 171, 2007, pp. 1137–1160.
32 See Lewis Mumford, *Technics and Civilization*, New York and Burlingame: Harbinger, 1962. Leo Marx, *The Machine in the Garden: Technology and the Pastoral Ideal*, Oxford: Oxford University Press, 2000. Langdon Winner, 'Do Artefacts Have Politics.' *Daedalus*, 109(1), 1980, pp. 121–136. Thomas Hughes, *Human-Built World: How to Think about Technology and Culture*, Chicago: University of Chicago Press, 2004.
33 See Harry Collins, 'What Is Tacit Knowledge,' in T. R. Schatzki, K. Knorr Cetina and E. von Saviguy (eds.), *The Practice Turn in Contemporary Theory*, London and New York: Routledge, 2001. Alan Wolfe, 'Mind, Self, Society and Computer: Artificial Intelligence and the Sociology of Mind.' *American Journal of Sociology*, 95(5), 1991, pp. 1073–1096.
34 Bruno Latour, *Pandora's Hope*, Cambridge, MA: Harvard University Press, 1999. Bruno Latour, *Reassembling the Social*, Oxford: Oxford University Press, 2005.
35 See, for example, Michel Serres, *Hermes: Literature, Science, Philosophy*, Baltimore and London: John Hopkins University Press, 1982; Isabelle Stengers, *Cosmopolitics Ii*, Minneapolis: University of Minnesota Press, 2011.

36 One of the few studies in which Latour does address AI is: Bruno Latour, 'Social Theory and the Study of Computerized Work Sites,' in W. J. Orlinokowski, G. Walsham (eds.), *Information Technology and Changes in Organizational Work*, pp. 295–307. London: Chapman and Hall, 1996. For a sympathetic critique of the applicability of Latour's thought to the field of AI and robotics, see: Raya A. Jones, 'What Makes a Robot "social".' *Social Studies of Science*, 47(4), 2017, pp. 556–579

37 Lucy Suchman, *Human – Machine Reconfigurations*, Cambridge: Cambridge University Press, 2007; Paul Dourish and Genevieve Bell, *Divining a Digital Future*, Boston, MA: MIT Press, 2011; Judy Wajcman, *Pressed for Time: The Acceleration of Life in Digital Capitalism*, Chicago: The University of Chicago Press, 2015; Susan Leigh Star, 'The Ethnography of Infrastructure.' *American Behavioral Scientist*, 43(3), 1999, pp. 377–391.

38 Rosi Braidotti, *The Posthuman*, Cambridge: Polity, 2013, p. 42.

39 See Nigel Thrift, *Knowing Capitalism*, New York: SAGE Publications, 2005, and Nigel Thrift, *Non-Representational Theory: Space, Politics, Affect*, New York: Routledge, 2007.

40 Thrift, *Non-Representational Theory*, p. 30.

41 See Anthony Giddens, *The Consequences of Modernity*, Cambridge: Polity Press, 2013; Anthony Giddens, *Modernity and Self-identity: Self and Society in the Late Modern Age*, Stanford: Stanford University Press, 1991; Ulrich Beck and Elisabeth Beck-Gernsheim, *Individualization: Institutionalized Individualism and its Social and Political Consequences*, New York: SAGE Publications, 2001; Zygmunt Bauman, *Liquid Lives*, Cambridge: Polity Press, 2005; Zygmunt Bauman, *Liquid Modernity*, Cambridge: Polity Press, 2000.

42 Giddens, *The Consequences of Modernity*, p. 38.

43 Anthony Giddens, 'Off the Edge of History: The World in the 21st Century.' *London School of Economics and Political Science*, www.youtube.com/watch?v=bbkyiRCef7A.

44 See Anthony Elliott, *Reinvention*, New York: Routledge, 2013; Cornelius Castoriadis, *The Imaginary Institution of Society*, Cambridge: Polity Press, 1987; Anthony Elliott, 'DIY Self-design: Experimentation Across Global Airports,' in *Identity Troubles: An Introduction*, New York: Routledge, 2015.

45 See Anthony Elliott and Charles Lemert, *The New Individualism: The Emotional Costs of Globalization*, 2nd edition, London and New York: Routledge, 2009; Anthony Elliott and John Urry, *Mobile*

Lives, London and New York: Routledge, 2010; Anthony Elliott and Bryan S. Turner, *On Society*, Polity Press, 2012; Anthony Elliott, Masataka Katagiri and Atsushi Sawai (eds.), *Contemporary Japanese Social Theory*, London and New York: Routledge, 2013.

46 I have drawn from, and sought to contribute to the further development of, these theoretical approaches in some of my recent writings also. See Elliott, *Reinvention*; Anthony Elliott, *Identity Troubles*, London and New York: Routledge, 2016.

The rise of robotics

1 John Maynard Keynes, 'Economic Possibilities for our Grandchildren,' in J.M. Keynes (ed.), *Essays in Persuasion* (with a new Introduction by Donald Moggridge), pp. 321–333. Basingstoke: Palgrave Macmillan, 2010 (1930).

2 Karl Marx, *Capital (Volume 1)*, New York: International Publishers, 1987.

3 Karl Marx, *Grundrisse: Introduction to the Critique of Political Economy*. Trans. Martin Nicolaus, New York: Random House, 1973, p. 704.

4 Ibid., p. 705.

5 See for example M. Betancourt, 'Automated Labor: The "New Aesthetic" and Immaterial Physicality.' *CTheory*, 2013, pp. 2–5; T. Morris-Suzuki, 'Robots and Capitalism.' *New Left Review*, (147), 1984, pp. 109–121.

6 For one of the first social-theoretical engagements with, and sociological critique of, contemporary debates over technological innovations in robotics and AI see: Ross Boyd and Robert J. Holton, 'Technology, Innovation, Employment and Power: Does Robotics and Artificial Intelligence Really Mean Social Transformation?' *Journal of Sociology*, 2017 (Online First) doi.org/10.1177/1440783317726591

7 Joel Mokyr, Chris Vickers, and Nicolas Ziebarth, 'The History of Technological Anxiety and the Future of Economic Growth.' *Journal of Economic Perspectives*, 29(3), 2015, pp. 31–50; Joel Mokyr, 'The Past and the Future of Innovation: Some Lessons from Economic History.' *Explorations in Economic History*, 2018 (Online First), https://doi.org/10.1016/j.eeh.2018.03.003.

8 A far more pessimistic strain of scepticism argues that all of the most important inventions (steam, electricity, internal combustion engine) have occurred, and future innovations will not make

sufficient impact against the 'economic headwinds' (population aging, rising inequality or high public and private debt) that are the key job killers. See Robert J. Gordon, *The Rise and Fall of American Growth*, Princeton: Princeton University Press, 2016.

9 Geoff Colvin, *Humans Are Underrated: What High Achievers Know That Brilliant Machines Never Will*, New York: Penguin, 2015.

10 Ibid., p. 4.

11 See also David Autor and Anna Salomons, 'Is Automation Labor Displacing? Productivity Growth, Employment and the Labor Share.' *Brookings Papers on Economic Activity*, 2018, www.brookings.edu/wp-content/uploads/2018/03/1_autorsalomons.pdf; David Autor, 'Why Are There Still So Many Jobs?' *Journal of Economic Perspectives*, 29(3), 2015, 3–30; David Autor, Frank Levy and Richard Murnane, 'The Skill Content of Recent Technological Change.' *Quarterly Journal of Economics*, 118(4), 2003, pp. 1279–333.

12 Georg Graetz and Guy Michaels, 'Robots At Work.' 2015, http://cep.lse.ac.uk/pubs/download/dp1335.pdf.

13 Ibid., p. 4.

14 See J. Wajcman, 'Automation: Is It Really Different this Time?' *The British Journal of Sociology*, 68(1), 2017, pp. 119–127.

15 Erik Brynjolfsson and Andrew McAfee, *The Second Machine Age: Work, Progress, and Prosperity in a Time of Brilliant Technologies*, New York: WW Norton & Company, 2014, p. 8.

16 Martin Ford, *The Rise of the Robots: Technology and the Threat of a Jobless Future*, New York: Basic Books, 2015. See also Ursula Huws, *Labor in the Global Digital Economy: The Cybertariat Comes of Age*, New York: Monthly Review Press, 2014.

17 Klaus Schwab, *The Fourth Industrial Revolution*, Geneva: World Economic Forum, 2016.

18 Richard Susskind and Daniel Susskind, *The Future of the Professions: How Technology Will Transform the Work of Human Experts*, Oxford: Oxford University Press, 2015.

19 See Jeremy Rifkin, *The End of Work: The Decline of the Global Labor Force and the Dawn of the Post-Market Era*, New York: Putnam, 1995.

20 My thanks to Sven Kesselring for helping me grasp the significance of such impacts on the corporate scale.

21 Henry Mintzberg, 'Power in and Around Organizations,' in *The Theory of Management Policy Series*, Englewood Cliffs, NJ: Prentice-Hall, 1983.

22 See: www.bmw-connecteddrive.com.au/app/index.html#/portal

23 Anthony Giddens, *Runaway World*, London: Profile Books, 1999.

24 See Stephen Bertman, *Hyperculture: The Human Cost of Speed*, London: Praeger Publishers, 1998; Thomas Hylland Eriksen, *Tyranny of the Moment: Fast and Slow Time in the Information Age*, London: Pluto Press, 2001.

25 See S. E. Black and L. M. Lynch, 'What's Driving the New Economy?: The Benefits of Workplace Innovation.' *The Economic Journal*, 114(493), 2004; K. Kelly, *New Rules For the New Economy: 10 Radical Strategies for a Connected World*, New York: Penguin, 1999.

26 There have been multiple treatments of the sociological implications of the global financial crisis of 2008. See for example: Robert J. Holton, *Global Finance*, London: Routledge, 2012; D. Bryan and M. Rafferty, 'Financial Derivatives as Social Policy Beyond Crisis.' *Sociology*, 48(5), 2014, pp. 887–903.

27 See John Saul, *The Collapse of Globalism*, New York: Atlantic, 2005.

28 Offshoring, of course, is a complex and multifaceted issue, which I am unable to provide a full treatment of here. For a more in-depth sociological account of offshoring, please consult John Urry, *Offshoring*, London: Polity, 2014.

29 Gene M. Grossman and Esteban Rossi-Hansberg, 'The Rise of Offshoring: It's Not Wine For Cloth Anymore.' *The New Economic Geography: Effects and Policy Implications*, pp. 59–102, 2006.

30 Richard E. Baldwin, *The Great Convergence: Information Technology and the New Globalization*, Cambridge: Harvard University Press, 2016.

31 www.huffingtonpost.com/entry/telerobotics_us_5873bb48e4b02b 5f858a1579

32 A glimpse of the complex ways that management of employment at-a-distance through AI and telerobotics might be systematized can be discerned through the 'gig economy'. The gig economy – either through crowdwork (where online platforms locate and organize labor for the completion of a range of microtasks) or work-on-demand via apps – shifts the large bulk of the burden of economic risk onto labor. See Valerio De Stefano, 'The Rise of the Just-in-Time Workforce: On-Demand Work, Crowdwork, and Labor Protection in the Gig-Economy.' *Comparative Labor Law and Policy Journal*, 37, 2016, pp. 471–503.

33 World Economic Forum, 'The Future of Jobs: Employment, Skills and Workforce Strategy for the Fourth Industrial Revolution,' 2016.

34 See www.theguardian.com/technology/2017/jan/11/robots-jobs-employees-artificial-intelligence

35 Again, it is important to stress that the poorer parts of the world will also be seriously impacted by AI and robotics, as well as the developed countries. Whilst the large bulk of public and academic debate has addressed the likely impacts of robotics on employment in the industrialized countries, there is important social policy research on the consequences of robotics for developing countries. The research on AI, robotics and developing countries is largely concerned with the impact of the deployment of robots in the industrialized societies on the traditional labor cost advantages of developing countries. From this angle, robots deployed in the developed countries impact work and employment in both developed and developing countries. These analyses tend not to take into account the potentials of telerobotics, as discussed by Baldwin and others. See, for example, UNCTAD, *Robots and Industrialization in Developing Countries: Policy Brief*, United Nations Conference on Trade and Development, 2016, http://unctad.org/en/PublicationsLibrary/presspb2016d6_en.pdf

One notable exception to this is China, which is now the world's largest operator of industrial robots. In China, there is instead some evidence of a shift from economic organization based on the exploitation of a 'demographic dividend' or 'labour dividend' towards economic organization which leverages a prospective 'robotic dividend'. See Yu Huang and Sharif Naubahar, 'From "Labour Dividend" to "Robot Dividend": Technological Change and Workers' Power in South China.' *Agrarian South: Journal of Political Economy*, 6(1), 2017, pp. 53–78. My thanks to Ross Boyd for drawing my attention to this research.

36 On discontinuist interpretations of modern history, see Anthony Giddens, *The Nation-State and Violence*, Cambridge: Polity Press, 1985, pp. 31–34.

37 Jeffrey Sachs, 'How to Live Happily with Robots,' http://jeffsachs.org/wp-content/uploads/2016/06/Sachs-American-Prospect-August-2015-How-to-Live-Happily-with-Robots.pdf

38 Jeffrey D. Sachs, 'R&D, Structural Transformation, and the Distribution of Income,' in Ajay K. Agrawal, Joshua Gans and Avi Goldfarb (eds.), *The Economics of Artificial Intelligence: An Agenda* (Proceedings of the 2017 NBER Economics of AI Conference).

Chicago: University of Chicago Press, 2018, www.nber.org/chapters/c14014.pdf

39 Daron Acemoglu and Pascual Restrepo, *Robots and Jobs: Evidence from US Labor Markets*. Cambridge, MA: MIT Department of Economics, 2017.

40 I have developed the theory of the new individualism in a number of works. See A. Elliott and C. Lemert, 'The Global New Individualist Debate,' in A. Elliott and P. du Gay (eds.), *Identity in Question*, pp. 37–64. London: Sage Publications, 2009a; A. Elliott and C. Lemert, *The New Individualism: The Emotional Costs of Globalization* (revised edition). New York: Routledge, 2009b; A. Elliott, *Making the Cut*, London: Reaktion, 2008. The theory has subsequently been built on and refined by other studies, such as E. L. Hsu, 'New Identities, New Individualism,' in A. Elliott (ed.), *The Routledge Handbook of Identity Studies*, pp. 129–148. London and New York: Routledge, 2011.

41 For instance, in Australia the Foundation for Young Australians has repeatedly called for greater resources to help develop the skills they need for jobs of the future. www.fya.org.au/wp-content/uploads/2015/08/The-New-Work-Order-FINAL-low-res-2.pdf. In the United States, a report issued by the Executive Office of the President near the end of the Obama Presidency recommended that education and retraining initiatives were key to addressing the challenges posed by automation. https://obamawhitehouse.archives.gov/sites/whitehouse.gov/files/documents/Artificial-Intelligence-Automation-Economy.PDF

42 L. Bellmann and U. Leber, 'Economic Effects of Continuous Training,' in J. Addison and P. Welfens (eds.), *Labor Markets and Social Security*, pp. 345–365. Berlin: Springer, 2004.

Digital life and the self

1 'Mother Urges Internet Awareness After Daughter's Suicide.' *BBC News*, January 23, 2014, www.bbc.co.uk/newsbeat/article/25845273/mother-urges-internet-awareness-after-daughters-suicide (accessed September 4, 2017).

2 Following up on the Lisbon Strategy, the Digital Agenda for Europe (DAE) was conceived as one of the seven flagship initiatives of the Europe 2020 strategy adopted by the European Commission. See http://eige.europa.eu/resources/digital_agenda_en.pdf

3 See Anthony Elliott, *Identity Troubles*, London and New York: Routledge, 2016.

4 For a more in-depth discussion of how technologies and personal life are intertwined, see Anthony Elliott and J. Urry, *Mobile Lives*, New York: Routledge, 2010 and Mike Michael, *Technoscience and Everyday Life: The Complex Simplicities of the Mundane*, New York: Open University Press, 2006.

5 There are numerous accounts which have explored how Freudian theory has captured the complexities of selfhood. See Anthony Elliott, *Psychoanalytic Theory: An Introduction*, 3rd edition, London: Palgrave, 2015. Anthony Elliott, *Concepts of the Self*, 3rd edition, Cambridge: Polity Press, 2014. Stephen Frosh, *Identity Crisis: Modernity, Psychoanalysis and the Self*, New York: Routledge, 1991.

6 D. W. Winnicott, *Playing and Reality*, London: Tavistock, 1997.

7 There are of course notable exceptions to this tendency. See for example Knafo, Danielle, and Rocco Lo Bosco, *The Age of Perversion: Desire and Technology in Psychoanalysis and Culture*, New York: Routledge, 2017; and Anthony Elliott, 'Miniaturized Mobilities: Transformations in the Storage, Containment and Retrieval of Affect.' *Psychoanalysis, Culture & Society*, 18(1), 2013, pp. 71–80.

8 Sherry Turkle, *Alone Together: Why We Expect More From Technology and Less From Each Other*, New York: Basic Books, 2011.

9 Ibid., 16.

10 Sherry Turkle, *Life on the Screen: Identity in the Age of the Internet*, New York: Simon & Schuster, 1995.

11 Turkle, *Alone Together*, xii.

12 Ibid., 31.

13 See, for example, Sven Birkerts, *Changing the Subject: Art and Attention in the Internet Age*, Minneapolis: Minnesota Graywolf Press, 2015; Nicholas Carr, *The Shallows: How the Internet is Changing the Way We Think, Read and Remember*, London: Atlantic Books, 2010 and Rob Cover, *Digital Identities: Creating and Communicating the Online Self*, London: Academic Press, 2015.

14 Turkle, *Alone Together*, p. 36

15 See Elliott, *Identity Troubles*.

16 Work undertaken in the field of science and technology studies (STS) has done much to elaborate this understanding of technology. See, for example, Judy Wajcman, 'Addressing Technological Change: The Challenge to Social Theory.' *Current Sociology*, 50(3),

2002, pp. 347–363 and Wenda K. Bauchspies, *Science, Technology, and Society: A Sociological Approach*, Malden: Blackwell, 2006.

17 Roger Burrows makes a similar point. He has observed that our 'associations and interactions are now not only mediated by software and code they are becoming constituted by it'. R. Burrows, 'Afterword: Urban Informatics and Social Ontology,' in M. Foth (ed.), *Handbook of Research on Urban Informatics*, pp. 450–454. Hershey, PA: Information Science Reference, 2009.

18 Turkle, *Alone Together*, p. 61.

19 See E. Hargittai, 'The Digital Reproduction of Inequality,' in D. Grusky (ed.), *Social Stratification*, Boulder, CO: Westview Press, 2008 and Wenhong Chen and Barry Wellman, 'Charting Digital Divides: Comparing Socioeconomic, Gender, Life Stage, and Rural-urban Internet Access and Use in Five Countries,' in *Transforming Enterprise: The Economic and Social Implications of Information Technology*, pp. 467–497. Cambridge, MA: MIT Press, 2005.

20 Barry Wellman, 'Little Boxes, Glocalization, and Networked Individualism,' in *Kyoto Workshop on Digital Cities*, pp. 10–25. Springer Berlin Heidelberg, 2001.

21 Don Tapscott, *Growing Up Digital the Rise of the Net Generation*, New York: McGraw-Hill, 1998.

22 Marc Prensky, 'Digital Natives, Digital Immigrants Part 1.' *On the Horizon*, 9(5), pp. 1–6, 2001.

23 See, for example, Chris Davies, John Coleman, and Sonia Livingstone, *Digital Technologies in the Lives of Young People*, New York: Routledge, 2015.

24 See Paul DiMaggio, Eszter Hargittai, Coral Celeste, and Steven Shafer, 'From Unequal Access to Differentiated Use: A Literature Review and Agenda for Research on Digital Inequality.' *Social Inequality*, pp. 355–400, 2004 and Karine Barzilai-Nahon, 'Gaps and Bits: Conceptualizing Measurements for Digital Divide/s.' *The Information Society*, 22(5), 2006, pp. 269–278.

25 See, for example, Eszter Hargittai, 'Digital na (t) ives? Variation in Internet Skills and Uses Among Members of the "net generation".' *Sociological Inquiry*, 80(1), 2010, pp. 92–113.

26 Susan Greenfield, *Mind Change: How Digital Technologies Are Leaving their Mark on Our Brains*, New York: Random House, 2015.

27 V. Bell, D.V.M. Bishop and A. K. Przybylsk, 'The Debate Over Digital Technology and Young People.' *BMJ*, 2015.

28 Turkle, *Alone Together*, p. 30.

29 Donald W. Winnicott, 'The Use of an Object.' *The International Journal of Psycho-Analysis*, 50, 1969, p. 711.
30 Turkle, *Alone Together*, 56.
31 Ibid., 59.
32 Christopher Bollas, *Being a Character: Psychoanalysis and Self Experience*, New York: Hill and Wang, 1992.
33 Sigmund Freud, *Beyond the Pleasure Principle*, London: Penguin UK, 2003.
34 Bollas, *Being a Character*, p. 59.
35 George E. Atwood and Robert D. Stolorow, *Structures of Subjectivity: Explorations in Psychoanalytic Phenomenology and Contextualism*, New York: Routledge, 2014.
36 Ibid., 69.
37 Elliott and Urry, *Mobile Lives*.
38 See, for example, Indeok Song, Robert Larose, Matthew S. Eastin, and Carolyn A. Lin, 'Internet Gratifications and Internet Addiction: On the Uses and Abuses of New Media.' *Cyberpsychology & Behavior*, 7(4), 2004, pp. 384–394, and Daria J. Kuss and Mark D. Griffiths, 'Online Social Networking and Addiction – A Review of the Psychological Literature.' *International Journal of Environmental Research and Public Health*, 8(9), 2011, pp. 3528–3552.
39 Pew Research Center, 'Millennials in Adulthood: Detached from Institutions, Networked with Friends.' March 2014.
40 Theresa M. Senft and Nancy K. Baym, 'Selfies Introduction – What Does the Selfie Say? Investigating a Global Phenomenon.' *International Journal of Communication*, 9, 2015, p. 19.
41 David Nemer and Guo Freeman, 'Selfies| Empowering the Marginalized: Rethinking Selfies in the Slums of Brazil.' *International Journal of Communication*, 9, 2015, p. 16.
42 The experimentalist qualities of identities has been further explored in other works, such as E.L. Hsu, 'New Identities, New Individualism,' in A. Elliott (ed.), *Handbook of Identity Studies*, London and New York: Routledge, 2011, pp. 129–147, and in Elliott, *Identity Troubles*.

Digital technologies and social interaction

1 Ben Bajarin, 'Are you Multitasking or Are you Suffering from Digital-Device-Distraction Syndrome?' *TIME*, November 12, 2012, http://techland.time.com/2012/11/12/are-you-multitasking-or-

are-you-suffering-from-digital-device-distraction-syndrome/ (accessed October 17, 2016).

2 In important ways, the culture of AI bears out the prediction Mark Weiser, former chief scientist at Xerox PARC, famously made of ubiquitous computing: namely, that it has now disappeared into the texture of lived, woven itself "into the fabric of everyday life . . . [to become] indistinguishable from it" (p94). See Mark Weiser, 'The Computer for the 21st Century.' *Scientific American*, 265(3), 1991, pp. 94–104. As Paul Dourish and Genevieve Bell point out, however, this has not necessarily led to the types of outcomes anticipated by the engineers developing such technologies. See Paul Dourish and Genevieve Bell, *Divining a Digital Future: Mess and Mythology in Ubiquitous Computing*, Cambridge, MA and London: MIT Press, 2011.

3 This strand of research has tended to form around the concept of 'meetingness'. It is useful to consult Yolande Strengers, 'Meeting in the Global Workplace: Air Travel, Telepresence and the Body.' *Mobilities*, 10(4), 2015, pp. 592–608; John Urry, 'Social Networks, Mobile Lives and Social Inequalities.' *Journal of Transport Geography*, 21, 2012, pp. 24–30; and Anthony Elliott and J. Urry, *Mobile Lives*, New York: Routledge, 2010.

4 This facet of the self is explored in depth in: Anthony Elliott, *Concepts of the Self*, 3rd edition. Cambridge: Polity Press, 2014.

5 Erving Goffman, *The Presentation of Self in Everyday Life*, New York: Doubleday, 1959.

6 See Erving Goffman, *Presentation of Self*, New York: Penguin Books, 1971; also of relevance, see *Relations in Public*, New York: Penguin Books, 1971; *Interaction Ritual*, New York: Penguin Books, 1972.

7 Erving Goffman, *Behaviour in Public Places*, New York: Free Press, 1963, p. 92.

8 See Philip Manning, *Erving Goffman and Modern Sociology*, New York: Polity Press, 1992.

9 Goffman, *The Presentation of Self in Everyday Life*.

10 See, amongst others, J.B. Thompson, *Ideology in Modern Culture*, Palo Alto: Stanford University Press, 1990; J. B. Thompson, *The Media and Modernity: A Social Theory of the Media*, Palo Alto: Stanford University Press, 1995.

11 Thompson, *The Media and Modernity*, p. 89.

12 See Karin Knorr Cetina and Urs Bruegger, 'Global Microstructures: The Virtual Societies of Financial Markets.' *American*

Journal of Sociology, 107(4), 2002, pp. 905–950; Karin Knorr Cetina and Urs Bruegger, 'Inhabiting Technology: The Global Lifeform of Financial Markets.' *Current Sociology*, 50(3), 2002, pp. 389–405.

13 Cetina and Bruegger, 'Global Microstructures,' p. 908.

14 The practice of 'media multitasking' has been well explored across many different fields in the social sciences. Research has not only focused on its prevalence (Ulla G. Foehr, 'Media Multitasking among American Youth: Prevalence, Predictors and Pairings.' *Henry J. Kaiser Family Foundation*, 2006; Se-Hoon Jeon and Martin Fishbein, 'Predictors of Multitasking with Media: Media Factors and Audience Factors.' *Media Psychology*, 10(3), 2007, pp. 364–384, but its multiple impacts (Jennifer Lee, Lin Lin, and Tip Robertson, 'The Impact of Media Multitasking on Learning.' *Learning, Media and Technology*, 37(1), 2012, pp. 94–104 and motivations (Fleura Bardh, Anrew J. Rohm, and Fareena Sultan, 'Tuning In and Tuning Out: Media Multitasking among Young Consumers.' *Journal of Consumer Behaviour*, 9(4), 2010, pp. 316–332; Zheng Wang and John M. Tchernev. 'The "myth" of Media Multitasking: Reciprocal Dynamics of Media Multitasking, Personal Needs, and Gratifications.' *Journal of Communication*, 62(3), 2012, pp. 493–513).

15 I thank Tony Giddens for highlighting some of these social changes in "Norms of Co-Presence" and for discussing their possible impacts with me.

16 John Urry, 'Mobility and Proximity.' *Sociology*, 36(2), 2002, pp. 255–274. See P. Evans and T. Wurstler, *Blown to Bits. How the New Economics of Information Transforms Strategy*, Boston, MA: Harvard Business School Press, 2000, for more detail.

17 Beerud Sheth, 'Forget Apps, Now the Bots Take Over,' September 29, 2015, https://techcrunch.com/2015/09/29/forget-apps-now-the-bots-take-over/ (accessed October 24, 2016).

18 David Beer, 'The Social Power of Algorithms.' *Information, Communication and Society*, 20(1), 2017, pp. 1–13.

19 Douglas Hofstader, *Fluid Concepts and Creative Analogies: Computer Models of the Fundamental Mechanisms of Thought*, New York: Basic Books, 1996.

20 Ray Kurzweil in Ethan Baron, 'Google Will Let You Turn Yourself into a Bot, Ray Kurzweil Says,' May 31, 2016, www.siliconbeat.com/2016/05/31/google-chat-bot-coming-year-renowned-inventor-says/ (accessed October 20, 2016).

21 For an informative discussion of 'techno-optimism', it is useful to consult: Katherine Dentzman, Ryan Gunderson, and Raymond Jussaume. 'Techno-optimism as a Barrier to Overcoming Herbicide Resistance: Comparing Farmer Perceptions of the Future Potential of Herbicides.' *Journal of Rural Studies*, 48, 2016, pp. 22–372.

22 Deirdre Boden, *The Business of Talk: Organizations in Action*, London: Polity Press, 1994, p. 82, p. 94.

23 Anthony Giddens, *Modernity and Self-Identity*, Stanford: Stanford University Press, 1991, p. 120.

24 Brian Christian, *The Most Human Human: What Artificial Intelligence Teaches Us About Being Alive*, New York: Anchor Books, 2015, p. 25.

25 Jason Del Ray, 'Here's Amazon's Explanation for the Alexa Eavesdropping Scandal.' *Recode*, May 24, 2018, www.recode. net/2018/5/24/17391480/amazon-alexa-woman-secret-recording-echo-explanation

26 Christian, *The Most Human Human*, pp. 25–26.

27 Barry Wellman, 'Physical Space and Cyberplace: The Rise of Personalized Networking.' *International Journal of Urban and Regional Research*, 25, 2001, p. 238.

28 The phenomenon of desynchronization has especially been investigated the prism of work: Koen Breedveld, 'The Double Myth of Flexibilization: Trends in Scattered Work Hours, and Differences in Time-sovereignty.' *Time & Society*, 7(1), 1998, pp. 129–143; Manfred Garhammer, 'Changes in Working Hours in Germany: The Resulting Impact on Everyday Life.' *Time & Society*, 4(2), 1995, pp. 167–203.

29 Anthony Elliott and Charles Lemert, *The New Individualism: The Emotional Costs of Globalization*, New York: Routledge, 2009.

30 Milan Kundera, *Slowness*, New York: HarperCollins Publishers, 1995, p. 2.

31 Zygmunt Bauman, *Liquid Love: On the Frailty of Human Bonds*, John Wiley & Sons, 2013; Zygmunt Bauman, *Liquid Modernity*, John Wiley & Sons, 2013. See also Eric L. Hsu, 'The Sociology of Sleep and the Measure of Social Acceleration.' *Time & Society*, 23(2), 2014, pp. 212–234 and Eric L. Hsu and Anthony Elliott, 'Social Acceleration Theory and the Self.' *Journal for the Theory of Social Behaviour*, 45(4), 2015, pp. 397–418 for a more complex account of how speed manifests in the contemporary social world.

32 Paul Virilio 1986, quoted in Thomas Erikson, *Tyranny of the Moment*, London: Pluto Press 2001, p. 51.
33 Michael Harris, *The End of Absence: Reclaiming What We've Lost in a World of Constant Connection*, New York: Penguin Books US, 2014.
34 Ibid., p. 203.
35 This outline is informed by the discussion set out by John Thompson in 'The Media and Modernity.'

Modern societies, mobility and artificial intelligence

1 See, for example, David Z. Morris, 'At Uber, Troubling Signs Were Rampant Long Before a Fatal Self-Driving Crash.' *Fortune*, March 24, 2018, http://fortune.com/2018/03/24/uber-self-driving-program-troubles/
2 See Sam Levin, 'Uber Crash Shows "Catastrophic Failure" of Self Driving Technology.' *The Guardian*, March 22, 2018, www.theguardian.com/technology/2018/mar/22/video-released-of-uber-self-driving-crash-that-killed-woman-in-arizona
3 Richard Priday, 'Uber's Fatal Crash Shows the Folly of How We Test Self-driving Cars.' *Wired*, March 24, 2018, www.wired.co.uk/article/uber-crash-autonomous-self-driving-car-vehicle-testing
4 Nicholas Carr, *The Glass Cage: Automation and Us*, New York and London: W. W. Norton and Co., 2014.
5 Ibid., pp. 43–63.
6 See Sydney J. Freedberg Jr., 'Artificial Stupidity: When Artificial intelligence + Human = Disaster.' *Breaking Defense*, June 2, 2017, https://breakingdefense.com/2017/06/artificial-stupidity-when-artificial-intel-human-disaster/. Sydney J. Freedberg Jr., 'Artificial Stupidity: Fumbling the Handoff from AI to Human Control.' *Breaking Defense*, June 5, 2017, https://breakingdefense.com/2017/06/artificial-stupidity-fumbling-the-handoff/
7 Kingsley Dennis and John Urry, *After the Car*, Cambridge: Polity Press, 2009.
8 It is also instructive to consult Fabian Kröger's (2016) brief historical overview of how driverless car futures have developed in the cultural sphere, starting from the first half of the twentieth century. Kroger identifies some of the cultural narratives which have informed efforts to develop driverless vehicle technologies and systems.

9 Jitendra N. Bajpai, 'Emerging Vehicle Technologies & the Search for Urban Mobility Solutions.' *Urban, Planning and Transport Research*, 4(1), 2016, p. 84.

10 Ibid.

11 A more in-depth outline of the Google car and its functionality can be found in Michelle Birdsall's account of Google cars. Michelle Birdsall, 'Google and ITE: The Road Ahead for Self-driving Cars.' *Institute of Transportation Engineers. ITE Journal*, 84(5), 2014, p. 6. Research on Google cars, it should be noted, has been embryonic. How and the extent to which it will be utilized remain key points of discussion. See Lee Gomes, 'When Will Google's Self-driving Car Really be Ready? It Depends on Where You Live and What You mean By Ready [News].' *IEEE Spectrum*, 53(5), 2016, pp. 13–14.

12 Thomas Halleck, 'Google Inc. Says Self-driving Car Will be Ready by 2020.' *International Business Times*, January 14, 2015, www.ibtimes.com/google-inc-says-self-driving-car-will-be-ready-2020-1784150.

13 Bajpai, 'Emerging Vehicle Technologies & the Search for Urban Mobility Solutions.' pp. 83–100.

14 Numerous works have made predictions about these potential benefits of driverless transport systems, including Daniel J. Fagnant and Kara Kockelman, 'Preparing a Nation for Autonomous Vehicles: Opportunities, Barriers and Policy Recommendations.' *Transportation Research Part A: Policy and Practice*, 77, 2015, pp. 167–181 and Austin Brown, Jeffrey Gonder, and Brittany Repac, 'An Analysis of Possible Energy Impacts of Automated Vehicle,' in G. Meyer and S. Beiker (eds.), *Road Vehicle Automation*, pp. 137–153. Cham, Switzerland: Springer, 2014. However, there is some dispute as to the extent to which these benefits can even be realized, such as Brian Christian and Tom Griffiths, *Algorithms to Live By: The Computer Science of Human Decisions*, London: HarperCollins, 2016.

15 http://asirt.org/initiatives/informing-road-users/road-safety-facts/road-crash-statistics

16 M. Mitchell Waldrop, 'No Drivers Required.' *Nature*, 518(7537), 2015, p. 20.

17 See Nidhi Kalra and Susan M. Paddock, 'Driving to Safety: How Many Miles of Driving Would it Take to Demonstrate Autonomous Vehicle Reliability?' *Transportation Research Part A*, 94, 2016, pp. 182–193.

18 For further discussion, see James M. Anderson, Nidhi Kalra, Karlyn D. Stanley, Paul Sorensen, Constantine Samaras, Oluwatobi A. Oluwatola, *Autonomous Vehicle Technology: A Guide for Policymakers*, Santa Monica, CA: RAND Corporation, RR-443-2-RC, 2016. www.rand.org/pubs/research_reports/RR443-2.html   (accessed January 24, 2016).

19 Gary Silberg, Richard Wallace, G. Matuszak, J. Plessers, C. Brower, and Deepak Subramanian, 'Self-Driving Cars: The Next Revolution.' White paper, KPMG LLP & Center of Automotive Research, 2012, p.36.

20 Sebastian Thrun, for example, describes the potential of driverless cars to transform how parking is allocated and managed this way:

> cars are only utilized 4% of their lifetime. What if we could, on the click of a button, order a rental car straight to us? And once at our destination, we wasted no time looking for a parking; instead we just let the car drive away to pick up its next customer. Such a vision could drastically reduce the number of cars needed, and also free up important other resources, such as space consumed by parked cars.
>
> Sebastian Thrun, 'Toward Robotic Cars.' *Communications of the ACM*, 53(4), 2010, p. 105

21 Eric Laurier and Tim Dant, 'What We Do Whilst Driving: Towards the Driverless Car,' in M. Grieco and J. Urry (eds.), *Mobilities: New Perspectives on Transport and Society*, pp. 223–243. Farnham: Ashgate, 2012.

22 There are, however, a few notable exceptions. David Bissell has articulated how the act of commuting by railway can be framed as a productive act. David Bissell, 'Travelling Vulnerabilities: Mobile Timespaces of Quiescence.' *Cultural Geographies*, 16(4), 2009, pp. 427–445. And building off this work, Eric Hsu has indicated how the practice of sleeping in transit does not just have to be framed as 'wasted' time. Eric L. Hsu, 'The Sociology of Sleep and the Measure of Social Acceleration.' *Time & Society*, 23(2), 2014, pp. 212–234.

23 See Eric Laurier, 'Doing Office Work on the Motorway.' *Theory, Culture & Society*, 21(4–5), 2004, pp. 261–277; Michael Bull, 'Mobile Spaces of Sound in the City,' in Nick Couldry and Anna McCarthy (eds.), *MediaSpace: Place, Scale, and Culture in a Media Age*, pp. 275–293. London: Routledge, 2004.

24 On the skills and strategies people develop to organize and manage the demands of being a mobile person see: Sven Kesselring, 'Pioneering Mobilities. New Patterns of Movement and Motility in a Mobile World.' *Environment and Planning A*, 38(2), 2006, pp. 269–279.

25 For an informative discussion of automated automobilities, see John Urry, *Mobilities*, Cambridge: Polity, 2007.

26 Laurier and Dant, 'What We Do Whilst Driving: Towards the Driverless Car,' p. 237.

27 John Urry, 'Inhabiting the Car.' *The Sociological Review*, 54(s1), 2006, pp. 17–31.

28 See Malene Freudendal-Pedersen and Sven Kesselring (forthcoming) 'Mobilities, Futures and the City. Changing perspectives and policies through transsectoral intersections,' in *Mobility Intersections*, Special Issue in Mobilities, co-edited by Monika Büscher; Mimi Sheller and David Tyfield.

29 See Urry, *Mobilities*.

30 For a greater understanding of PackBot's military applications, see Brian M. Yamaguchi, 'PackBot: A Versatile Platform for Military Robotics.' *Defense and Security*, 2004.

31 Peter W. Singer, 'Military Robots and the Laws of War.' *The New Atlantis*, (23), 2009, p. 33.

32 www.cbsnews.com/news/south-korea-woman-hair-stuck-in-robotic-vacuum-cleaner/.

33 www.therobotreport.com/news/latest-robotic-vacuum-product-launches-change-industry-from-niche-to-mainst

34 Nigel Thrift, 'Lifeworld Inc. – and What To Do about It.' *Environment and Planning D: Society and Space*, 29(1), 2011, p. 11

35 Ibid., 11–12.

36 See also James Der Derian, *Virtuous War: Mapping the Military-industrial-media-Entertainment Network*, New York: Routledge, 2009.

37 Max Weber, 'Politics as a Vocation,' in H. H. Gerth and C. Wright Mills (eds.), *Max Weber: Essays in Sociology*, pp. 77–128. New York: Oxford University Press, 1958.

38 Benedict Anderson, *Imagined Communities: Reflections on the Origin and Spread of Nationalism*, London and New York: Verso, 1991.

39 For a more detailed sociological and historical account of the development of globalization, see Charles C. Lemert, Anthony Elliott, Daniel Chaffee, and Eric Hsu, *Globalization: A Reader*, Routledge London, 2010.

40 James Der Derian writes: "war is no longer a mere continuation of politics (Clausewitz); nor, for that matter, is politics a continuation of war (Michel Foucault). In parallel universes . . . wars that defy fixed definition (Syria: civil or international?), empirical verification (Yemen: open or secret?) and normal legal standing (drones: sub- or extra-judicial?) take on a multispectral, densely entangled, phase-shifting character." Reference James Der Derian, 'From War 2.0 to Quantum war: The Superpositionality of Global Violence.' *Australian Journal of International Affairs*, 67(5), 2013, pp. 570–585. The quote is from p. 575.

41 The work of Paul Virilio adds a much-needed layer of complexity to our understanding of the social consequences of satellite-based forms of warfare. Virilio's book, *Speed and Politics*, finds that automated satellite weapon systems – such as those found in the Cold War period – have the potential to decrease human autonomy and people's capacity to produce informed thought and discussion. With the arrival of satellites, wars move away from being a contest for land. Instead, wars become a contest for time. According to Virilio, who strikes first and fastest is the one who triumphs in the social order.

42 Manuel De Landa, *War in the Age of Intelligent Machines*. Cambridge: MIT Press, 1991, p. 1.

43 Ibid., p. 2.

44 www.defense.gov/UAS/

45 www.theguardian.com/news/datablog/2012/aug/03/drone-stocks-by-country
     This covered 807 drones in active service around the world – and should be considered a huge underestimate: data was not available for China, Turkey or Russia.

46 See Clay Dillow, 'All of These Countries Now Have Armed Drones.' *Fortune*, February 12, 2016, http://fortune.com/2016/02/12/these-countries-have-armed-drones/

47 See: www.aero-news.net/index.cfm?do=main.textpost&id=3769e102-dd30-4ed7-95b5-5341c14f4e93

48 Peter M. Asaro, 'The Labor of Surveillance and Bureaucratized Killing: New Subjectivities of Military Drone Operators.' *Social Semiotics*, 23(2), 2013, 196–224.

49 Derek Gregory, 'From a View to a Kill: Drones and Late Modern War.' *Theory, Culture & Society*, 28(7–8), 2011, p. 193

50 Neal Curtis, 'The Explication of the Social: Algorithms, Drones and (Counter-) terror.' *Journal of Sociology*, 52(3), 2016, pp. 522–536.

51 Colleen McCue, *Data Mining and Predictive Analysis: Intelligence Gathering and Crime Analysis*, Oxford: Butterworth-Heinemann, 2007, p. 220.

52 Simon Jenkins, 'Drones Are Fool's Gold: They Prolong Wars We Can't Win.' *The Guardian*, January 11, 2013, www.theguardian.com/commentisfree/2013/jan/10/drones-fools-gold-prolong-wars.

53 Grégoire Chamayou, *A Theory of the Drone*, New York: New Press, 2015, p. 14.

54 G.R. Ian Shaw, 'Predator Empire: The Geopolitics of US Drone Warfare.' *Geopolitics*, 18(3), 2013, p. 537.

55 www.defense.gov/News/News-Releases/News-Release-View/Article/1044811/department-of-defense-announces-successful-micro-drone-demonstration/

56 www.livescience.com/57306-un-addresses-killer-robots-in-2017.html?utm_source=feedburner&utm_medium=feed&utm_campaign=Feed%3A+Livesciencecom+%28LiveScience.com+Science+Headline+Feed%29

57 https://thenextweb.com/us/2016/01/21/40-countries-are-working-on-killer-robots-and-theres-no-law-to-say-how-we-use-them/#.tnw_35IqjjXw

58 The UN recently convened a forum on how to set guidelines for autonomous warfare.

59 See Olivia Solon, 'Killer Robots? Musk and Zuckerberg Escalate Row Over Dangers of AI.' *The Guardian*, July 26, 2017, www.theguardian.com/technology/2017/jul/25/elon-musk-mark-zuckerberg-artificial-intelligence-facebook-tesla

60 See: www.theguardian.com/technology/2016/jun/12/nick-bostrom-artificial-intelligence-machine

61 See: www.bbc.com/news/technology-30290540

62 For a summary of these developments see: https://futurism.com/lethal-autonomous-weapons-pledge/

AI and social futures

1 Ray Kurzweil, 'The Law of Accelerating Returns.' 2001, title http://www.kurzweilai.net/the-law-of-accelerating-returns

2 R. Kurzweil, *The Singularity Is Near*, New York: Penguin Books, 2005.

3 Research on the utopian elements of Kurzweil's work has produced a number of novel insights. Some work has sought to establish how the theory of singularity bears resemblance to some religious movements: Roberto Paura, 'Singularity Believers and the New Utopia of Transhumanism.' *Im@ go. A Journal of the Social Imaginary*, 7, 2016, pp. 23–35; Oskar Gruenwald, 'The Dystopian Imagination: The Challenge of Techno-utopia.' *Journal of Interdisciplinary Studies*, 25(1/2), 2013, p. 1. This line of analysis often charges that Kurzweil and others often invest too much into the power of technologies without appreciating the complexities of human culture and experience.

4 For further discussion of the importance of complexity to the analysis of adaptive systems, see John Urry, 'The Complexity Turn.' *Theory, Culture & Society*, 22(5), 2005, pp. 1–14; John Urry, *Global Complexity*, Cambridge: Polity, 2003. See also on the co-evolution of technology, economy and society Brian Arthur, *The Nature of Technology: What It Is and How It Evolves*, New York: Simon and Schuster, 2009.

5 Jenny Kleeman, 'The Race to Build the World's First Sex Robot.' *The Guardian*, April 27, 2017, www.theguardian.com/technology/2017/apr/27/race-to-build-world-first-sex-robot

   In addition to *Harmony*, Kleeman also discusses *Roxxy*, touted as the world's first sexbot and previewed at a high profile launch at the February 2010 Las Vegas Adult Entertainment Expo. It is worth noting that no commercial models of Roxxy have appeared on the market as of 2018.

6 Various debates have circled around the asymmetrical dimension of human-sex robot relationships. See, for example, Matthias Scheutz and Thomas Arnold, 'Are We Ready For Sex Robots?' in *The Eleventh ACM/IEEE International Conference on Human Robot Interaction*, pp. 351–358. Piscataway, NJ: IEEE Press, 2016.

7 David Levy, *Love and Sex with Robots*, New York: HarperCollins Publishers, 2009.

8 See also Riley Richards, Chelsea Coss, Jace Quinn, 'Exploration of Relational Factors and the Likelihood of a Sexual Robotic Experience,' in Adrian David Cheok, Kate Devlin and David Levy (eds.), *Love and Sex with Robots*, Proceedings of the Second

International Conference, LSR 2016, London, UK, December 19–20, pp. 97–103. Cham, Switzerland: Springer, 2017.

9 But see Levy's more cautionary notes on the research and development required to develop software to the point where 'realistic emotion driven behaviours' in robots is attained. This is developed in Adrian Cheok, David Levy, Kasun Karunanayake, Yukihiro Morisawa, 'Love and Sex with Robots,' in Ryohei Nakatsu, Matthias Rauterberg and Paolo Ciancarini (eds.), *Handbook of Digital Games and Entertainment Technologies*, pp. 833–858. Singapore: Springer, 2017.

10 See Kathleen Richardson, 'The Asymmetrical "Relationship": Parallels Between Prostitution and the Development of Sex Robots,' published in the ACM Digital Library as a special issue of the ACM SIGCAS newsletter. *SIGCAS Computers & Society*, 45(3) (September 2015), pp. 290–293, https://campaignagainstsexrobots.org/the-asymmetrical-relationship-parallels-between-prostitution-and-the-development-of-sex-robots.

11 Kathleen Richardson, *Sex Robots: The End of Love*, Cambridge: Polity Press, 2018.

12 John Danaher, Brian Earp, Anders Sandberg, 'Should We Campaign Against Sex Robots?' in John Danaher et al. (eds.), *Robot Sex: Social and Ethical Implications*, Cambridge, MA: MIT Press, 2017.

13 Eva Wiseman, 'Sex, Love and Robots: Is this the End of Intimacy?' *The Guardian*, December 13, 2015.

14 Maartje M.A. de Graaf, Somaya Ben Allouch, Tineke Klamer, 'Sharing a Life with Harvey: Exploring the Acceptance of and Relationship-building with a Social Robot.' *Computers in Human Behavior*, 43, 2015, pp. 1–14.

15 This research forms part of a project I lead in Japan at Keio University, and which is funded by the Toyota Foundation: '*Assessment of socially assistive robotics in elderly care: Toward technologically integrated aged care and well-being in Japan and Australia*', 2017–2019 (D16-R-0242). The interdisciplinary research team includes Atsushi Sawai, Masataka Katagiri and Yukari Ishii in Japan, and Eric Hsu and Ross Boyd in Australia.

16 Mark Coeckelbergh. 'Care Robots and the Future of ICT-Mediated Elderly Care: A Response to Doom Scenarios.' *AI and Society*, 31, 2016, pp. 455–462. Quote from p. 461.

17 www.accenture.com/t20171215T032059Z__w__/us-en/_acnmedia/PDF-49/Accenture-Health-Artificial-Intelligence.pdf

18 www.kingsfund.org.uk/sites/default/files/field/field_publication_
   file/A_digital_NHS_Kings_Fund_Sep_2016.pdf
19 https://spectrum.ieee.org/robotics/medical-robots/would-you-
   trust-a-robot-surgeon-to-operate-on-you
20 https://spectrum.ieee.org/robotics/medical-robots/would-you-
   trust-a-robot-surgeon-to-operate-on-you
21 For an informative discussion of the advances, limitations, potentials of haptic technologies, consult: Abdulmotaleb El Saddik, 'The
   Potential of Haptics Technologies.' *IEEE Instrumentation & Meas-
   urement Magazine*, 10(1), 2007, pp. 10–17.
22 Kurzweil, p. 323.
23 Ibid., p. 300.
24 Nikolas Rose, *The Politics of Life Itself: Biomedicine, Power, and Subjectivity in the Twenty-First Century*, Princeton: Princeton University Press, 2009, p. 17
25 Ibid., p. 20.
26 Ibid., p. 20.
27 Manuel Castells, *The Internet Galaxy*, Cambridge: Polity Press,
   2010.
28 See, for example, John Dunn (ed.), *Democracy: The Unfinished Journey, 508 BC to AD 1993*, Oxford: Oxford University Press, 1992;
   John Keane, *The Life and Death of Democracy*, New York: Norton,
   2009.
29 See David Held, *Democracy and the Global Order*, Cambridge: Polity
   Press, 1995; David Held, *Models of Democracy*, Cambridge: Polity
   Press, 2007.
30 A classical account is C. B. Macpherson, *The Political Theory of Pos-
   sessive Individualism: Hobbes to Locke*, Oxford: Oxford University
   Press, 2010.
31 John B. Thompson, *Media and Modernity: A Social Theory of the
   Media*, Cambridge: Polity Press, p. 240, 1995.
32 See, among others, Jamie Susskind, *Future Politics: Living Together in
   a World Transformed by Tech*, Oxford: Oxford University Press, 2018.
33 On the behavioral science theory of nudging see R. Thaler and C.
   Sunstein, *Nudge* (revised edition), London: Penguin, 2009.
34 Most treatments of the Russiagate scandal have been developed in
   the media, with the quality press providing in-depth investigation
   of these developments. A useful, but partial, overview of Russiagate
   is Luke Harding, *Collusion: How Russia Helped Trump Win the White
   House*, London: Guardian Faber Publishing, 2017.

35 www.nytimes.com/2017/01/06/us/politics/russia-hack-report.html

36 For a recent analysis see Darren E. Tromblay, *Political Influence Operations*, Lanham, Maryland: Roman and Littlefield, 2018.

37 James R. Clapper and Trey Brown, *Facts and Fears: Hard Truths from a Life in Intelligence*, New York: Viking, 2018.

38 Special Counsel Mueller's investigation uncovered evidence of crimes committed by, among others: Michael Flynn, former national security adviser and a key Trump campaign figure, who pleaded guilty to making false statements to federal investigators; Paul Manafort, Trump's campaign chair, who in 2018 was convicted of five counts of tax fraud, two counts of bank fraud and one count of failure to disclose a foreign bank account; Rick Gates, a senior aide on the Trump campaign; George Papadopoulos, a foreign policy adviser on the Trump campaign, who pled guilty to making false statements to federal investigators; and, 13 Russian nationals and three Russian companies that were indicted on conspiracy charges, and some on identity theft charges, related to Russian social media and hacking efforts.

39 James Comey, *A Higher Loyalty: Truth, Lies and Leadership*, Basingstoke: Palgrave Macmillan, 2018.

40 See Andrew Popp, 'All of Robert Mueller's Indictments and Plea Deals in the Russia Investigation So Far.' Vox: www.vox.com/policy-and-politics/2018/2/20/17031772/mueller-indictments-grand-jury

It is also worth noting that, in March 2018, the United States Treasury Department formally sanctioned various Russian "cyber actors" for interference in the 2016 election and various malicious intrusions targeting critical infrastructure. See: https://home.treasury.gov/index.php/news/press-releases/sm0312

41 www.nytimes.com/2017/09/07/us/politics/russia-facebook-twitter-election.html

42 See Clarence Page, 'Why Nobody Complained When Obama Used Facebook Data.' *Chicago Tribune*, March 23, 2018, www.chicagotribune.com/news/opinion/page/ct-perspec-page-facebook-zuckerberg-obama-20180323-story.html

43 The Computational Propaganda Research Project, based at the Oxford Internet Institute at Oxford University, investigates the interaction of algorithms, automation and politics. See http://comprop.oii.ox.ac.uk

44 See, for example, Kofi Annan, 'How Information Technology Poses a Threat to Democracy.' *The Japan Times*, February 19, 2018, www.japan times.co.jp/opinion/2018/02/19/commentary/world-commentary/ information-technology-poses-threat-democracy/

45 https://ec.europa.eu/digital-single-market/en/news/experts-appointed-high-level-group-fake-news-and-online-disinformation

46 See the classic discussion of R.A. Dahl, *Polyarchy*, New Haven: Yale University Press, 1971.

47 There are a range of associated debates concerning democratic politics, algorithmic power and the rise of web 2.0. See the following contributions, which raise cognate issues and make related points: David Beer, 'Power through the Algorithm? Participatory Web Cultures and the Technological Unconscious.' *New Media & Society*, 11(6), 2009, pp. 985–1002; C. Fuchs, 'Web 2.0, Prosumption, and Surveillance.' *Surveillance & Society*, 8(3), 2011, p. 288; and, Christian Fuchs, 'Social Media and the Public Sphere.' *tripleC: Communication, Capitalism & Critique. Open Access Journal for a Global Sustainable Information Society*, 12(1), 2014, pp. 57–101.

48 See the Report issued by the Future of Humanity Institute, the University of Oxford and the Centre for the Study of Existential Risk, 'The Malicious Use of Artificial Intelligence: Forecasting, Prevention, and Mitigation,' https://arxiv.org/pdf/1802.07228.pdf
    The development of such counter-measures have included scientific experts from such organizations as the Electronic Frontier Foundation, the Center for a New American Security, and OpenAI.

49 An example of such structural ambivalence pervading the digital revolution, and which in turn manufactures many second-order societal risks and insecurities, is the so-called 'Dark Web'. As Eric Jardine argues, the Dark Web affords anonymity to both users and hosts of 'hidden service' websites. While most commonly associated with sinister uses – weapons selling, drug dealing, terrorist activities and the distribution of extreme child abuse imagery – the Dark Web has also been a redeeming feature for women and men living under repressive regimes, enabling them to communicate with each other and the wider world, as well as gain access to information free from surveillance, censorship and persecution. See Eric Jardine, *The Dark Web Dilemma: Tor, Anonymity and Online Policing*. GCIG Paper Series No. 21. London: Centre for

International Governance Innovation and Chatham House, 2015, www.cigionline.org/sites/default/files/no.21_1.pdf

My thanks to Ross Boyd for this insight.

50 I am indebted to Sven Kesselring for this insight.

51 I refer here to work of scholars including Manuel De Landa, Benjamin H. Bratton, Sven Kesselring, Deborah Lupton, Thomas Birtchnell, Judy Wajcman, Mark Poster, Eric Hsu and Ross Boyd.

52 Felix Guattari, 'Regimes, Pathways, Subjects,' in Jonathan Crary and Sanford Kwinter (eds.), *Zone 6: Incorporations*, Cambridge, MA: MIT Press, 1992, p. 18.

53 Jean-François Lyotard, *The Postmodern Condition: A Report on Knowledge*. Trans. Geoff Bennington and Brian Massumi, Minneapolis: University of Minnesota Press, 1984, p. 67.

54 Jamie Bartlett, *The People Vs Tech: How the Internet is Killing Democracy (And How We Save It)*, London: Edbury Press, 2018, p. 1.

55 Bruce Schneier, *Data and Goliath: The Hidden Battles to Collect Your Data and Control Your World*, New York: Norton, 2015, p. 279.

56 Zygmunt Bauman, *The Individualized Society*, Cambridge: Polity Press, 2001, p. 204.

57 For example, Paulo Gerbaudo highlights the transformation of the class-based mass political party into today's new model based on online participatory platforms and social media, thus underscoring the crucial role of digital skills. See Paulo Gerbaudo, *The Digital Party: Political Organisation and Online Democracy*, London: Pluto, 2018.

58 See https://hansard.parliament.uk/Lords/2017-09-07/debates/666 FC16D-2C8D-4CC6-8E9E-7FB4086191A5/DigitalUnder standing

59 'Digital Skills in the United Kingdom,' House of Lords, Library Briefing, August, 2017: http://researchbriefings.parliament.uk/ ResearchBriefing/Summary/LLN-2017-0051

60 The law is called Netzwerkdurchsetzungsgesetz – NetzDG for short. See: www.bmjv.de/SharedDocs/Gesetzgebungsverfahren/ Dokumente/RegE_NetzDG.pdf?__blob=publicationFile&v=2

61 On the importance of ensuring transparency in an age of big data and intelligent algorithms see Roger Taylor and Tim Kelsey, *Transparency and the Open Society*, Bristol: Bristol University/Policy Press, 2016.

62 See www.bloomberg.com/view/articles/2017-10-20/russian-trolls-would-love-the-honest-ads-act

63 See, for example, Jimmy Wales, 'With the Power of Online Transparency, Together We Can Beat Fake News.' *The Guardian*, February 4, 2017. www.theguardian.com/commentisfree/2017/feb/03/online-transparency-fake-news-internet

64 See Damian Tambini, 'Fake News: Public Policy Responses.' *Media Policy Brief 20*, London School of Economics Media Policy Project, 2017, http://eprints.lse.ac.uk/73015/1/LSE%20MPP%20Policy%20Brief%2020%20-%20Fake%20news_final.pdf

65 See, for example, Michael Grynbaum and Sapna Maheshwari, 'As Anger at O'Reilly Builds, Activists Use Social Media to Prod Advertisers.' *New York Times*, April 6, 2017, www.nytimes.com/2017/04/06/business/media/advertising-activists-social-media.html

66 John Cook, 'Technology Helped Fake News. Now Technology Needs to Stop It.' *Bulletin of the Atomic Scientists*, November 17, 2017, https://thebulletin.org/technology-helped-fake-news-now-technology-needs-stop-it11285

67 See David Cox, 'Fake News Is Still a Problem. Is AI the Solution?' *NBC News Mach*, February 16, 2018, www.nbcnews.com/mach/science/fake-news-still-problem-ai-solution-ncna848276

68 See, for example, Bruno Lepri et al., 'Fair, Transparent, and Accountable Algorithmic Decision-making Processes.' *Philosophy & Technology*, 2017, pp 1–17.

Bruno Lepri et al. 'The Tyranny of Data? The Bright and Dark Sides of Data-Driven Decision-Making for Social Good,' in T. Cerquitelli, D. Quercia and F. Pasquale (eds.), *Transparent Data Mining for Big and Small Data: Studies in Big Data*, vol. 32, Cham: Springer, 2017.

69 See, for example, Aylin Caliskan, Joanna J. Bryson and Arvind Narayanan, 'Semantics Derived Automatically from Language Corpora Contain Human-like Biases.' *Science*, 356(6334), 2017, pp. 183–186, DOI: 10.1126/science.aal4230. Here Princeton University researchers developed a machine learning version of the Implicit Association Test (a psychological test designed to measure the associations human subjects make between mental representations of objects). They used this to map the links machine learning systems forge between concepts and words. In addition to

categorizing "flower" and "music" as more pleasant than "insects" and "weapons", what was far more revealing was the way the system categorized European-American names as more pleasant than African-American names, as well as the association of the terms "woman" and "girl" with the arts, rather than science and mathematics. In effect, the AI replicated the bias found in the Implicit Association Test studies of human subjects.

70 See Julia Angwin, Jeff Larson, Surya Mattu and Lauren Kirchner, 'Machine Bias.' *ProPublica*, May 23, 2016, www.propublica.org/article/machine-bias-risk-assessments-in-criminal-sentencing

71 See Mara Hvistendahl, 'Can "Predictive Policing" Prevent Crime Before it Happens?' *Science*, September 28, 2016, www.sciencemag.org/news/2016/09/can-predictive-policing-prevent-crime-it-happens

72 Thus the phenomenon of enabling AI (being maths based) to replicate bias unchecked, and the organizations using AI to disavow responsibility for such bias – known in some quarters as 'mathwashing': www.mathwashing.com/ Helga Nowotny, in her brilliant *The Cunning of Uncertainty*, discusses evidence based policy, and particularly the application of computational resources (including machine learning) to massive data-sets, as an attempt to scientize politics and thus enhance the capacity for policy-making certitude when coping with uncertainty. She suggests this computational reinvention of politics is, however, highly problematic. Referencing the story of Google Flu Trends – an innovation where Google researchers claimed they could track the spread of influenza more effectively and economically than the US Centers for Disease Control and Prevention through tracking people's online searches for flu symptoms, treatment recommendations and so forth – Nowotny finds ample evidence of "data hubris". She underscores that Google Flu Trends persistently overestimated flu levels, at times by more than 50%. In spite of having access to enormous amounts of data, all that the Google algorithms did was establish non-causal correlations, which without hypotheses or searches for cause-effect linkages did not yield any form of meaningful knowledge. See Helga Nowotny, *The Cunning of Uncertainty*, Cambridge: Polity, 2016, pp. 120–124.

73 Cathy O'Neill provides an important analysis of the socially destructive impacts of algorithms, considering specifically how

inequalities can and have been aggravated through the application of algorithms to filtering job applications, setting insurance premiums, teacher evaluations and US college rankings. See Cathy O'Neil, *Weapons of Math Destruction: How Big Data Increases Inequality and Threatens Democracy*, New York: Crown, 2016.

74 See Giddens's Lecture of this title: www.youtube.com/watch?v=bbkyiRCef7A

75 www.theguardian.com/science/2016/oct/19/stephen-hawking-ai-best-or-worst-thing-for-humanity-cambridge

76 www.wsj.com/articles/the-key-to-smarter-ai-copy-the-brain-1523369923

INDEX